More Than Words

More Than Words provides an accessible introduction to communication theory and practice. It covers essential areas of communication, including communication between individuals and groups, in organizations and through mass media and new technologies. This fourth edition of the best-selling text has been fully revised and updated to take into account new developments in technology and developments in media, culture and communication studies.

The fourth edition includes case studies, assignments and key questions, all designed to help students understand the central concepts in communication studies. Sections on practical communication and media skills offer guidance on listening skills, interpersonal and social skills, writing skills, leaflet design, working in audio-visual media and the basics of Web design.

More Than Words is illustrated with new models and photographs and has checklist summaries for easy revision purposes. Clear and practical, it is an essential text for students of communication studies.

Richard Dimbleby is a former Principal of Bournemouth and Poole College and now works as a writer, trainer and consultant.

Graeme Burton is a freelance author and part-time lecturer at the University of Teesside. He has written several books on communication and the media, most recently *Media and Society: Critical Perspectives* (2004) and, with Richard Dimbleby, *Between Ourselves: An Introduction to Interpersonal Communication* (third edition, 2006).

More Than Words

An introduction to communication

Fourth edition

Richard Dimbleby
and
Graeme Burton

Routledge
Taylor & Francis Group

LONDON AND NEW YORK

First published 1985
by Methuen & Co. Ltd

Second edition first published 1992
by Routledge
2 Park Square, Milton Park, Abingdon, Oxon OX14 4RN

Simultaneously published in the USA and Canada
by Routledge
270 Madison Ave, New York, NY 10016

Third edition 1998
Reprinted 2000, 2001, 2004, 2005

Fourth edition 2007

Routledge is an imprint of the Taylor & Francis Group, an informa business

© 1985, 1992, 1998, 2007 Richard Dimbleby and Graeme Burton

Typeset in Janson and Futura by
Keystroke, 28 High Street, Tettenhall, Wolverhampton
Printed and bound in Great Britain by
MPG Books Ltd, Bodmin

British Library Cataloguing in Publication Data
A catalogue record for this book is available from the British Library

Library of Congress Cataloging in Publication Data
Dimbleby, Richard.
  More than words : an introduction to communication / Richard Dimbleby
and Graeme Burton. – 4th ed.
    p. cm.
  Includes index.
  ISBN 978–0–415–30382–8 (hardback : alk. paper) -- ISBN 978–0–415–30383–5
(pbk. : alk. paper) 1. Communication. I. Burton, Graeme. II. Title.
  P90.D53 2007
  302.2–dc22

                              2006034337

ISBN10: 0–415–30382–6 (hbk)
ISBN10: 0–415–30383–4 (pbk)

ISBN13: 978–0–415–30382–8 (hbk)
ISBN13: 978–0–415–30383–5 (pbk)

Contents

Illustrations

Figures

All images were reproduced with kind permission. While every effort has been made to trace copyright holders and obtain permission, this has not been possible in all cases. Any omissions brought to our attention will be remedied in future editions.

Table

Preface

Just as toothpaste and mouthwash are really not the key to social success, nobody can give you a communication pill which will automatically transform you into a communication star.

(Gail E. Myers and Michele T. Myers,
Dynamics of Human Communication, 1992)

Why study communication?

If you're looking at this book, we assume you're interested in knowing more about 'communication' and interested in learning how to communicate more effectively.

Whether we like it or not, we spend every moment communicating. We depend on this activity in our personal, social and working lives. So, it makes sense to find out *what* we're communicating, *how* we're communicating and *why* we're communicating.

We believe the study of communication is about:

- **knowing** – what happens when people communicate with themselves and with each other;
- **understanding** – how that knowledge can be used to explain and interpret the processes of communication in everyday life;
- **skills** – using this knowledge and understanding to enable us to communicate more effectively.

What is communication studies?

Many school and college courses carry the label 'communication studies' in some form. Increasingly, people recognize that being an effective communicator is an asset.

In the past, the art of effective communication (being able to express your ideas and opinions and understand other people's) was thought to be based on 'correct' uses of language. However, communication studies goes beyond 'correct' uses of language to include 'appropriate' uses of both language and other forms of communication. These are studied to enable us to understand and deal with people.

Communication studies embraces the use and analysis of media technologies, including information technology, video, films and audio materials.

The art of communicating is not a natural process or an ability we are born with. **We learn how to communicate**. Therefore, we may study what we learn in order to use our knowledge more effectively.

All communication involves the creation and exchange of meanings. These meanings are represented through 'signs' and 'codes'. Communication studies is concerned with the business of making and understanding 'signs'.

People seem to have a need to read meaning into all human actions. Observing and understanding this process can lead us to be more aware of what we are doing when we are communicating.

What this book offers

This book helps you to develop skills and techniques of communicating. It describes theories about communication in order to understand why and how the processes of communication work.

Our aim has been to produce a readable book. We have simplified and abbreviated a good deal. We have not attempted to include discussion of all possible theories about communication. Readers who wish to follow up the ideas of this book with more factual detail and background information will find suggestions for further work at the end of each chapter and in the resource lists at the end of the book.

How to use this book

The *general reader* may like to go from first to last page. Alternatively, you may prefer to dip into sections that particularly interest you. You may wish to use the book as a source of reference.

The *teacher of communication* may want to use it as a course book and as a source of ideas and discussion, presentations and practical activities.

The *student* will find sections that provide an account of key concepts and understandings of communication, with examples and suggestions for your own practical work. Whether you work on your own or in a group, we hope you will gain ideas for analysing other people's communication and for creating your own communications.

All chapters will follow a similar pattern:

- brief summary of the whole chapter;
- a personal story attached to some sections;
- general concepts and ideas;
- particular examples, applications and cases;
- review of the main elements of the chapter;
- assignments to develop analytical and creative skills, with suggestions for further reading.

We hope that readers will explore the meanings of our illustrations as they relate to the sections and topics that follow them. In particular, these pictures may say something about people's values and views of others in terms of gender, age, status and occupation.

Why another book about communication?

There are many books about communication. Some are about personal communication skills, some about the mass media, some about use of language, some about business communication. We have brought all these topics together in one book to provide a general introduction.

Many of the available books are rather difficult to read because they contain a good deal of jargon and are aimed at graduate-level readers. We have tried to explain some of the jargon, to create a book that is accessible to people in the final years of school, to students at colleges and to any interested reader.

Richard Dimbleby
Graeme Burton
June 2006

Acknowledgements

It is said that a cat has nine lives; perhaps this book will turn out to be the proverbial cat, with as many lives. Anyway, we are happy to have reached our fourth life with this edition – and thank our loyal readers out there. We are trying to give you what you want and need.

We are grateful to our families for being the home front back-up. The younger members have literally grown up through the editions of this book. Thank you to Judy and Gill for living as writers' widows. Thank you to Rachel Horner, Barbara Dunphy and Carol Childs at Prior Pursglove College, for giving comment and advice for the mass-communication chapter. Thanks to Tom Burton at wearebeef.co.uk for some timely technical advice and comment on the Web.

Every effort has been made to trace copyright holders. Where this has not been possible, we apologize to those concerned.

Most of all, we would like to say thank you to the editorial and production people at Routledge, who have brought the book into being. There was patient nagging over deadlines – our apologies. But with your help we have done it. So, a well-deserved vote of thanks to Natalie Foster and Charlotte Wood, in particular.

Chapter 1

What is communication?

Votre communication n'est pas un jeu d'hasard.
(Your communication is not a matter of luck.)

(From a French T-shirt, 2006)

This chapter provides a general introduction and background to the whole book by explaining three important aspects of communication:

1   How we experience communication, and how this experience can be analysed.
2   How communication serves our personal, social, economic, creative and play needs.
3   Ways of describing and explaining communication processes.

FIGURE 1   From 'Be a Bloody Train Driver', © Jacky Fleming, 1991

1 How do we experience communication?

CATHY'S STORY

Cathy was a bouncy kind of person. Even her hair, which caused her private despair, was springy and irrepressible. One of her friends had nicknamed her 'Tigger'. Cathy wasn't sure if that was a compliment or not. But it didn't stop her being disgracefully cheerful in the morning. This one was no exception. Most of her friends were sitting at the table in the college canteen like a scene from Return of the Zombies. *Cathy was punching buttons on the jukebox and then chatting to the assistant on the till before she came bouncing back to the table. Tom was out of it anyway. You could hear his music even though it was coming through his iPod, and he was frantically texting someone as well. Jacob had his head in his hands, but was not dying, only looking at a music mag. Sarah was reading a chapter for the next class, which she should have done a week ago. Cathy felt guilty at this, and pulled out her folder. She was looking at her notes, but not really concentrating. She had put in for entertainments officer in the union elections and this was very much on her mind. She wouldn't say anything to the others, but she really wanted to win the election. She had run her own poster campaign and had even made a CD for the college radio, with Jacob's help – only the lecturer running the course had vetoed electioneering on the radio. Cathy glanced at her watch. She had just remembered that she wanted to photocopy something, and the class time was coming up. Tom waved his hand languidly as Cathy bounced out of the canteen.*

ABOUT CATHY'S STORY

If you were asked to spot references to communication in this story, you would probably refer to objects that communicate: things like magazines or television are what many people immediately associate with the word 'communication'. In fact, we also experience communication through other things such as talk and gestures. One could say that all such examples are, in one way or another, means of communication. See what you can find in the story, and see whether you can guess what affects how the people in it communicate, or don't, as the case may be.

1.1 Means of communication

In this case, communication is defined in terms of the means by which it takes place. It seems that if we are talking about radio, or painting, for example, then we must be talking about communication. But this isn't good enough, because it doesn't tell us how the means of communication is being used. It doesn't tell us why the communication is happening. In fact, it doesn't tell us a lot of things, all of which partly answer our main question, what is communication?

Still, we have to start somewhere, and it is useful to sort out how one describes the many means of communication that we use and experience. Not all of them are, strictly speaking, individual and separate forms. So, we suggest that you use the following three terms:

(a) **Form of communication is a way of communicating such as speaking or writing or drawing.**

   Forms are distinct and separate from one another in so far as they have their own system for putting the message across. So, when marks are made on paper according to certain rules (such as those of grammar and spelling), then we create words and the 'form' of writing.

   As a generalization, many of what we would call 'forms' are ways of communicating which we control directly, such as non-verbal communication (gestures, facial expressions, etc.).

(b) **Medium of communication is a means of communicating which combines different forms.**

   A medium often involves the use of technology that is beyond the control of most of us. So, for example, a book is a medium that uses forms of communication such as words, pictures and drawings.

(c) **The media are those examples of mass communication that have come to be a distinct group of their own.**

   We are going to discuss the media in chapter 5, and say something about what they have in common and how they communicate with us. Examples of these are radio, television, cinema, newspapers and magazines.

   These media are also distinctive in the way that they may include a number of forms of communication. For example, television offers words, pictures and music.

   Again, the term 'media' often identifies those means of communication which are based on technology that makes a bridge between the communicator and the receiver.

Comment

Some qualities of forms or media of communication are 'built in'. So, something like speech is necessarily transient. There is no permanent record of what is said. A magazine, on the other hand, has the quality of storing what it communicates: there is a permanent record on the page and we can go back to the communication any time we want to.

   Some qualities of forms or media of communication are imposed. For example, cartoons, whether in a newspaper or on television, would probably be described as funny, but they don't have to be. Serious cartoon films have been made. Commercial interests and film-makers have imposed a habit of using the medium in a particular way.

To take another example, we tend to think of radio as a broadcast medium. But this quality is also imposed, and is not a natural consequence of the technology of radio. Setting aside problems of crowded airwaves, there is no technical reason why radio should not be used by us for exchange of messages, as much as for transmission. Radio telephones are of course such a use, but we think of them as telephones, not as a form of radio.

All forms or media of communication extend the power of our senses. All the communication that we give or receive must pass through our five senses, especially those of sight and hearing. This is true even when we use some piece of technology to aid our communication. A public address system extends the range of the human voice. A recording on CD or DVD extends our ability to communicate over distances, or even through time. It can be carried from place to place and can be kept for many years.

Computers are interesting because they are also extending human powers such as that of memory. A computer never forgets what it has been 'told', and can do the same job over and over again. The Internet provides personal access to a global network of information from all sorts of reliable and unreliable sources. We may feel able to give more trust to the information on a site from the BBC than to a personal weblog.

Most means of communication are intentional. That is to say, someone created them with the intention of communicating a message. Even a church spire may be regarded as a means of communication. It is an unusual example but it can be argued that it is intended to draw attention to the building, to its function and to a religion.

However, it is important to recognize that messages and meanings can also be understood in some cases where the means of communication is used unintentionally. For example, every day we deal with a flood of messages about our environment. Neighbours may not intend to tell us about their activity when they are using a lawnmower. But of course we do take a message about what they are doing and where they are from the sound of the lawnmower.

In chapter 2 we will see that this question of intention can be particularly important when understanding people's non-verbal messages. They may send these to us unintentionally.

1.2 Communication makes connections

In everyday experience we find that **communication is something that makes connections**.

The connections are made between one person and another, or between one group of people and another. Sometimes the connection is immediate, as when we talk face to face. Sometimes it is 'delayed', as when advertisers communicate with us through street posters. But still a connection is being made, mainly through what we have called forms or media.

What flows through the connection are the ideas, beliefs, opinions and pieces of information that are the material and the content of communication. Our television set links us with the world at large through news programmes. Speech links us with each other.

But bear in mind the fact that being able to speak to someone doesn't mean that we can get across what we want to say. Having made the connection, we then have to learn how to use it to the best of our ability.

1.3 Communication is an activity

We experience communication as an activity.

It is something that we do, something that we make, and something that we work on when we receive it from others. In this sense, communication is not just about speech, but about speaking and listening; not just about photography, but about photographing and viewing photographs.

When we are talking to someone, we are actively engaged in making sense of what the other person is saying, as much as talking ourselves. For the same reason, it isn't true to say that watching television is passive. On the contrary, just as a group of people have been actively engaged in putting a programme together, so we are actively engaged in making sense of the programme.

1.4 Communication is learnt

Communicating is something that we learn to do.

In fact, not only do we learn how to communicate, but also we use communication to learn how to communicate. This is what is happening in schools and colleges at the moment. It is what is happening as you read this book – we hope.

Our earliest experiences as babies include others talking and gesturing to us. We learn how to do the same thing, by practice and trial and error. There are some people who believe that we are born with some basic skills that help us learn how to talk and to understand what we see. Nevertheless, most of our communication skills must be learnt. An English baby, born in Britain but brought up in Japan, will be Japanese in all but appearance. That is to say, that person will learn to communicate in the ways that a Japanese person does.

So, abilities such as talking or writing are not natural. They are taught us by parents, friends and school. And, as growing creatures, we want to learn at least some of these communication skills because we can see that they are useful – for example, to explain to others what we want.

The fact that we experience communication as something which we learn to do has important consequences for anyone studying the subject. It means that we should consider important questions such as why we learn, how we learn and what effect this has on us. Answers to these questions help explain other aspects of communication study, such as what effect television may have on us, or why we may have problems in communicating with others. So, when we examine examples of communication in given situations, there is more to them than what is going on at the time. We must also examine what is behind the communication, what came before, what comes afterwards.

1.5 Categories of communication

We can divide our experiences of communicating into four categories.

These categories are loosely based on the numbers of people involved with the act of communication. They are a useful way of trying to define our field of study, like the terms 'form' and 'media'. Some forms or media belong more to one category than another, though there is no absolute rule. The remaining sections of this book are based on these categories.

(a)   **Intrapersonal communication is communication within and to the self.**

When we think, we are communicating within ourselves. We could be reflecting on the events of a day, or working out a problem in our heads. Arguments about how we think, for instance whether we use words or pictures when we think, have not been resolved.

We also talk to ourselves, and write diaries for ourselves. Again, the person making and receiving the communication is us.

(b)   **Interpersonal communication is communication between people.**

Usually this category is taken to refer to two people interacting face to face. There are 'odd' examples that could fall within this category, such as a telephone conversation. And it is worth remembering that face-to-face communication takes place in situations where there are more than two people present. Examples of familiar interpersonal situations are an interview, a salesperson talking to a client and a conversation between friends in a café. It is the fact of face-to-face contact and the emphasis on speech and non-verbal forms of communication that make such situations in this category distinctive.

(c)   **Group communication is communication within groups of people and by groups of people to others.**

In this case it is convenient to make two more divisions: small groups and large groups. Small groups behave differently from pairs, but they still interact face to face. More will be said about them in chapter 3. A family is a small group; so is a group of friends out for an evening together, or a committee meeting at work.

Large groups behave differently from small groups, not only because they are bigger but because they are often brought together or come together for purposes that are rather different from those of small groups. Examples include an audience at a concert and some kind of business organization or company. It is this last example that we will concentrate on in chapter 4.

(d) **Mass communication is communication received by or used by large numbers of people**.

In making a definition based on numbers, we don't have to be specific. An open-air concert for a thousand people might reasonably be called mass communication. The point is that the numbers involved at any one time are much bigger than anything we would reasonably call a group. It is the fact of large numbers being involved that makes this category special, in terms of who is able to control the means of communication, and in terms of what its effect may be. This will be explored in chapter 5.

There are two kinds of examples to cite. The mass media form one subdivision, where obviously we are talking about large audiences. A particularly popular TV programme may be watched by several million people. Similarly, millions a day may access a particular website or read a particular newspaper.

The telephone and postal systems are examples of the other kind of mass communication. There may not be large audiences for the kinds of communication that are sent out. But such systems are used on a large scale, by thousands of people at any one time, so they do fit this category on general grounds of number.

1.6 Communication is used for a range of different purposes

We use communication in different ways regardless of what means of communication are used in these ways. Examples of such uses are:

- to warn others (e.g. road safety signs or a warning shout);
- to inform others (e.g. mobile phone text or a fact sheet);
- to explain something (e.g. a manual or the write-up for an experiment);
- to entertain (e.g. telling jokes or a film);
- to describe (e.g. a TV documentary or telling someone about a holiday);
- to persuade (e.g. a trailer for a radio programme or a poster for a charity).

These uses are talked about from a different angle, as functions of communication, in section 3.2 of this chapter.

1.7 Communication is culture

How we communicate and what is 'said' through our communication helps define what is 'our culture'.

Linguists have long argued that spoken languages, their words, say a lot about how a given set of people see the world. In the case of Hopi Indians it is literally the case that they have their way of seeing the world because they have a few words for colours which other people don't have. But culture is a very broad term for describing the beliefs of a people as represented through their arts, their religion, their social customs, and so on. The point we would make is that one only knows art, religion, customs through acts of communication – therefore culture is communication and vice versa. And of course this means communication in the widest sense; it includes forms other than just words.

Cultures often have dominant symbols or icons, such as the turban for Sikhism or the tartan for Scottishness. But there is more to both these cultures than recognizable items of clothing. We suggest that you try making a list of verbal, visual and non-verbal communication for a culture of your choice, in order to work out what seems typical of that culture. Then you should try to describe what sort of beliefs and attitudes your list represents. In this way you will have worked out one example of how communication does define culture.

What is it about different forms of communication that makes them useful in doing different jobs of communicating?

Hint: think about reasons why you would choose to use video or would talk to someone face to face.

---

2 Why do we communicate?

SARAH'S STORY

It was Friday night and a bad time for Sarah. The mirror was no help, so she took it off her wall. The darkening evening outside her window was cheerless, so she drew the curtains. She tripped over her sports bag as she turned away from the window, so she kicked it.

What would be the third thing to go wrong, she wondered. Last week she had lost her Saturday job. Not enough customers coming to the wine bar, O'Rourke had said. Business is bad. Not so bad, she had found out, that he couldn't keep on the other part-timer. And we all know why he kept her on, thought Sarah darkly to herself.

And now she had broken up with Neil. She had to admit that they hadn't been getting along so well. But she hadn't expected him to actually break it up. It wouldn't have been so bad if it had been her idea. . . . So here she was looking at the wallpaper, bored as hell, and not feeling good about herself.

'Is there something wrong with me?' she wondered. 'I just couldn't stand him sulking every time I wanted to go off and do something different, maybe go out with

some girlfriends. Still, maybe I should have been more considerate. Maybe there's something about me that puts them off. After all, he's not the first to go.'

Sarah's morale sank again. She looked at the clothes that she had put out to wear before that abrupt phone call.

'I'd better do something before I commit suicide,' she thought.

It was then that she remembered that O'Rourke had given her a further day's pay in lieu of notice. Not that he had to, she thought, to be fair. But it meant that she could go shopping in town. Because she had some money, and because now she wouldn't be working tomorrow.

'I'll ring Julie,' she decided. 'Perhaps I can go round there and talk things over with her. That's what I need to do – talk to someone – get it all in proportion. And Julie might want to come to town tomorrow as well. New clothes and a day out . . . and who knows who we might meet,' thought Sarah.

ABOUT SARAH'S STORY

Sarah's story tells us something about what communication does for us. There has to be a reason why we decide to communicate in the first place. If we consider what Sarah did, and what she was going to do, then it is clear that her thinking was a piece of 'intrapersonal communication', and that when she rang Julie she would be within the category of 'interpersonal communication'. And when Sarah talked over her situations and her feelings with herself, she was impelled to communicate by something within herself. The same could be said of her conversation with Julie – when it took place. Sarah wanted to feel better about herself, she wanted someone to talk to. We all want something to happen through communicating. In other words, we have needs, which communicating can help to satisfy. Having recognized a need to express ourselves, we identify aims or purposes to fulfil those needs through communicating with other people.

2.1 Needs and purposes for communication

Needs and purposes can therefore be seen as mirror images: a need is felt from within, a purpose recognizes the outcome we want.

People must have a reason for communicating. It is worth remembering that when people communicate, they may be fulfilling more than one purpose at the same time. For example, someone may tell you something that you want to know; their purpose may be to inform you, but at the same time, perhaps, to impress you with their knowledge.

The concept of purpose helps explain what people intend to achieve when they communicate. In our working lives at least, it helps to be clear about our own purposes when we communicate.

Purposes relate to needs in that our purpose is what we intend to get done through communicating in order to satisfy our needs.

We may not always be conscious of our purposes. In the example given above, the person might not be aware that they were 'showing off'. But by examining how they use words, gestures and tone of voice, we might be able to understand that this was indeed what they were doing. When we communicate face to face, it is the non-verbal forms of communication that often reveal our unconscious purposes or needs.

Similarly, communication outcomes may be intentional or unintentional. If we hurt or upset people through what we say or do, we may not have intended to do so. An owl hooting outside my window does not intend to tell me that it is there and that it is night-time. That is not its purpose. For communication to have purpose, it must (even unconsciously) be directed from one person to another, or indeed from one animal to another. The people who manufacture a newspaper intend to communicate with their readers. The company that issues a report on its trading over the previous year intends to communicate with its shareholders.

There are several common purposes and needs of communication which are described below.

Survival

We communicate to survive.

In wealthy Northern countries it seems strange to talk about survival, especially in its basic senses of warmth, food and shelter. Yet some of our communicating is still about these physical needs. For example, we would communicate in order to rent a flat (shelter). The flat might be rather different from a village hut, but it still does the same job. If we felt ourselves in physical danger, we would also communicate with others to try to get help.

Co-operation

We communicate in order to work with others.

It could be argued that co-operation between people is the single greatest need and purpose in communication. It is obvious that our need to form social groups actually comes from our need to co-operate with each other in order to survive. Organized groups of people in any society work together to provide basic needs and also less basic needs. We use communication to get along with other people and to work with other people.

Chapters 3 and 4 provide further information on this.

Personal needs

We communicate to satisfy personal needs.

This reminds us that, just as survival was about more than physical things, so also our needs are not merely physical.

We have a personal need to feel secure within ourselves. This leads to other needs: to have a good opinion of ourselves, to feel that we are wanted and valued by other people.

In the story above, Sarah had begun to feel badly about herself, to feel that there might be something wrong with her. She wanted to be wanted and valued, and so was turning to a friend for comfort. Communication with and from others helps to satisfy these security needs. All of this underlines the important fact that communicating isn't just about practical things like buying 6 kilos of potatoes. It is also about non-physical things such as emotions, feelings and ideas.

These personal needs are behind acts of communication such as dressing in the right way for an occasion; having a cry on somebody's shoulder; or giving people presents.

Relationships

We communicate to be involved with other people, to form and maintain relationships.

This follows naturally from the last two points. We need to have friends, because friends support each other. We need to get along with our workmates, because working with people is about more than job tasks: it relates to needs for co-operation.

When one talks about being involved with others, this could be in terms of number (pairs or groups); in terms of what binds those involved (friendship or love); and in terms of what description we may give the involvement (family or social club).

Persuasion

We communicate to persuade other people to think in the way that we do or to act in the way that we want them to.

The most obvious example of this is advertising. The advertiser intends to persuade a certain category of people – car owners or pensioners, for instance – to buy a given product or service. Communication makes the connection with these people persuasively. It usually seeks to change the opinions or attitudes of those people regarding the advertised product or service.

However, persuasive communication is more common than we may realize and is not confined to flamboyant examples of advertising. We may want to persuade someone to loan us some money, or to join our drama group, or to help us with repairing our car. It is true that the word 'persuasion' has a certain sense of manipulation – to get what we want. But in this sense we are all manipulators, every day.

Power

We communicate to gain or exert power over other people.

To a certain extent this may seem to be like persuasion – our purpose is to get someone else to do something we want. But the word 'power' introduces something new into the situation. It suggests that the communicator intends to put the other person in a submissive or helpless position. It can suggest that the communicator has special privileges in terms of what they know or the means of communication they can use.

For example, a blackmailer has power. This person may possess such significant information about another that we call this other person a victim. If the blackmailer threatens to reveal this information to others, then their purpose in communicating is to exert their power, usually to get money.

Propaganda is communication used to control or manipulate others, usually large groups of people. It involves the control of sources of information and of the means of communication. This control represents power. The Union of Soviet Socialist Republics used propaganda to reinforce its economic and military power for some seven decades of the twentieth century.

Mass communications are particularly well suited to this exertion of power because they can broadcast or distribute information and opinions to great numbers of people from a central source. Those who have power control that central source. That is why there is always concern about who controls the media in any country. The media can exert power over their audiences. It is argued that the most important way in which they do this is in shaping people's attitudes and beliefs.

Even in democratic societies, information about the state and about defence issues is often closely guarded. In the United Kingdom in recent years the Freedom of Information Act has provided somewhat more access to information about national and local government.

Social needs

We communicate to hold our society and our organizations together.

The bigger the society or the organization, the more communication is needed. It is the practical problems of running large businesses, for example, that have led to the development of new forms and media of communication. Data processing with computers seeks to solve the problems of handling huge amounts of information quickly by using new means of electronic communication.

These more practical social needs are to do with what goes on outside ourselves. They are to do with making the whole system work for us. Hospitals, schools, manufacturing organizations and government organizations all rely on effective means of communication in order to function.

Information

We communicate to give and receive information.

We are exchanging information with other people almost constantly. We may need to find out the time when a bus leaves. We may be keen viewers and readers of the news because we want to know about other people, events and places in the world. On a smaller scale, we are great gossips and conversationalists because we want to find out what is going on around us.

Making sense of the world

We use communication to make sense of the world and our experience of it.

We suggest that making sense of the world is about four important things:

- what we believe in;
- what we think of ourselves;
- what we think our relationships are with other people;
- what we think is real.

These ideas map out the physical world, our social world and the world inside our heads.

When a child asks questions in order to find out, for example, how granny is also mummy's mummy, he or she is making sense of the world of family relationships. When we watch a television documentary on the forests of South America, then we are making sense of another piece of the physical world. If we become involved in a discussion about the rights and wrongs of the way we treat animals (as when we use experiments on animals), then we are making sense of the world of our values and beliefs.

Self-expression

We communicate to express our imagination and ourselves to others. We like to be creative with our communication in words, pictures, sounds and other forms.

Self-expression is an important kind of need because it covers the creative aspects of communication. This creative expression of the imagination includes the kind of reasoning seen in a book on the possibilities of life existing on other planets, as well as that seen in a television play.

We use our imaginations to cover an infinite range of possibilities. One could argue that drawings representing the design concept for a new car show communication being used in the cause of self-expression. If stories are made up through the powers of our imagination, then so is our view of ourselves.

Under this heading of self-expression comes the whole range of urges that all people have to express themselves through dress and body adornment. These may be regulated through social conventions. On certain occasions certain sorts of dress are considered appropriate: for example, if we attend a funeral, then we wear dark clothes. These serve to express our feelings in socially accepted ways. However, we may seek to dress and adorn ourselves in ways that we think challenge social conventions.

It seems that humans have an innate urge to use their imagination and to be creative. Clearly, there is more to life than merely surviving or doing business. We use communication for more than carrying out transactions with other people. Our use of forms of communication, especially those using words and pictures, enables us to make up things that might happen, or create situations that will never happen. In particular, we love stories and dramatic creations – fictions that give us amusement and pleasure and explore possibilities. Through a story we can be in places that we may never visit or meet people whom we would fear to meet. We can be involved with a relationship which reminds us of one that we once had, or one that we would like to have.

Each of us, then, communicates for a whole variety of needs and purposes. We could list other reasons in addition to those mentioned above. But all of them could perhaps be organized under four main headings: **personal needs, social purposes, economic necessities and artistic expression.**

Having seen why we communicate, in the next section we want to see what happens when we communicate.

2.2 Maslow's hierarchy of needs

One much-used version of needs is that of Abraham Maslow, in which he describes people as being driven by sets of needs in a hierarchy, from the most basic at the bottom, to the most refined at the peak of a triangle (see figure 2).

Basic needs are about wanting food, shelter, sex. Just above these come the needs for safety: having a roof over one's head and knowing that one belongs to some group, like one's family. Then there are the social needs for things like love and friendship, which urge us into relationships. These are followed by ego and esteem needs, which are about us as individuals wanting self-respect, recognition, even power. Finally, at the top of the triangle comes the most sophisticated need: for self-actualization. This is about self-fulfilment, about finding and being oneself. Certainly these needs get more complicated and personal as one goes up the hierarchy. This sense of development also loosely relates to our growing up and becoming more complex human beings. But in

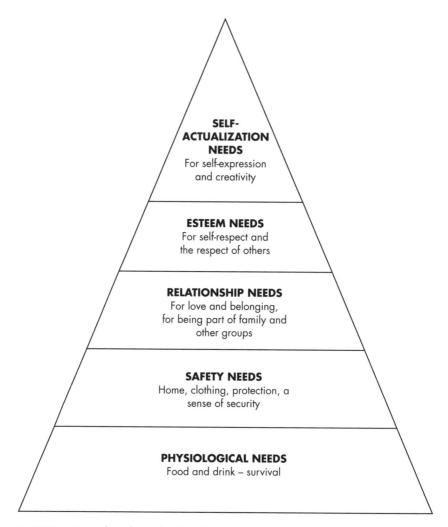

FIGURE 2   Maslow's hierarchy of needs

terms of our lives and actions one cannot really say that we simply move away from 'baser' needs. They are always there somewhere. Why we are driven by different needs at different times very much depends on circumstances, on how we are feeling at a given time, on personality. In one case a boxer is driven by needs that cause him to bite through his opponent's ear. In another case a sailor is driven by needs that urge him to rescue a fellow sailor a thousand miles from land and with the near loss of his own life. You can discuss what drives such different people in different ways.

Maslow's hierarchy is simply a theory or model to try to explain needs that people have. These needs then act as motivators for action. Such a model is not rooted in experimental research that seeks to prove it is true. Indeed, one writer at least has suggested that there is 'precious little evidence in favour of it' (Furnham 2005). Do you think that Maslow's model is a useful way of trying to explain what motivates people? Do you think it is culture based or universal to all people?

2.3 Nature or nurture?

Does the ability to communicate come from learning or from our genes?

You should relate what follows to section 1.4. As a species, we are biologically privileged by our relatively huge brains. It seems likely that to some extent this development is a survival or selection characteristic in which the ability to use speech and to visualize space and movement has helped us a great deal. But what we have done with this talk and this visualization, in respect of socialization or of creativity, is another matter. It is not apparent that anyone is born with special creative skills. We are not born talking.

Some linguists, particularly Noam Chomsky, have theorized that we are born with 'deep structures' in our brains. These are supposed to enable us to make sense of the conventions of speech, to learn to speak as babies. This was a theory that tried to explain how we learn to talk, but there is no biological or physical evidence for these structures. There is plenty of evidence, however, that people learn communication skills by imitating others and by practising. Where writers or artists seem to run in families, this is most probably not because of some inherited gene; rather, it is because the children grow up in an environment that encourages one form of communication. It may also be because those children feel challenged by their parents' skills, and need to match these in order to satisfy their personal needs.

Education is a great nurturer of communication skills. Plainly, those who don't have certain kinds of education are not able to write, or cannot draw, and so on. This is why we believe that communication skills can be learnt and developed. Our society has education because it believes that, apart from other knowledge and skills, it is useful and desirable to be able to communicate effectively in various forms. Communication is nurtured in children by family and the school. It (particularly speech) is the means by which we satisfy our needs, through which we function socially and economically.

Why is it that we don't think it is appropriate to communicate at times?

Hint: think of the times when you feel you should speak up and those when you should keep quiet.

---

3 What happens when we communicate?

LUCY'S STORY

It had been a tough day for Lucy. She had had a row with Janet Capstick, her supervisor at work, and now she was worrying about whether she would get the sack. Like many arguments, it had started with something apparently trivial and then got out of hand. The trouble was that Mrs Capstick, it seemed to Lucy, was a bossy woman. She wasn't that much older than Lucy herself, but seemed to think a lot of her position. And she was a great one for the rules. Lucy was on contract work, with thirty others, operating a telephone answering service for this insurance company. The rules were tight. If you were even a minute late in logging on, it counted against your pay. Today had been too much for Lucy. She had started on at Lucy in the first tea break.

'Could I have a word with you, Miss Johnson?' she had said, with that insincere smile on her face.

Lucy felt herself go all brittle. She followed her supervisor out of the tea room into the corridor. She really couldn't think what the problem was. But she felt resentful already. It wasn't the first time that they had had words.

'I wish to point out to you that you are improperly dressed,' Janet Capstick almost hissed into Lucy's ear. Lucy thought that she would laugh, but then realized that she would have to take it seriously. This person had no sense of humour.

'But I thought we sorted this out the other day,' she said. 'I'm wearing tights, I'm wearing an ordinary skirt. What's the problem?'

Capstick went a little pink. 'Your blouse. Too see-through. Too low. Not enough buttons.'

'Too much for who?!'

'It's the company's rules. They are quite clear. And indeed this is the third time that I have spoken to you about your dress.'

'Mrs Capstick, I'm working in a room full of women. I don't deal with the public. And as it happens, I was going to wear an ordinary top, only it's in the wash. I'll have it tomorrow.' I'm not going to strangle her, thought Lucy. I'll be polite. I need the money.

'Well, I'm afraid that is not good enough.' Janet Capstick stared at Lucy steadily and unnervingly. Lucy wondered if she would try it on if Lucy were as tall as her. 'I would like you to go home and change now, and be back in half an hour.'

Lucy couldn't believe her ears. 'You aren't serious, are you?!'

'I will be making a note of this incident on your file. I'd advise you to do what I ask – now.'

Lucy felt her eyeballs beginning to bulge. 'This is ridiculous. You really are a power freak.' She turned on her heel, and tried to walk away with dignity.

ABOUT LUCY'S STORY

You may have noticed that this story suggests that people do think about communicating, not only after the event but also while it is going on. Things that matter to the exchange are clothes, words, surroundings – the physical context. Phrases like this are the communication terms that we use to describe what communication is and how it happens.

You may also have noticed how the story of this communication is about a developing, changing situation, with various factors coming in. The relationship between Lucy and Mrs Capstick develops. It still isn't over: we don't know what will happen next.

We have already talked about communication being dynamic. Whether we are making the communication or we are taking it in, something is happening continuously. Communication, even reading a magazine, is an activity; it is a doing experience, it is a process.

3.1 Communication as a process

When we are in a conversation, there is a continuous exchange going on.

Ideas or facts or opinions are being turned into words and shifted from one person to the other through speech. In chapter 2 we will look at how, in another part of the process, non-verbal communication is also conveying messages.

So, when we talk about the communication process, we are talking about this active flow.

And what we want to do is to explain what's happening, why and how. We want to know what is going on in the process, so that maybe we can improve our handling of it. Through knowledge come understanding and the possibility of change. We look at the communication process from various angles in this book in order to become better communicators.

We use communication terms to describe various aspects of the process, breaking it down into stages and parts. We use terms to identify factors that may affect how communication is carried on. We interpret the evidence thus produced and try to make sense of it. Interpretation is not only about making deductions, but also about saying why these deductions are significant.

For example, if we see context as a factor in the process, then what is important is to say why it matters in the examples that we are looking at. Theory needs to be applied.

FIGURE 3   Communication processes

One of the earliest and still one of the most useful attempts to describe the communication process in separate parts was made by Harold Lasswell in 1948. He said the process of communication could be described in these terms:

Who says What
in which Channel
to Whom and with what Effect

This is the same as saying that every example of a communication process can be broken down into the following terms:

A Sender
directs a Message
through some Form/Medium
to a Receiver
with some Effect

One may add other points to this list. These points are all examples of communication terms, or concepts, which identify different aspects of the process.

Context refers to the idea that every act of communication must happen in some sort of surroundings. Only what we mean by this is actually quite complicated. Most obviously there is the *physical context* – whether we are talking to someone in our living room or on the terraces at a football match. But then there is the *social context*, which is to do with the occasion involved and the people in it. This might be a group of friends in a club or a family meal or a group of mourners at a funeral. And then there is the *cultural context*, which refers to an even broader set of circumstances and beliefs, which still may affect how we talk. For example, it would matter whether the funeral was in a Hindu or an Anglican context. It is particularly important to see that **the media are part of the cultural context in which we operate**. How we talk, what we talk about, what music we listen to, has a lot to do with the influence of the cultural context of the media.

Purpose and need are also factors in the process. They refer to the basic question of why any act of communication takes place. Everyone has a need that causes them to communicate, and everyone has a purpose in communicating.

Audience refers to the receiver mentioned above. This idea focuses on where messages go to, on the person or people to whom the communication is addressed. **The nature of the audience always affects the treatment of the message**. You don't talk to teachers in the same way that you talk to friends. You don't talk to one person in the same way that you talk to a group. You don't write a letter to a relative in the same way that you would write to your local councillor.

Of course there are other factors at work, such as the important question of what you are trying to say anyway. You need to look at all these factors, including audience, as you try to describe process and the nature of communication.

So, communication is a process, and this process can be broken down into parts that help explain what is happening, how and why.

When we use certain terms to explain parts of the communication process, we will try to suggest what they mean and give examples. But also remember that there is a glossary near the back of this book which you can use to check out special words.

3.2 Exchange of messages

One dominant idea is that when we communicate, we exchange messages.

We give messages and we receive them. These messages are taken into our minds, interpreted, stored or acted upon.

The messages can be about all sorts of things. They could be about something that is happening – a fire in the house next door; or about someone's feelings – they are very unhappy because a relative has just died; or about opinions – we tell someone that we think a certain film is well worth seeing.

In this sense we can also list certain functions of messages (and of the act of communication which puts them across). These functions could be:

- to warn;
- to advise;
- to inform;
- to persuade;
- to express opinions;
- to amuse.

You will recognize some of these words from elsewhere in this chapter. So, rather than our giving you examples this time, see if you can devise word messages that do the sort of jobs we have just listed.

The idea of message, in its broadest sense, is held to cover a wide range of communication forms and media. Maps give us messages about the area of land they depict. Graphs can give us messages about things like the increase in the number of goods that we import into our country. Photographs can give us messages about what people look like in countries that we have never been to. It is even argued that a piece of music is a kind of message from its composer – perhaps about an experience, a mood or feelings.

When we receive such messages, we are involved in an exchange process with their makers, just as we are when we make messages ourselves.

Sharing

When we communicate we are also part of a process of sharing.

Communication forms and media carry messages that allow us to share thoughts, feelings, opinions, information and experiences with others. This makes the point that communication, especially in our everyday dealings with others, isn't just about facts. It is about emotions, attitudes and beliefs. These are important to us. They are bound up with the personal and social needs that we have already described.

Such sharing, especially on a personal basis, affects many aspects of our lives, including the time we spend at work. It is all too easy to see work as a business of handling messages of a factual nature. But if our jobs involve dealing with people, then this cannot be the whole truth.

At work, for example, we are frequently concerned about what people think of us, and we of them. We spend time, however briefly, exchanging messages about personal background and experience. Indeed, there is evidence to suggest that how well we deal with 'job messages' depends on how well we are exchanging 'personal messages'.

So, sharing is an important aspect of the exchange of messages.

Neutrality of messages

Messages are rarely neutral.

It is possible to argue that simple messages of fact are neutral. For example, a message expressed in word form, such as 'There are two wheels on my motorcycle', seems quite objective.

But then such messages rarely come on their own. In the example just given, there would probably be other verbal and non-verbal messages around that sentence. It would be said in a particular situation and could be said in a particular way. In this case, the speaker could be addressing a friend whose motorcycle is laid up with a smashed front wheel. In that case, the message is not just a statement of fact. It is also saying something like, 'My bike's OK but yours isn't. Hard luck!'

The cartoon at the start of this chapter (page 2) may be a simple question and answer. But the apparent tone, the situation, the unexpected reply and the nature of the relationship that seems to be portrayed (as well as comment on male and female cultural attitudes and behaviour) show that this little interaction is not neutral.

And, of course, messages in advertisements are never neutral. Even a factual list of functions in a car advertisement is not just a neutral list. It is a selected set of messages about the good points of the car. We don't hear about any possible bad points. We shouldn't be surprised about this lack of neutrality. Any student of communication who examines the purpose behind the message in the communication can see very well why the messages are not neutral.

This is not to make a moral judgement on the purposes of messages. People may say things with the best of intentions. But we should understand that they do have intentions and are dishonest, or unconscious of what they are doing, if they say that they don't. This leads on to the idea that messages we exchange may be overt or covert.

Overt or covert messages

Some messages are clear and obvious; some are hidden and not so obvious.

This is another argument for the study of communication. It means that we should look carefully at what is actually being expressed in any example of the communication process.

Sometimes a piece of communication actually intends to hide some of its messages. How good it is at doing this depends on how sharp the receiver is at decoding the communication. For example, an advertisement could be saying overtly, this is a good fabric conditioner that makes your clothes feel soft. But it may also be saying covertly, you aren't a very good parent to your family unless you buy this fabric conditioner.

Sometimes there are hidden messages in a piece of communication which may not be intended by the sender. For example, a friend might tell you overtly that she has not been out for the past two weeks and hasn't seen many other friends. What she could be saying covertly is that she is lonely and wants some company.

Multiple messages

Communication usually involves the exchange of more than one message at a time.

This is implied by what we have just said. If there are overt and covert messages in a piece of communication, then clearly, when we communicate we don't just pass back and forth single, simple messages. Indeed, there is another proposition that goes with this. Communication usually takes place through multiple channels. In the examples given above, we can see that the advertisement probably communicates through pictures and words and the people communicate through speech and non-verbal communication. Indeed, where people are concerned, it is often the non-verbal channel that carries the covert message.

The nature of messages

We shall discuss messages under the heading of linear models later. But it is worth emphasizing the fact that **messages are not just about what is said.**

They are about how things are said, and about what channel (or code/ codes) is used.

Our knowledge, attitudes, communication skills and cultural background affect how we communicate with others. In other words, our effectiveness as communicators depends on what we know, our attitudes, how good we are at communicating and how we have been brought up to communicate.

Whatever happens when we communicate is something that we have learnt to do, in certain ways, for certain reasons. As the quotation at the head of this chapter says, communication is not a matter of luck or chance. We are effective communicators because we have learnt to use communication to convey messages.

However, there are other ways of explaining what happens when we communicate.

Communication and meaning

Although we are going to talk about meaning in the next section, with reference to signs, the idea of meaning is important enough to comment on now.

Messages are really about meanings. We use the word 'message' as a convenience. It makes some kind of sense when for example one is talking about passing memos around an organization. But in fact communication is not really about passing around little 'packages' from one person to another through talk or pictures or whatever. It is rather more complicated than that.

Every piece of communication, whether it is a conversation or a photograph, means something to those involved in creating it or receiving it. What those involved think the communication means is, however, not cut and dried. Most pieces of communication mean more than one thing to most people (see 'Multiple messages', page 24). What is more, they may not mean the same thing to everyone. Even an invitation to a party 'starting at 8.00' won't mean the same thing to everyone (see figure 4). People will arrive at different times.

Some forms of communication tend to be more ambiguous in their meanings than others. So, one is more likely to argue about the meanings in a photograph than about what is meant by the write-up of a physics experiment.

When we 'take in' some example of communication, when we decode it, what we are really doing is to deconstruct it and reconstruct meanings in our mind (see figure 5). A lot of this book is really about the factors that affect how we construct those meanings. If someone yells at us 'Look out!', what do we do? We work out that we are being warned about something. We work out that we should use our eyes. But do we look behind us? Or look up? Do we duck? Do we yell back? What do we assume the warning is about? There may be factors in the situation that help narrow down the meaning of the message. But even when we have deconstructed the shouted words, still there are different

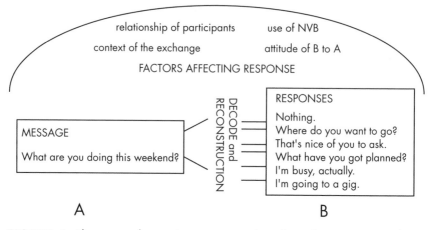

FIGURE 4 The response that we give to a message depends on what it means to us. There may be many possible responses, affected by a variety of factors

meanings that we may reconstruct in our heads. And that is important to remember: that the meanings are in our heads. Communication may involve physical objects or physical activity. But ultimately it is all in the mind.

3.3 Communication as signs

Communication is all about the giving and receiving of signs that have meanings attached to them.

This is one of the most convincing views of what happens when communication takes place, because it seems to apply to all examples in all situations.

So, the idea is that when you speak to someone, you are making signs at them. As long as they know what these signs mean, then they can decode them and the message will have been put across. The same could be said of any form of communication. A non-verbal sign might be a wink, meaning 'Keep quiet, it's a secret between us.'

A picture sign might be a low camera angle, meaning 'this person is important and dominating'. A musical sign might be a black mark between lines on the score which means 'play this note for a specific length of time'. And this page is covered with signs, called letters and words. We hope that they mean something to you.

Signs and meanings

But a sign can only be a sign for us if we assign meaning to it. And there are four problems here:

(a) To say that something is a sign doesn't tell you what its meaning is.
(b) The same sign can have different meanings in different places or at different times.
(c) One sign can have more than one meaning.
(d) The same sign can mean different things to different people.

The answer to the first problem is that **we learn to connect a sign with a meaning**. Mainly, we learn to do this through parents and friends, as part of growing up. We are also taught formally in school, college and university. And we should go on learning something about signs and their meanings for the rest of our lives.

If we want to learn the word signs of the spoken French language, then we go on a course where we are taught to make the signs, and are taught to attach meanings to the signs. This second point is important because, of course, being able to say a French word correctly doesn't tell one what it means. Signs are useless unless one knows the meaning – which is why archaeologists have spent years trying to decipher (decode) some ancient scripts.

The second problem must also be solved by **learning the 'rules' for the right place and the right time**. Don't tell an American that you want to wash up if you mean that you want to help with the dishes. An American will think that you want to wash yourself. And beware especially of non-verbal signs. You might, as a British person, raise your hand casually, palm outwards, in greeting to someone whom you pass by at work. But for a Greek, the same sign looks suspiciously like an insult! Even within our own culture, we know that putting an arm around someone's shoulders signals different things according to the situation that we are in (and who is involved).

The third problem is obviously connected with the last one. Indeed, the last example could also apply here. But place, time or person doesn't have to be involved in this case.

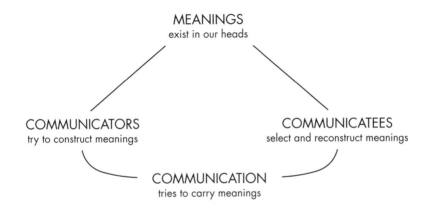

FIGURE 5 Communication and meaning: it's all in the mind

Take a written word sign such as 'bow'. As a sign on its own it could refer to the action of bending the body, and an object which projects arrows, and an object which is drawn across the strings of musical instruments. Knowing all the possible meanings of the sign doesn't help, even though it is a lot better than having no idea at all of what the word means.

From this example we learn that **we often understand the meaning of a sign from other signs around it**. A sentence (string of signs) such as 'She raised the bow and loosed off an arrow at the target' helps pin down the meaning of the word.

Or, to take the example of a party game such as charades, we know that the more dress and gesture signs the player gives us, the more likely we are to guess the character being portrayed.

So, if communication is about exchanging signs, or giving and receiving meanings, then the ability to use a wide range and number of signs is likely to aid communication.

It may also appear that in some cases we have more than one sign for the same meaning. The sets of words 'naked, nude, starkers' and 'slim, thin, slender' are examples. But in fact, because in the first case the words mean rather more than 'without clothes', one can say that they are not just different signs for the same thing. You work out exactly what they do mean.

But the point is that **even when people are speaking the same language in the same place at the same time, signs can still mean different things**. Take the word 'disgusting'. A dictionary might have us believe that it means something like loathsome or nauseating. But, for example, do parents really mean this when they express their disapproval of the state of their child's room by saying it is disgusting? They probably don't mean that the room actually repulses them. More likely they mean that they disapprove of its untidiness. And if we use a sentence such as 'It's a disgusting state of affairs when you can't rely on the buses to run on time' we aren't really talking about physical loathing. We mean that the situation is very annoying and unsatisfactory, so far as we are concerned.

So, we really do have to learn a wide variety of possible meanings for signs, and be careful about choosing the meaning that seems to best fit the communicator's intentions. The reverse is also true, of course: we must be careful about picking the signs we use, in order to be able to express what we really intend. It is not easy to say what we mean.

Codes

When we communicate through signs, we use codes.

A code is a system for using signs. This system is based on rules and conventions shared by those who use the code.

Morse code identifies itself literally. It is a code of long and short electrical signals (dots and dashes) that stand in place of other codes and signs – such as the alphabet and writing, or numbers.

Speech is a series of sound signs which forms a code that we know as spoken words. A photograph of a person represents two forms of communication and two codes. One is the non-verbal code composed of the various dress and body language signs which we see represented in the picture. The other is the pictorial code composed of signs such as defocused background or close-up on head and shoulders.

The forms and codes of communication are bound by certain 'rules' as to how they are used. These 'rules' are called conventions.

In some instances the conventions are quite strong. One has an organized system of signs. Here the best example is that of spoken or written language. We have all been taught the rules of spelling and grammar; and if we haven't, then we must have learnt them from others. The act of speaking involves knowing which sign goes where. And just as we share knowledge of signs, and more or less agree what they mean, so also we more or less agree on these conventions. Without the organizing power of these conventions, we wouldn't be able to communicate at all. Anyone who mispronounces or mis-spells a word badly, fails to communicate that word and so fails to communicate what they mean. And when someone mis-spells a word only slightly and is still understood, then it is still the organizing power of those conventions that has saved the day for them and got the meaning across. Because we know how words should be spelt, we can work out what a mis-spelt word is probably intended to represent.

Codes are sets of signs. Conventions are rules for using these signs (see figure 6).

It is possible to divide a code into *primary and secondary codes*. A secondary code is a particular form of the primary main code. The primary codes represent the main set of signs for a given form: verbal, non-verbal, pictorial, and so on.

Secondary codes are composed of special sets of signs that work within the primary code. Secondary codes are often related to work (computer talk), or social/subcultural groups (bikers). These secondary codes may also have conventions governing their use. We slip into them on many occasions because we think they are appropriate (people baby-talking to young children). Our use of codes is not always appropriate to the occasion or to those present. You might consider the arguments for and against using babytalk with children as an example.

3.4 Communication as behaviour

This view suggests that the act of communication is a kind of behaviour. It also suggests that we communicate with others in order to modify their behaviour.

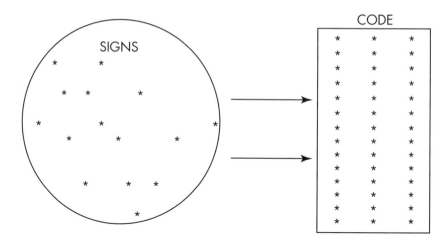

FIGURE 6   Signs form a code when organized by conventions

The first proposition suggests that communication is as much a kind of behaviour as eating, or banging a nail in a piece of wood. Again, this raises the question of what we know how to do when we are born and what we learn to do afterwards. There are those who think that we learn to do everything after we are born. Others would say that, in the case of speech, for example, we are born with a certain *competence* to make speech. Then they would say we develop *performance*, or the skills of speaking.

Either way, there certainly is a lot of learning involved. And it is true that just as we may learn to use a knife and fork or chopsticks to eat with, so we learn to use words in certain ways to put over what we mean, whichever language we may be talking about. And it may be said, just as we learn to behave in different ways according to our upbringing, so **we learn to communicate in different ways according to our upbringing**. So, the idea that communication is a kind of behaviour helps us look at why we communicate as we do. If we aren't much good at drawing, it could be said that this is because we haven't been taught this particular form of behaviour. Or even if we aren't much good at apologizing to people, this is because we haven't learnt much about how to do this.

The second proposition – about modifying the behaviour of others – is easy to understand if, once more, one looks at the example of advertising. Generally speaking, an advertisement wants to change our attitudes so that we then change our behaviour. For example, it might want us to feel favourably disposed towards a certain company's life insurance policy, so that we then go and take out a policy with that company. However, the proposition can be applied to a wider range of examples. For instance, it could be said that a baby cries in a certain way because it has found out that this will cause its mother to give it food. It has changed the mother's behaviour.

The idea that communication changes behaviour doesn't have to be confined to simple examples, where something is seen to happen immediately. It could be said that everything we learn, every piece of information that we acquire, changes our behaviour to some extent in the end. Every piece of communication which we experience may affect our attitudes and beliefs in some small way.

We cannot help but change others and be changed by others when we communicate. So, for example, a person might choose a career in social work because he or she had read a publicity booklet intended to persuade readers that this is a good and worthwhile occupation. On the other hand, someone might choose this career simply because of the many things heard, read or watched about it on television. No one was intending to change this person's attitudes and behaviour. But it happened because of an accumulation of messages.

This idea of communication as something that acts as a stimulus and that evokes a response relates to behaviourist psychology. This may be briefly described as *S–R (stimulus–response) theory*.

People like B.F. Skinner were convinced that all creatures' lives were defined by the responses that they gave to various kinds of stimulus, and that these responses could be modified by changing the stimulus. At its most simplistic, the approach proposed that anyone could be made to do anything provided you could find the right stimulus. Primary stimuli would be forms of pain or pleasure.

Propagandists might like to believe this! If one can only find the right kind of communication, then people can be persuaded to do and to believe anything. Fortunately, it is not that simple. People make sense of stimuli (such as words or pictures) in different ways for different reasons (see figure 7). Communicating is not like pressing buttons.

Nevertheless, when one is looking at communication between people, it can be quite illuminating to hang on to some idea of response, to look at why people make the responses that they do. For example, in social interaction, we now know that there is a lot of cueing of responses – in taking turns to talk, or in getting to like someone. So, one should not ignore S–R theory either.

3.5 Models of communication

Another way of describing the communication process is to use a model.

A model is a simplified description of a communication process, usually set out in graphic form as a diagram. It can show the elements of a communication process and the relationships between those elements.

A model is a medium which is mainly graphic. The parts of the process are laid out, for example to describe what comes first, second, and so on. And the parts are labelled using communication terms. Models are useful because

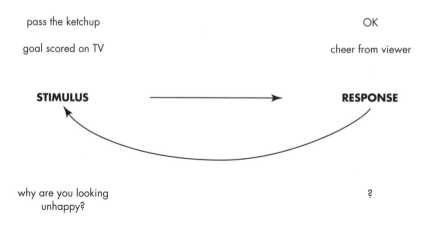

FIGURE 7   A stimulus–response model for communication. But is it that simple?

they lay out the process, or a view of what the process is like, in a simple, visual way.

Because there are different terms and different views of what makes up the communication process, so there are different models.

And one can change the terms of a communication model without changing the layout. For example, we can talk in general terms about the receiver of a message, whatever the situation. But in fact, if we were referring to receivers of music at a concert or receivers of a radio programme, then it is more appropriate to use the term 'audience'. And this is what models for mass communication tend to do. They do this because the term 'audience' draws attention to the fact that there is often more than one receiver for a piece of mass communication, and to the fact that such receivers are not engaged in the communication process in the same way as people talking face to face.

Models and the terms used in models may be changed to emphasize particular points about a situation – for example, the difference between making a speech and reading a book.

There are a variety of models used in this and other books. You will find some models worked out by other people useful. But remember that communication studies is about doing. Be prepared to make up your own models. Models can be more or less complicated, according to the number of terms used, and the ingenuity of the layout.

We will start with the simplest style of model.

Linear models

Linear models lay out parts of the process in a line, as if communication is all about sending messages from A to B. In fact, communication is rarely that simple, but it is a good enough way to begin. This model, shown

FIGURE 8 Basic linear model of communication

in figure 8, with a simple situation indicated below it, suggests a few terms and ideas.

Source and *destination* make the point that communication always comes from someone and goes to someone. But it matters as to who exactly the source and destination are. For example, one would want to take into account whether person B is male or female.

The idea of *codes* has been described on pages 28–9. Communication has to be expressed through some form or medium, and these all have their own codes. For example, the message in figure 8 could have been encoded through a non-verbal sign, such as touching. This is a different code from that of speech. In any case, thoughts or feelings have to be expressed in some form to be 'decoded' and understood by someone else.

And then there is the term *message* – what is said, or expressed one way or another. An American writer on communication, D.K. Berlo, has broken this term 'message' down into three parts: content, code and treatment. In the example given above, the content is 'I like you', the code is that of speech and the treatment depends on how it is said – warmly, lovingly, factually, and so on.

Exchange models

Exchange models indicate that communication is at least a two-way process.

In the case of a group of people, it may seem to be more than two-way. In the case of someone watching television, it may be difficult to see how there is a response to the messages coming from the television set. This will be discussed in the last chapter of the book. But for situations to be discussed in chapter 2, this kind of model, shown in figure 9, is very useful. This model makes the point that messages go both ways in a conversation. It also says that everyone is a decoder and an encoder. That is to say, we have to find some way of putting together and expressing what we have to say, as well as some way of taking in what the other person says.

But then, we also have to make sense of what is said. This is where the term *interpreter* comes in. We are all interpreters of messages, all day and every day. How we interpret messages is another matter, and will be discussed later. But we will find that there are reasons why people may interpret the same message in different ways. Here is a fundamental reason for studying communication. If we all got our messages across exactly as we intended, there would be fewer problems between people. But this doesn't happen. When we

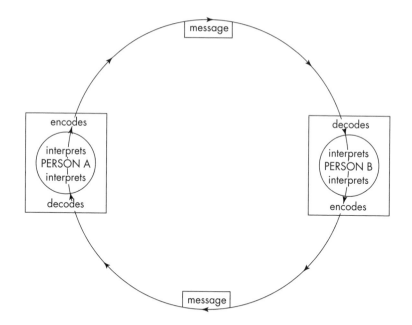

FIGURE 9   An exchange model of communication

examine the idea of perception, we will see that because we all have different kinds of experience, and make different kinds of assumption, so we interpret messages in different ways.

Sometimes the difference isn't great. Sometimes it is, and it matters.

For example, looking back to the situation of the first model, if the person who is the source of the message (person A) is female and the person who is the destination (person B) is male, and if person B interprets the message as loving when it was meant to be just friendly, then the two people concerned have got problems. We will return to examples of problems throughout this book.

Contextualized models

Contextualized models add the dimension of situation or surroundings.

This matters more or less to how communication takes place according to the particular example. But **context always affects the act of communication**.

For example, we would communicate differently in the situation of a formal dinner party with our boss, as compared with eating fish and chips in the kitchen with friends. This example shows that context has both physical and social aspects.

Figure 10 is a model that includes context. One other term is important: *feedback*. It reminds us that communication is often two-way: that there are

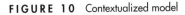

CONTEXT OR ENVIRONMENT

FIGURE 10 Contextualized model

responses to messages sent. And that we adjust the way that we carry on a conversation, for example, according to the feedback that we get from the other person. The channel that conveys feedback does not have to be speech but may be non-verbal – for example, a bored expression or a movement of the feet in readiness to leave.

You will also notice that we have changed the words 'source' and 'destination' in figure 8 to 'sender' and 'receiver'. You may come across these terms in other books. Try to decide for yourself which words are most useful.

Conclusion

We have argued that the act of communication is one in which meanings are exchanged through signs. We have made a number of suggestions about what happens when we communicate. And explaining what happens when we communicate helps explain what communication is.

Generally, in this chapter we have given ways of:

- explaining why we communicate;
- describing how we communicate.

Now you can check what we have said by looking at the summary that follows. After that, we shall suggest some activities that will bring out some of the points we have made, and that will encourage you to check our ideas and explanations as to what communication is.

Do we know what we are doing when we communicate?

Hint: when are you conscious or unconscious of the effect of what you are saying?

Review

This review is intended to help you check on the main points of this first chapter, 'What is communication?'

First we said that communication is something that we experience in various ways. So then we asked ourselves:

1   HOW DO WE EXPERIENCE COMMUNICATION?

1.1   Through various means of communication which you should be able to define and give examples of, from the list that follows:

- forms;
- medium;
- the media;
- other kinds.

1.2   As a connection between people, joining friend with friend, or newspaper reporter with newspaper reader.

1.3   As an activity, because it is something that we do. We make communication in order to make things happen in our lives.

1.4   As something that we have learnt to do, like other skills and abilities which we have.

1.5   Within four main categories of communication activity. Again, you should be able to define and give examples of these from the list that follows:

- intrapersonal communication;
- interpersonal communication;
- group communication;
- mass communication.

1.6   As something we use, e.g. to inform, persuade and entertain.

1.7   As a means of expressing our culture and our beliefs.

Second, we said that there has to be a reason for communicating to take place. So then we asked the question:

2 WHY DO WE COMMUNICATE?

2.1 To satisfy needs that we have within us;

to survive, physically and as social beings;
to feel secure and valued by others;
to be involved with others, in relationships;
to conduct the everyday business of our lives;
to give and receive information;
to play with ideas and stories;
to express ourselves;
to make sense of the world.

2.2 Maslow sees needs as ranging from the simple to the complex.

2.3 We may ask ourselves whether communication comes from learning (nurture) or from genetic inheritance (nature).

3 WHAT HAPPENS WHEN WE COMMUNICATE?

3.1 We are involved in a process in which many things are happening at the same time. The process can be broken down into various parts, according to a given situation, which can be described through special terms. This process is all about making sense of the world, making meanings in our heads.

3.2 We exchange messages, which may be about facts, opinions or beliefs. This means that we share information, feelings and ideas with others. But we have to take account of the fact that messages are rarely neutral, that messages may be overt or covert and that messages are usually multiple (more than one is exchanged at a time). The term 'message' can be divided into three parts: content, code and treatment.

3.3 We are giving and receiving signs and their meanings, but signs can have more than one meaning: they mean different things to different people; they change their meaning according to time and place; and meanings only belong to a sign because we agree that they do. Together the signs in a form of communication make up codes. These codes depend on conventions that govern how they are used, which we learn and which help the communication to make sense.

3.4 We are involved in a kind of behaviour that may well be a way of trying to change the behaviour of others. Some people see behaviour as a process of stimulus leading to response, and so on.

3.5 We can see this process very clearly through the use of models. These fall into various types. You should be able to define and give examples of the following types:

- linear;
- exchange;
- contextualized.

Debates

How do we draw a line between communication that is intentional and communication that is not?

- One problem is knowing or finding out what was in the mind of the sender (purpose).
- Another problem is that communication may take place even without the intention or knowledge of the sender (non-verbal leakage).
- Another problem is that the effect of the communication may not match its intention (perception).
- Another problem is that communication will have some effect, whatever it was or was not intended to do by the sender (one cannot help communicating).

WHAT DO YOU THINK?

Is it true that most communication is designed to change the behaviour of others in some way?

- Points about intentionality also apply here.
- One issue is about whether those communicating need to be in the same place at the same time as others in order to affect the behaviour of those others (context).
- Another issue is about one's general approach to communication: a behaviourist psychologist would probably agree with the point of the question (S–R theory).
- Another issue has to do with what you would define as behaviour (forms of communication).

WHAT DO YOU THINK?

How far is communication defined by one's culture or subculture?

- One point of view suggested by the question is that the way we talk depends on the way we are brought up.
- Another view would be that the way we talk (communicate) actually defines the culture we belong to.
- Another view would be that the real point is not about how we communicate but about how we think.

WHAT DO YOU THINK?

Do we learn to communicate or are we born with some ability to do this anyway?

- This question is all about what is known as the nature–nurture debate – what are we born with (genetic inheritance) and what are we nurtured into (socialization)?
- One problem is that babies can't talk, so it is hard to work out what they 'know' or don't know.
- Another problem is in deciding when communication is intentional or not.
- Another problem is in trying to separate out environmental influences from what we may be able to do naturally.

WHAT DO YOU THINK?

Assignments

Assignment 1

Draw a diagram using any of the communication models in this chapter – or adapt one for yourself – to describe the process of communication through contrasting examples such as a photograph from a family album, a radio programme, a telephone conversation, a job application form.

You should cover factors such as source, audience, purpose, context, feedback.

Assignment 2

Write an explanation of how the ideas of sign, meaning and conventions relate to the fact that the words 'great' and 'grate' sound the same; and the fact that the word 'spirit' can refer to different things.

Using magazines, make a collage of photographs to bend or break the conventions for showing women in perfume advertisements, and for showing politicians in news articles.

Assignment 3: Cartoon – serious or funny?

Refer to the cartoon at the beginning of this chapter as source material.

(a) Do you think this cartoon is funny? Give a few reasons.
(b) What does the cartoon seem to be saying about the relationship between this man and woman?
(c) What does this cartoon seem to be saying about the process of communication here?
(d) Write a short dialogue for these two people to say after this incident.

Suggested reading

Beck, A., Bennett, P. and Wall, P., *Communication Studies: the essential resource*, London: Routledge, 2004 Part 1, 'Texts and meanings in communication', contains a useful range of extracts that explore the nature of communication, including models and meanings.

Ellis, R. and McClintock, A., *If You Take My Meaning* [2nd ed.], London: Hodder Arnold, 1994.

Fiske, J., *Introduction to Communication Studies* [2nd ed.], London: Methuen, 1990. See the introduction and chapters 1–4 (but be warned that some of this book is written for an advanced level).

Myers, G.E. and Myers, M.T., *The Dynamics of Human Communication* [6th ed.], New York: McGraw-Hill, 1992. See chapters 1, 2 and 5.

See also the resources list at the end of this book.

Chapter 2

Interpersonal communication

Think of someone whom you like talking to. What do they do to make the conversation enjoyable? They probably make you feel that they really are listening and interested in what you are saying. They do this by giving you encouragement, perhaps smiling, nodding, etc. Contrast this picture with someone whom you dislike talking to. What do they do to make it unpleasant? Perhaps they seem to ignore you (the boss who shuffles his papers while insisting that he is listening), or perhaps they try to dominate proceedings.

(Peter Hartley, *Interpersonal Communication*, 2nd edition, 1999)

This chapter provides information about communication between individual people. It includes accounts of how speech and non-verbal communication enable us to relate to one another. There is also comment on how we present ourselves to others, how we perceive other people, and on barriers to communication.

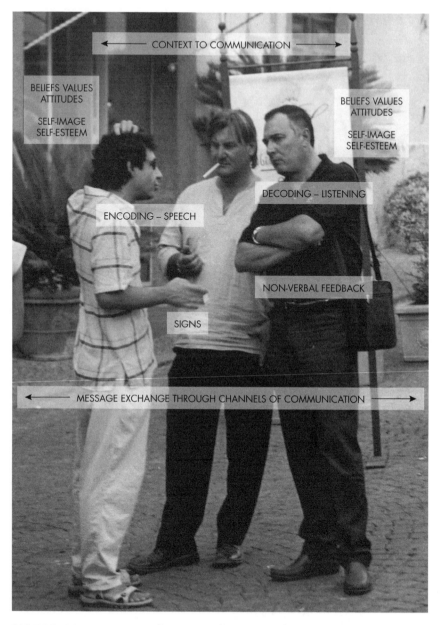

FIGURE 11 Communication between people is active and continuous, and works at a non-verbal level as much as through speech

1 Means of contact

HAZEL'S STORY

The Spanish beach was crowded and as hot as a warm bath. Hazel tipped her straw hat back a little. The cries of children sounded like complaining seagulls. Only there weren't any seagulls around this beach. Hazel shifted position on her beach towel and opened one eye. There wasn't even the noise of the cicadas, which could usually be heard scraping away. It was too hot and too near the town for them. Hazel opened the other eye, wide. The children were gone.

She sat up abruptly. Ten minutes ago Laura and Tim had been playing at the water's edge, in a straight line with her big toe. Hazel scanned along the waterline anxiously. Surely they must be all right. After all, Laura was 6 years old and Tim was 8. And two kids can't go far in ten minutes or less. She looked around the encampments filling the beach. A dark-haired, handsome youth grinned at her, encouragingly. Hazel scowled at him. Another time, Don Juan, she thought. Panic began to set in when she stood up and still saw no familiar blond heads. Pauline and Roger will go mad, she thought. I'll murder those kids. Aunty Hazel is not going to be popular.

Within twenty-five minutes she was at the local police station and wishing that she had learnt some Spanish before they came on this holiday. Luckily, someone had helped her on the way, when she was trying to find the word for 'police'. That, and some determined gestures, had got her to the right place. But the kids were still missing. And she felt silly, clutching a striped beach bag and with only a beach robe over her bikini.

The Spanish policeman who was trying to help her was courteous and charming, but he didn't speak any English. Hazel tried a few simple words and then gave up, as they smiled at one another uncomprehendingly. There was plenty of goodwill on both sides, but that was all at the moment. Hazel wished that her brother-in-law was there. He spoke a little Spanish. Even the word for 'child' would be a help. Something had to be done. She was beginning to believe that something terrible could have happened to the children. Perhaps she should just go back to the beach and wait.

Hazel looked the policeman in the eye and took a deep breath. She made a flat-handed gesture, with her palm, about the height of Laura's head from the floor. Then she shrugged her shoulders and tried to look anxious. The policeman looked on with interest and then pointed suddenly to a picture on the wall. It was a photograph of a child.

ABOUT HAZEL'S STORY

This tells us about the different ways of making contact with other people. We tend to take things like words and gestures for granted – until they don't work the way we want them to. These verbal and non-verbal forms of communication are in fact the channels through which we pass messages to others. Most of us have forgotten the experience of early years, when we were learning the signs that belong to these forms, and what they mean. It is only when we are stuck in a situation like Hazel's that we may rediscover what it was like to be a young child, cut off from others, without means of contact. But even a young child who cannot speak still has some ways of getting through to others. Hazel got through to the policeman when she smiled at him, and when she used her body and her hands to express what she meant. For interpersonal communication to happen, there must be some means of contact with the other person. There are two principal means of contact: non-verbal communication and speech.

1.1 Non-verbal communication (NVC)

We make and receive non-verbal signs whenever we are with others.

These signs are not words, but they are often used with words. They affect the meaning of what we say. They are produced by various uses of our bodies, by the way we dress ourselves and by the ways in which we can utter the words that make up speech. They say a lot about our feelings and our attitudes towards others. And they can be used apart from words. We become well aware of this when a policeman raises his hand to stop our car at a junction, or if an angry driver waves his fist at us.

These non-verbal signs can be placed under three main headings: (a) body language; (b) paralanguage; (c) dress.

(a) Body language

Body language tells us a lot about people's feelings, attitudes and intentions.

Actors understand this very well when they put on non-verbal signs in order to convince the audience of the part that they are playing. Some books try to convince their readers that the key to success with the opposite sex lies in the use of non-verbal signs. This is only partially true. People may like us if we are pleasant and friendly towards them; and a lot of this friendliness is shown through body language. But it is not the only thing that matters. There are a great many signs that we give off when we are talking to someone. It is the meaning of all of these together that counts. And meaning varies according to the situation and who is involved. That said, it is also true that we are capable of paying more attention than we do to what other people are saying to us through their body language. And we are capable of controlling our body signs more carefully than we do, so that, for example, we get on with people better. In other words, our communication skills are learnt, and we can learn more – in which case it is useful to have some idea of what we are doing.

Body language includes five main elements, as follows:

Gesture: the way we use our arms and hands.

It is common to see people wave across a crowded room to attract attention, and then beckon someone to them. We use gesture to express things like the height and width of objects we are describing. But there are more subtle signs, such as the steepling of fingers to express confidence. And for some people, gestures are part of their job – the tick-tack men at a racecourse, signalling bets and results. There are some complete languages of gesture – codes: the sign language used by deaf people, for example.

Expression: the way that we signal with our faces.

Expression usually says a lot about mood and emotion. The eyes and the mouth dominate expression signs. These are the signs that people look for first when they are trying to weigh up someone. We are capable of distinguishing subtle variations in smile or look. If someone gazes at you a lot, then it means they are interested in you. If two people gaze at one another a lot, then it means that they have a positive and trusting relationship. Or again, we are able to distinguish between the raised eyebrow of surprise, of fear or of acknowledgement when we meet a friend. In short, we do a lot of looking during the process of encoding and decoding body signs.

Body posture: the way that we hold our bodies.

A relaxed posture expresses confidence in the person whom we are talking to. On the other hand, at an interview you would be well advised to sit up straight and look interested! To take another example, when one talks about a confrontation, it means just that: bodies positioned front to front. Together with closeness and direct gaze, this signals mutual aggression. So, it isn't surprising to find that, in the West at least, people normally stand with their bodies slightly averted from one another when having a conversation. This is considered polite. It signals that your intentions are friendly or neutral.

Body space and body proximity: how near to others we stand or sit.

First, everyone needs a certain space around them, to feel comfortable. Factors such as the age or the sex of people involved in an exchange can make a difference to this. But generally, adults won't let another person get within arm's reach unless they know them pretty well. Indeed, one can guess the degree of people's friendship from the way that they treat each other's body space. It may be possible to get on good and friendly terms with someone by 'dipping' into their body space. But it is advisable to think hard about the person and the situation, because doing so may upset them instead. This is when one starts talking about body proximity. People often rate their status according to proximity. So, while it may be all right to get close to friends and loved ones, the boss may take a dim view of what could be seen as 'familiarity'. The meaning of body proximity, like that of other non-verbal signs, varies from culture to culture.

Touch: is about who we touch, when, where and how.

Touching tells us a lot about relationships, status and degrees of friend-liness. Women tend to do more touching with women, just as young children do more touching than adults. But obviously there are all kinds of special situations with special rules, such as those concerning lovers. It is also notorious that the British are one of the least 'touching' nations in the world, which can provide serious problems in Britons' relationships with those from other cultures. There is some evidence that more touching – within the broad social rules – would help us get on better with others, including those from our own culture. Usually, when we are touched (however briefly) by the other person during an interaction, we feel more friendly towards them. Salespeople have been known to exploit this reaction.

(b) Paralanguage

Paralanguage tells us a lot about how to interpret the meanings of words during a conversation. It describes the non-verbal signs that accompany speech.

There are those signs that are separate from the words themselves. They are often about immediate reactions and emotions. We may whistle or gasp in surprise. People making public speeches are fond of 'er' and 'um', which is really a sign for 'Hold on, I'm thinking up the next bit.' We may scream with fright or groan with pain.

There are those signs that are represented through ways in which the words themselves are pronounced. They are signs such as pitch, stress and volume. We don't speak like robots, in a flat and even way. So, when the voice rises at the end of a sentence, for example, it may tell us that this is a question. Try delivering this set of words as a statement and as a question and you will see what we mean: 'You'll meet me at eight o'clock tonight.' Another example of this kind of paralanguage is to be seen in the fact that we often know that a person is angry when they begin speaking loudly. And again, it would be impossible for people to be sarcastic or speak ironically without the aid of these special signs.

Paralanguage can suggest things about a person's state of mind or their emotions. When we say that a person is calm or excitable or nervous, then it is the way that they deliver their words which can tell us this. So, if we want to present ourselves well at an interview, we could try to use the calm and even tones of someone who is confident and who is thinking about what they are saying. At the same time, we would try not to speak in a flat, monotonous manner, because that would suggest that we are boring or bored.

(c) Dvess

The third kind of non-verbal communication that we use is to do with dress, hair, jewellery and make-up.

This one says a lot about personality, role, job and status. For example, characters in television comedy and advertisements are given certain kinds of dress to make them easily identified. An extrovert type may be given wild and colourful hair, with bright clothes. Housewives are put in aprons. Businessmen wear dark jackets and pin-stripe trousers. And important people are seen in a Rolls-Royce, wearing expensive clothes.

You could try making your own analysis of the dress of a policewoman, a priest, a nurse and a teacher.

Dress also signals people's identity. When we group people by class or job (soldier) or subculture (goths), often it is clothes which first identify them with the group.

As well as dress and personal adornment of various kinds, we use objects and possessions to reflect or express ourselves. Obviously, your desire to create a particular personal statement through the clothes you wear, or the bike or the car you own, or the furniture with which you surround yourself, may be limited by the amount of money you possess. But other people are likely to interpret all of these as reflections of you. All of us have a tendency to read meanings into objects.

Comment

NVC has a number of characteristics and functions. Some functions occur when it is used with language. For example, it may reinforce something that is being said, as when a speaker chops one hand down upon the other in an emphatic gesture. Or it may elaborate on what is said, when, for example, a speaker uses a level hand, palm down, to add to a description of the height of a child. Sometimes a non-verbal sign can have the function of modifying what is said. For example, it is possible to smile at someone at the same time as 'telling them off'. The smile takes the edge off the spoken disapproval.

NVC is a primary code of communication, as much as written language. It also has its share of secondary codes. For example, the floor manager of a television production has a special set of signs by which he or she communicates with programme presenters.

NVC is also controlled by conventions (rules) in the way it is used. These conventions are not as exact as the rules of grammar that control our use of language. But they do make it probable that, for example, we will look at someone just before we smile, just before we shake hands with them.

Ritual kinds of non-verbal behaviour are also common. Chanting and flag-waving fans at the football match every Saturday show this. Some rituals are well known and public, such as those in a church service. But others may be less obvious, if no less a matter of habit. See if you can think of any examples of ritual NVC that you know of, at home, at school, at work.

Non-verbal cues may be involuntary or intentional. Signs such as blushing are considered to be reflexes which we can't control. It is in fact quite difficult to control many non-verbal signs. But it can be done to an extent; politicians practise such control for their public appearances. It is an interesting question as to whether NVC is intentional or not. We learn to use the signs subconsciously in most cases, yet they are not produced by accident, and so it would seem that there is some intention there to communicate. Perhaps we should all try to be more conscious of what our intentions are.

NVC is specific to nations or cultures. A culture or subculture is a collection of people who have strong beliefs and values in common. They may have a certain religion, recognizable arts of their own, what we would call a way of life of their own. Cultures can often cut across national boundaries, as is the case with Jewish people. But also, cultures can exist within nations, as is the case with West Indian communities in Britain.

Television and travel have helped carry non-verbal signs (and words) across national boundaries in the world today, so that people are tempted to think that gestures and expressions mean the same everywhere. This is not so. One may see the same signs in other places, but they don't necessarily mean the same thing as they do in Britain.

Even though a very few signs are used quite widely, such as the lifted eyebrow flash to express surprise, many other signs do not travel well. Men from Middle Eastern cultures like to stand close and face the person whom they are talking to. Men from Western cultures don't like this directness and closeness, so they are inclined to dance away from an Arabic speaker, who of course quicksteps after them in order to show what he considers to be polite signs of conversation.

Precisely because this is an age of international travel, we should think about our NVC as much as our words when on holiday or business abroad.

So, NVC is a complex combination of signs through which we can communicate even when we aren't talking. These signs give rise to the proposition that we cannot help communicating, whether we like it or not. So, whatever clothes you put on, other people will be noting these, and to some extent trying to read something into them.

NVC relates to our perception of others (section 3 of this chapter). A significant part of what we perceive in others is in their non-verbal signs.

NVC helps build and maintain relationships. Because non-verbal signs say a lot about our attitudes towards one another, they influence the nature of our relationships. Positive relationships depend on positive attitudes. These attitudes can only be understood through appropriate uses of NVC.

NVC relates to the idea of feedback (section 2.7 of this chapter). We give off and make sense of these signs very rapidly indeed, even at the same time as we are talking or listening. So, it is hard to 'notice' everything that is going on. This is where it is useful to look at videotape recordings of people in conversation and slow them down so that one can see just how the people involved are signalling to one another.

For example, in an interview one could look at several units of interaction. In the first place there is the 'handshake' procedure, when the two people greet one another. Then there is the period of initial assessment, where usually insignificant questions are asked, but the two people are weighing each other up in terms of personality and attitude. And then there is a period of evaluation, where as well as handling a question-and-answer session on a verbal level, the two people are checking and confirming (or not) their first impressions of each other on a non-verbal level. And there is plenty of evidence that non-verbal impressions can strongly influence the outcome of an interview.

We have used the term 'non-verbal communication' in this context, which suggests an intention, conscious or not, to convey some message to other people through non-verbal signs. **It is useful to separate non-verbal communication from non-verbal behaviour (NVB); the latter phrase notes that we may act in various ways without any intention of communicating to other people. However, all human behaviour is likely to have meanings assigned to it by other people.** As many writers on communication comment, 'One cannot not communicate.' Whatever one does or does not do may be interpreted by other people as meaningful actions.

1.2 Speech

We have already seen that there is more to conversation than the acts of delivering and hearing words. The exact meaning of what we say depends on our use of paralanguage in particular. And of course other non-verbal signs accompany the words. A fist in the palm of the hand may help emphasize the importance of what we are saying. On the other hand, a mocking smile may accompany an apparently pleasant remark: it could contradict what we said, and point to an opposite, true meaning.

Spoken words are sound signs. We have a tendency to regard words as somehow natural and true, as if they are an absolute fact of life. In our last story, Hazel found out that this certainly isn't true, when she realized that she couldn't make the right sounds to communicate with the policeman. Actually, words themselves are made up of small units of sound called phonemes. We combine these to make a spoken word, and that word is only a sign. The fact that the signs mean something to us is the result of a long process of learning. The word 'dog' could just as well be the word 'bart'. If everyone thought of the same animal when the sound 'bart' was uttered, then it would do just as well as 'dog'.

And, as with other cases that we have looked at, we often need more than one of these sound signs to work out what they actually mean. For example, for most people the spoken words 'there' and 'their' and 'they're' all sound pretty much the same. Try saying them. It is only when they are uttered in the context of a sentence that we can be sure of which one is meant.

Speech is a code of signs, ruled by conventions. This follows what we have previously said. Many other forms of communication, such as NVC and pictorial images (film and photographs), consist of codes. The rules by which these codes are used are called conventions.

We expect words to appear in a certain order (called syntax) and to be combined in a certain way to produce 'proper' English (called grammar). What we call the English language is a primary code of communication. We learn its signs and conventions at an early age because it satisfies a lot of our basic human needs to be able to speak. We will also learn some of its secondary codes and their conventions because they also have special uses. For example, air traffic controllers and airline pilots have their own code within the main code of English, which uses special words in special ways. People who haven't learnt their code can't understand them.

Utterance is the formal term used to describe a collection of words that express an idea. This could be a phrase rather than a sentence. But it will put across meaning because it does use conventions. So, 'terrible weather yesterday' is an utterance, even though it is not a sentence with a verb. It also illustrates how the way that we talk, the way that we assume others understand us, does depend on a variety of factors such as shared experience.

Dialect is also an example of a code. It represents regional differences from 'standard' English. These differences are to do with vocabulary, or the collection of words that one uses, as well as to do with the ways in which those words are used. A common example is the shifting of pronouns, where a dialect speaker might say 'I' instead of 'me'. There are many examples of dialect words in use. In the west of England, where we are writing this book, people often talk about 'daps', where others might talk about gymshoes, or even plimsolls. Dialect is not improper English. It is another version of English. In a given region it may be the main spoken language code in use. Many people use more than one code anyway: standard and dialect. The reason that it is useful to be able to use 'standard' English is that it does provide a good chance that one will be clearly understood by English speakers wherever one may be.

Accent should not be confused with dialect. Certain accents may go with certain regional codes, but accent is part of the sign system of paralanguage. Everyone has an accent. It says a lot about our beliefs and values, especially in relation to class, that many people are brought up to think that there is a middle class which has no accent and that this is 'normal' and 'proper'. This is purely a matter of opinion. English people who have not been brought up to distinguish the relevant signs have no idea what a proper Scottish accent should be. The idea of 'proper' is just a meaning which we have chosen to associate with certain signs.

Received pronunciation (RP) is a phrase used to describe one accent which is associated with the 'correct' pronunciation of words. From one point of view it is not a bad thing if there is some notion of standard, if it means that people can speak English in such a way that they can understand one another easily. On the other hand, the phrase has strong cultural meanings that are not so desirable. RP is too often assumed to be good and right, and any deviation from it assumed to be wrong – which is nonsense. RP is associated with status, acceptance and even power within our culture. It becomes a sign for these attributes. This situation is undesirable, but has its equivalent in many languages and cultures (compare, for example, Parisians' attitudes towards southern French accents).

Register follows on from our last point. We have the ability to choose our speech from two kinds of broad code, labelled upper and lower register. The distinction is usually thought of in terms of the difference between ordinary English and 'posh' English. In fact, once more this is a rather snobbish way of looking at it. Upper register is simply a rather more careful kind of English with a wide vocabulary and formal syntax, which we use when we want to be careful about what we say – for example, if we are giving evidence in court. Self-conscious use of upper-register sounds strained and silly: for example, the policeman in the same court who is 'proceeding in a northerly direction', instead of walking down the road to where it meets the High Street. The point is that we need this careful upper register when we have to explain things accurately or argue things through logically. That is all. It is no good saying 'Put a bit of the yellow liquid in the brown stuff' when trying to explain something to a trainee in the laboratories of a chemical company. The result could be a bang!

Speech uses idiom and colloquialisms. It isn't necessary to have an English language lesson to be able to analyse and use spoken communication more effectively. But it is useful to have labels for some of the more common ways of handling language. Colloquialisms are the characteristics of everyday, casual speech. They appear in lower-register use. Simple examples are 'won't' and 'can't' for 'will not' and 'cannot'.

'Idiom' refers to some of the slangy and non-literal ways in which we use everyday speech: the sort of things that make it hard for people from other countries to learn English. We know what we mean when we tell someone to 'Belt up!', but it is an odd thing to say if you think about it from the point of view of, say, a German.

Speech is part of culture. That is to say, we develop the kind of spoken language that expresses the things our culture believes in, its ideas, even just the objects with which it is familiar. This is why translating from one language to another is so hard. The French, for example, don't have exactly the same set of ideas and objects as we do, with merely a different code of sound signs. They talk about *ennui*; we translate it as 'boredom'. But this isn't exactly what it means to them. It also says something about tiredness of the spirit. More obviously, it is hardly surprising to find that Eskimos have many different words for different kinds of snow. They need them in a land where their lifestyle and their very survival depend on different kinds of snow.

If the study of communication is a study of how we produce meanings from signs, then we should be aware that culture affects this process, and that spoken language helps define the culture. What people mean when they say something depends partly on their background, and their culture is very much part of this background. Because there are cultural variations within what we broadly call English culture, we can come up against problems even in one country. For a start, there is the question of England's so-called ethnic minorities. Someone whose background is Pakistani and who is being interviewed for a job may feel it necessary to say a lot about their qualifications. Their use of English might be 'good', but their intention and meaning would be subtly different from that of the average English person. In their subculture, it is a matter of status and sound argument at an interview to stress good qualifications. The interviewer may see this as slightly irrelevant and a little boastful. In this example, the cultural factor does matter. Also, different people from different backgrounds in different parts of one country may represent cultural variations. They may use language slightly differently, or mean different things by it. People often talk about the differences between the north and south of England. What are these differences? Are they to be seen in the use of spoken language?

Spoken language is very good at dealing with ideas, opinions and arguments – what we call abstracts; things to do with the world of the mind, as opposed to a physical and material world. Speech is quick, immediate, flexible, a form of communication that everyone has some ability to use and which doesn't require assistance from technology – not even a pen! Our relationships depend on speech because we have made it a tool for describing and discussing feelings. Our sciences depend on speech because we have made it a tool for explanation and reasoning. Words allow us to suggest things that might happen, but haven't, and to discuss things that have happened but aren't happening any more. All aspects of our working and social lives depend on being able to use words. But best of all, they allow us to reason and to deal with feelings.

Speech contributes to our social identities. How we talk gives us and others a sense of who we are. This is most obvious when we speak in some kind of role. So, the captain of a team is expected to be loud, firm and directive if they say anything while a game is in progress. In this way, speech is an expression of how we see ourselves at a given time. This ties in with what we say about self-presentation. So, apart from particular roles and specific situations, we may also see ourselves, for example, as a caring person – in which case, our paralanguage will support this self-image, and what we talk to people about will also express this sense of caring.

Speech gives social recognition. By this we mean that we use words and talk to acknowledge who it is we are talking to. Sometimes this is obvious in forms of address, such as calling someone 'sir', or 'Lady Brown'. But it is also common, though less obvious, in other ways. For example, one form of greeting may be 'How's it going?' You may or may not really want an answer to this. But uttering the phrase gives recognition to the other person. Similarly, it is important to talk 'properly' to children, perhaps about something they are doing, because this talk recognizes them as human beings with valid interests. Such recognition usually brings an equivalent response. Being recognized helps them to grow up.

Speech creates social meanings. The way we conduct a conversation in respect of words chosen, as well as non-verbal factors, says a lot about our understanding of the social circumstances of the conversation. Compliments from a male to a female at a party about her appearance will not just be about how she looks. Both people also know that what he says carries other implicit meanings such as – this is the kind of situation where I expect to be able to say things like that – I'm drawing attention to the fact that you are female – I'm starting to 'chat you up' – and so on (now see figure 12).

Do we mean what we say?

Hint: when have you unintentionally given someone the wrong message?

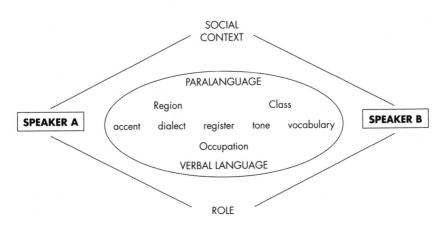

FIGURE 12 When speaking with others we have complex choices to make about our expression and what is appropriate

2 Dealing with others

2.1 Strategies

A strategy is a short piece of communication behaviour or interaction. It involves the deliberate use of verbal and non-verbal signs to achieve a communicative purpose.

We use these strategies the whole time, though we may not be aware of it. One of the earliest and simplest strategies that a baby uses, for example, is the hunger cry. What starts off as a reflex becomes a deliberate yell for food, and then perhaps for attention. The child learns to generate communication signs deliberately.

Salespeople are actually taught strategies for dealing with people so that they stand a better chance of making a sale. In effect, this involves learning a set of verbal and non-verbal signs that, it is hoped, will have the desired effect. Among other things, they may be taught to do a lot of smiling, to find excuses (such as the use of brochures) for getting inside the client's body space, to refer to details of the client's lifestyle or home approvingly, to agree (or to appear to agree) with everything the client says, to relate their product or service to the client's known or supposed needs. All this proves that communication can be controlled, can be used for an effect – whether or not we approve of what the effect is. And it comes about as a result of using one or more strategies.

Of course, not all strategies are persuasive. You might consider what you think people do when they use strategies for encouraging a child in its reading or for comforting a woman whose husband has been injured in a traffic accident.

We use the most common strategy every day in its various forms. This is the 'greetings strategy'. A strategy doesn't have to be a lengthy piece of interaction. Greetings can be quite short. But still, what happens is that various non-verbal signs and words are used to show that the people involved recognize one another and feel friendly towards one another, and to confirm the nature of their relationship.

Some strategies, like the greetings ones, can become a matter of habit. If the same pattern of communication is used again and again, then it becomes a ritual. Some strategies are used more consciously than others. Obviously, if we are not familiar with a given situation, then we have to think more consciously about what strategy is most useful. But if a general type of strategy has been tried once, then it is easier to think up variations on it. For example, pupils have quite a stock of useful excuses for being late for school, from 'The bus went early' to 'The cat was sick on my school bag'. But the basic strategy remains the same: it always includes elements such as the breathless arrival, the sincere, direct gaze and the verbal apology.

There are a great number of strategies that we use, so many that it is hard to categorize them. One way of doing so is to look at communication needs as mentioned in chapter 1, and place all strategies under one of these headings.

Other ways of describing strategies have already been mentioned, in effect, through examples in this section. So, we have strategies for persuading, for approving or disapproving, for making excuses and for avoiding people and problems.

Finally, one very common set of strategies that we have is to do with conversation. One could say this is the basic stuff of everyday interpersonal communication, but again, conversations don't just happen and develop by chance. We communicate because we want to. We use strategies to shape conversation. The most common ones are these: starting and finishing a conversation; interrupting people; keeping the conversation going; changing the direction of the conversation.

All these strategies may happen quite quickly, but still, the signs achieve the purpose. For example, in the case of interrupting we may use a sign such as a small cough to distract the speaker; we will use eye contact and perhaps a small finger movement to say that we are ready to speak; and we may nod our head vigorously to signal that we have taken in what the previous speaker has to say, and that he or she can now shut up!

2.2 Games

A game is an interpersonal strategy used to put someone down. The usage was coined by Eric Berne to describe one aspect of his theories of transactional analysis. His book *Games People Play* is all about the way that people misuse communication skills. He concentrates a lot on words, but games are also played through NVB. Games are often seen in relationships – friendship, marriages, boss–worker relationships. They are about the one person exerting power over the other, and trying to make the other person feel bad. Berne calls that other person the Victim. He describes different sorts of games and gives them titles.

The most basic game is called 'Yes, But'. This could be played by your friend on you, where you are trying to help them get through an assignment. Every time you make a helpful suggestion, they have another reason why it won't work – 'Yes, but I have to go and see my Gran that night.' Finally you get really cross with them blocking you, and then they say something like, 'Great friend you are!' Or, 'I told you it was impossible.' Then you feel guilty. That's what they want. Don't rise to it. Do your friend a favour: tell them to stop making excuses.

A more sophisticated version of this game is called 'Wooden Leg'. This is where someone has a genuine problem, perhaps a disability, but they exploit it. You have to be tough to break this game. We know a true story about a girl in a wheelchair at a school, who was forever using her condition to get what she wanted and to make others feel bad if they didn't give it to her. For instance, she would force her way to the computers in the IT room, though there weren't enough for the class, complaining that people were not thinking about her disability. Other pupils gave way, feeling guilty. What they should have done is to say, no, the fact that you are in a wheelchair has nothing to do with you taking your turn to get some machine time, so wait.

There are particular ways that the game player can lead the other on in a game, and can wind them up. You will need to follow this up with further reading if you are really interested.

2.3 Presentation of self

We present different personalities to other people according to the situation we are in.

The idea that we present ourselves to others in different ways at different times comes from a book by Erving Goffman. It provides a useful and entertaining account of how we play parts when communicating with others, whether in public or in private situations. He uses a number of terms to explain his ideas. The most useful of these can probably be included in one sentence. *We stage a performance through a persona.*

The idea of staging is that we do put on a show, especially in public situations. If a woman is paying for petrol at a filling station and then discovers that she has no money with her, she may well put on a performance to cover her embarrassment and to explain why she can't pay. In which case, the place and situation become the stage. And the stage does make a difference to the performance. For example, imagine a situation in which you are a motorist and your car won't start. If this happened at the air line in a filling station, you might mutter, but then you would look for a reason for the problem, and go back and ask for help. But if it took place in a driveway at home, then you might feel free to put on another performance involving strong language and banging of car doors to express feelings.

And again, staging can involve using the props on the stage. In the case of an interview, the interviewer can arrange props to assist in staging: an easy chair to relax the interviewee; folders in front of them to make them appear well informed; glasses to suggest intelligence and authority. Or, to take another example, a young man inviting a new girlfriend to his flat for a meal will tidy the place, perhaps put flowers on the table, choose some music. In fact, he will dress the stage for his performance, having regard for the needs and purposes of his communication.

The persona is the character that we adopt to play the part. Different parts in different situations require a different persona. A receptionist in a hotel would put on one kind of persona to do his job and another kind to talk to a girlfriend who takes him out for a meal.

Each persona in this case is defined by its characteristics, as one would define personality. The first one might be described as pleasant whereas the second one might be friendly. The persona is part of our way of dealing with people. It is the character out of which we communicate. In this sense it defines how we communicate. To decide (subconsciously) on using a particular persona is also to make a decision about communication style – how we talk to and use non-verbal cues with the other person.

The ability to shift from one persona to another, to choose one, is an important part of being an effective communicator. Some people believe that we have a fixed personality, or even that there is somehow something dishonest about adapting our behaviour to different situations. This is not so. We need to change. It would be absurd and insensitive for someone to present the same persona for dealing with a work colleague in a production meeting and when visiting the same person in hospital after an accident.

The use of persona tends to be most obvious when one is talking about public situations, whether they involve work or leisure. If there is such a thing as a basic personality, then we would probably agree that this is the self that we present to friends and family. But still one should note that persona and performance can describe how we make contact with others in some fairly private situations. A doctor examining a patient is, in one sense, having close and personal contact with that patient. But he communicates as a particular persona in a particular way so that they both understand the 'rules' of that situation.

Or there might be the case of a visit to relatives. They may be family and it may be a private situation, but still it is possible that we would adopt a persona for dealing with, say, an aunt or uncle.

The idea of a persona is very close to the idea of role, which we will be looking at again in chapter 3. Roles exist in groups. They are about personality, behaviour and position within the group. People have roles as a member of a group – family, or friends or work group. Sometimes these roles are recognized by labels such as daughter or supervisor. A persona goes with the role. A supervisor of a group of clerical assistants would communicate in a way that they saw as being appropriate to that role. But they would also adopt a persona which fitted the role. The way that they communicated would also be affected by this persona.

A performance is the act of presenting the self; it is the act of communicating. The term is meant to suggest an intentional use of speech and NVC.

The performance makes contact with the other person. A performance will probably involve some of the strategies that we have already referred to. There are some obvious and professional examples of performances. For instance, try watching a quiz show presenter on television. Watch the way that they glad-hand the game players, especially if these are members of the public. Watch the way they introduce and conclude the show. Watch the way they whip up excitement or produce laughter. This is all part of their performance. But then consider the example of parents telling off a child. This is also a performance. Watch for the way that they grab the child's attention, then enforce silence and stillness. Watch the way they hold that attention through the telling off that follows. Watch the way that this involves a mixture of disapproval, explanation and threats. Of course, the fine detail of the performance is composed of signs. Verbally, there may be phrases such as 'Don't do that!' or 'I'm not bringing you here again.' But don't miss the non-verbal aspects of the performance: gaze from beneath the brows, stiff body posture, threatening hand gestures. This is the stuff of the performance. This is how contact is made.

2.4 Communication skills

A communication skill is an ability to use a means of communication effectively, with regard for the needs of those involved.

It should be emphasized that when one is talking about interpersonal communication being 'effective', this is not the same thing as getting one's own way. The idea of effectiveness includes consideration for, and understanding of, the other person. It follows that any communication skill involves more than mere mechanical ability to use the means of communication concerned. To be literate and to be able to write a letter requesting particulars of a job requires one level of skill. One also has to know and use the conventions of the given format (the letter). But to be able to write a letter of application for a job that is persuasive and attractive enough to get one an interview requires deeper skills. In this case, effective communication involves a sense of style, among other things.

Making contact with others

Communication skills that require us to deal directly with people are based on the use of spoken and non-verbal communication. Initiating, managing and ending contact with others is a basic human experience of everyday life. It is so basic that we may not realize that we do learn skills in managing these contacts, whereas everyone is aware that they are taught to read. If you think of the number of situations in which you deal with other people every day, then it is also obvious that these skills of contact are tremendously important. How we manage them is not something 'natural'. Not everyone does it well. And we all have something to learn about getting on well with others. Peter Honey says of other people, 'their attitudes towards us and, more importantly, their behaviour towards us, are determined largely by our behaviour towards them' (Honey, *Face to Face Skills*, Aldershot: Gower, 1990).

We have already referred to strategies and self-presentation. Looked at another way, it is reasonable to say that:

It is a skill to be able to use strategies effectively.
It is a skill to be able to present the self effectively.

Before we write about feedback and perception, which are very much concerned with skills, it will be useful to comment on relationships in particular.

2.5 Shaping relationships

Interpersonal communication is most important in that it helps define our relationships with other people. It can make them or break them. It can help maintain them. And our lives are a network of relationships. The communication skills that we have already described are most influential in terms of making the contact that is to do with these relationships.

Relationships are not only to do with family, friends and lovers. We have some kind of relationship with everyone around us, not least those we work with. These relationships may not all be good ones. But even then, communication provides us with the means for a remedy. If we want to like and be liked, then we have to do something about it. Our skills in using verbal and non-verbal communication will be most important in this case. Since we cannot avoid having some kind of relationship with so many people in our everyday lives, it seems sensible at least to make these friendly and positive. We can work towards doing so by, for example, developing skills in giving signs of recognition and approval. We hope that others would do the same for us. When we begin to talk to another person, we begin to establish a relationship with them. It is up to us what the nature of this relationship is. But we cannot avoid this fact: communication is never simply about passing factual information, where two people are concerned. Nor is it just about having mechanical skills of communication – the practical ability to use words. It is about what we use those words for, about why and how we use them.

This is why people, even on matters of pure business, who are seeking information, say, over the phone, will start off their conversation with some enquiry about the other person's health or family. We would do well to remember that communication between people is basically about people.

Communication does not just define a relationship, it is also defined by it. As Peter Hartley says, 'any communication between two people will be influenced by the relationship which exists between them' (Hartley 1999).

A relationship is about the roles of those concerned; it is about shared experience. It has been noted that people starting a love relationship talk more than those who are well established. Those who don't talk so much don't love each other any the less, but the nature of their relationship defines how much they feel the need to talk and what they feel they need to talk about. In a secure relationship – friends, family, lovers – people may well talk more freely about feelings. But equally, people can be in a family relationship and feel insecure, and not talk freely. It doesn't matter that in principle they are, for example, sisters, and 'should' have a relationship. The way they talk will show what their relationship is really like.

Relationships also go through stages, in which those involved explore one another's knowledge, opinions, values. They can move from the experimental to a secure stage – or not. Again, the way talk is used will say something about the stage people are at.

Other aspects of interpersonal communication will also both help make a relationship and reflect on its nature at a given time. For example(self-disclosure – talking about your background and your beliefs – helps open up a relationship. It is a recognized skill in developing positive communication. If you can talk quite freely, it will help people trust you.)Hearing people talk freely may also tell listeners about the state of their relationship – good friends who trust one another.

Which relationships are most important to us?

Take a few minutes to list some of your key relationships (e.g. family, partner, friends, work colleagues, people you study with at school/college/university, neighbours, people you met on holiday, people you chat with on the Internet). Make a few notes about (1) the nature of each of the relationship, and (2) how you use various forms of communication to sustain it.

2.6 Defining social situations

It is possible to categorize interpersonal communication and the situations in which it occurs in terms of oppositions. These labels are quite useful because they suggest contrast in the way that communication is used, and because they offer a quick way of looking for a range of situations through which to discuss how we make contact with others.

Formal/informal: suggests a difference between calculated and sponta-neous use of communication. It suggests another contrast of public/private situations. It says something about how conscious we may or may not be of the effect of our communication on others. It would be the difference between a casual visit to the cinema with a friend and attending a première of a film where one had to talk to royalty and the famous.

Public/private: suggests a difference of context where the communica-tion takes place. This in turn suggests a difference of presentation and an awareness that others may be observing the communication. In public we tend to restrain our non-verbal cues, the messages about feelings. We do not say so much about ourselves. It would be the difference between discussing one's political views with the family and talking about them in a television interview.

Distant/intimate: suggests a difference of relationship between the people communicating – and also, possibly, a difference in the situation that they might be in. If there is distance between us and the person we are talking to, then we are inclined to be formal in the way that we use language. If the situation is intimate, then we reveal more of our real selves, and therefore build a closer relationship with more trust. It is the difference between discussing supply problems with the boss and discussing marriage plans with a partner.

Ritual/open: suggests a difference in the predictability of the communication used – and also, possibly, a difference in the familiarity with the situation of the people involved. Ritual situations often confirm relationships, attitudes and feelings of security. But they don't open up a genuine dialogue in which communication is used to explore feelings and ideas. It is the difference between a market researcher asking someone to answer questions for a standard questionnaire and meeting someone on a blind date.

Functional/expressive: suggests a difference in the quality and purpose of the language used. The two kinds of situation make different demands on the participants. In the one case the language suggests that there is a practical job to be done, in the other that the communication is needed in order to discuss and to speculate. It is the difference between trying to buy a spare part for a car and trying to interpret the results of an experiment carried out in a laboratory.

2.7 Feedback

Feedback was introduced in chapter 1 when we talked about contextualized models.

The idea of feedback has two main aspects. One is the idea that messages are sent through verbal or non-verbal channels in response to messages from another person. The other is that these response messages are acted upon: that an adjustment of the content and style of communication may take place as a result of feedback.

This is important, because it can be argued that if we are poor at giving off, recognizing or acting upon feedback, then we are that much poorer at communicating with others.

Feedback can, of course, be verbal as well as non-verbal. If a person invites someone to come round and see them, and the other person says that they can't do that, then that person has given verbal feedback.

But it is non-verbal feedback which is, if anything, more important. This is because it isn't always recognized, and yet research suggests that it is the most influential channel in terms of affecting our attitudes and emotions with regard to the other person. For example, simply smiling and nodding at the other person suggests that we like them and approve of what they are saying. This feedback will encourage them to talk.

In another instance, it could be that we give negative feedback to someone else. For example, we might unconsciously clench our fists while talking to this person, which suggests tension within us, and probably some feeling of aggression towards this other person. They will get the message and either respond with a degree of aggression themselves, or perhaps just keep quiet.

Remember that non-verbal signs are usually used unconsciously, which means that they can often be taken for a true sign of someone's feelings.

This should also remind us of the idea of *strategies*. These can also be used consciously or unconsciously. And again, it is often the non-verbal signs in the strategy that are the most useful in achieving whatever it is we want to get done. For example, if we sense from their feedback that someone is losing interest in what we are saying, then we can use a strategy to try to recover that interest. If we are talking about a television programme, then we will try to make it sound more exciting. In particular, we are likely to start using more large gestures to describe action, so that the eye of the other person is drawn. We will vary the pitch and tone of our voice, so that it doesn't sound too boring. We will look more at the other person, stand a little closer and perhaps touch them lightly.

Our strategy would be a response to their response. And this tells us that a conversation is a continuous process of feedback of messages and adjustment of each person's approach to communicating. Once more, the rule seems to be that effective communication is, in various ways, a matter of paying attention to the other person, of considering what they need. A good communicator is observant and sympathetic.

This can apply to many of life's situations and experiences. If a child is learning to tie his or her shoelaces for the first time, then approving pats and saying 'Well done' will encourage the child to stick at it.

If a supervisor is trying to get her clerical team to put in an extra half-hour in order to clear a job before the weekend, then she is likely to get them to do this by saying complimentary things about their work, reinforcing her words with smiles and nods, and other signs of interest in what they are doing.

Feedback regulates our contact with others. It helps decide how well a conversation will go. It is our reaction to other people's communication, and their reaction to ours.

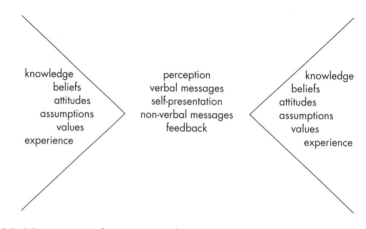

FIGURE 13   Interpersonal communication factors

2.8 Gender

Interpersonal communication both defines and is defined by gender. There are important debates going on now about the social roles of female and male. There are issues surrounding the treatment of women at work, and the equality of their opportunities. Understanding of how males and females see one another and talk to one another can help inform those debates and issues.

At the same time, questions of equality should not be confused with matters of difference. Gender differences and the social–biological interplay between these are represented through our uses of verbal and non-verbal communication. The ways in which a male talks to a female who is pregnant with their child may be a particular example of such gender difference.

In this area we are back to the important questions of meaning – what do we mean by what we say and how we talk to someone of another gender? Objections to some uses of language in particular by men towards women are in effect based on the belief that what is said means something objectionable. To use a cliché, the insertion by a male of the phrase 'my dear' into an utterance used towards a woman is taken to be condescending. It is considered to be an expression of a male sense of superiority and of a subconscious attempt by the male to diminish the woman.

These meanings and implied attitudes help explain the rather difficult word **discourse**. This describes how we have particular ways of using languages (codes) to produce particular meanings about particular topics. You can have a discourse about all sorts of topic areas – for example, the law, childhood, masculinity. The ways in which boys and girls talk about one another reveal that two gender discourses do exist. You can look at girls' magazines to discover some words, and indeed picture language, that are used by girls about boys. Even more revealing are some of the words used by men to talk about women, which are also reflected in the words and pictures of so-called 'lads' mags'. You could easily collect these for yourself and work out what they mean in terms of attitudes and values. This kind of communication is important because it is part of the process of socialization. Boys and girls grow up having a certain under-standing of what it means to be a male or a female because of the words that are used about them. It is one thing to use words that describe general gender differences – strength, for example. But it is another thing to use words that create unequal ideas about difference – about strength of mind or intelligence, for example.

Finally in this varied survey, we return to gender in conversations. A number of defining differences have been discovered here, especially those that are about women deferring to men. For instance, traditionally many women like to talk about feelings; many men do not. Stereotypically, many men like to talk about things – objects – such as cars; women are not as interested in such things. Men like to talk about themselves, about their achievements; women listen to them doing so when, as they have admitted in surveys, they would rather not. 'Women talk about family, friendships, feelings, clothes, health and food. Women engage in more self-disclosure, talk about more intimate topics, especially to other women' (Argyle 1992).

Kate Fox in her book *Watching the English: The Hidden Rules of English Behaviour* (London: Hodder & Stoughton, 2004) includes a chapter on grooming talk, which she describes as the verbal equivalent of picking fleas off each other or mutual back-scratching. She suggests that after the weather, English gossip turns to grooming talk. This may concern ourselves and people we know, but also includes 'celebrities', who are the mainstay of much newspaper, TV and magazine gossip.

Traditionally it has been asserted that women 'gossip' more than men. However, Kate Fox points out that

> contrary to popular belief, researchers have found that men gossip just as much as women. In one English study, both sexes devoted the same amount of conversation time (about 65%) to social topics such as personal relationships; in another, the difference was found to be quite small, with gossip accounting for 55% of male conversation time and 67% of female time.

Of course, these are general differences, and there will be exceptions to this kind of communication. Such differences are also changing rapidly, so that many more liberated men do talk about their feelings and relationships; and many women are equally keen on things and sport.

Some magazines seem to be stuck in old-fashioned gender stereotypes. Have a look at the language, pictures and advertisements in a range of magazines in your local shop to see what you think.

2.9 Culture

Interpersonal communication varies according to the culture in which it happens. We have just talked about gender (and discourses), but what these mean to us does depend on our culture. This is one of the problems about getting into issues of gender. Some spoken language and the language of dress codes for women in, say, Iran or Afghanistan may raise 'feminist' issues for at least some Westerners. It does not for many of the people in those countries. What they mean by what they say when they talk to one another is not what we may think is meant. Wearing a veil is seen as a sign of being a proper and modest woman, not a symbol of male repression. These are, yet again, differences of meaning, of beliefs, attitudes and values. They create problems when one culture tries to deal with another.

There are also often subcultures coexisting within one nation. Here again, the ways in which people communicate with one another both define and are defined by the subculture to which they belong. What is meant by culture can be quite complicated. It could be about being black Afro-Caribbean, but also male, and young. It could be about being Bangladeshi, but also female, and third generation born in Britain. It could be about being Irish, but Northern Irish, and Protestant.

The ways in which people talk to one another in cultures imply what they believe as part of that culture. The conventions of social interaction will be different.

In the previous section we quoted from Kate Fox's book *Watching the English: The Hidden Rules of English Behaviour* (2004), in which she sets out as a social anthropologist to define English culture and 'Englishness'. For students of communication, her conclusion regarding defining Englishness makes interesting and disturbing reading:

> The central 'core' of Englishness: Social Dis-ease. Social dis-ease is a shorthand term for all our chronic social inhibitions and handicaps . . . it is our lack of ease, discomfort and incompetence in the field (minefield) of social interaction; our embarrassment, insularity, awkwardness, perverse obliqueness, emotional constipation, fear of intimacy and general inability to engage in a normal and straightforward fashion with other human beings.

Not surprisingly, Kate Fox also sees 'class-consciousness' as another defining characteristic of Englishness.

2.10 Class

Class is also part of culture and varies from culture to culture. It describes people's status and power in a given culture. In some cultures, priests may be better regarded – seen as of a better class – than they are in others. Certainly class and status are recognized non-verbally. For example, high-status people are usually recognized by being given more body space and territory than others. Some institutions actually encourage class differences – or exploit them – through communication. For example, 'high-class' hotels will dress the staff in certain uniforms. These staff are expected to address guests as 'madam' or 'sir', to suggest such differences. Actually, they are trying to massage the self-esteem of their guests. Some public schools still allow pupils to play out class games – for example, letting younger boys work for the older ones, and even using classist language ('fag'). Some grammar school teachers may address pupils only by their surnames. This kind of interaction encourages class language and a sense of class/status when such people leave school.

It has also been suggested that there are different kinds of language for what people describe as the working class and the middle class. These have been called restricted and elaborated codes. Research in this area suggests, for example, that elaborated-code users ask more questions and give more explanations for what they do and say. This is especially seen in parenting behaviour. According to this analysis, restricted-code parents are more inclined simply to tell their kids what to do.

Certainly our use of language and of paralanguage are perceived as indicators of social class. Kate Fox captures some of this in *Watching the English* when she quotes comments from her anthropological research:

> Key phrases include: 'it is impossible for an Englishman to open his mouth without making some other Englishman hate him or despise him'; 'don't say serviette, dear, we call it napkin'; 'a bit naff/common/ nouveau/flashy/vulgar/unsmart/uncouth/Sharon-and-Tracey/suburban-semi/petit-bourgeois/mock-tudor . . .'; 'stuck-up posh tart (hurray/upper class twit/old-school tie/snob/public school yah-yah/green wellie/Camilla . . .) thinks she's better than us'; 'that nice little man from the shop'.

2.11 Conventions

Conventions keep on coming up when one talks about communication, because 'rules' for encoding or decoding are pervasive. They are everywhere, even though we may not realize that they exist. They are also present in interpersonal communication, sometimes referred to as *social interaction*.

These 'understood' rules affect how we deal with people under all circumstances: meeting them, carrying on conversations, interviewing them, arguing with them, trying to be friends with them. We have talked previously about conventions in a more formal sense, with reference to codes and signs. Here, we are referring to them in a more social sense, though not simply as rules for behaving 'properly'.

So, this section is not about etiquette, but it is, for example, about having learnt when to speak and when not to speak. This could be affected partly by rules relating to the status of the people involved – 'Don't interrupt your mother!' There would also be general conventions about taking turns in conversations, regardless of who was talking or what the occasion was. We have learnt not to talk over one another the whole time through using and noticing little bits of non-verbal behaviour, such as people glancing at the person they want to speak next just before they have finished speaking.

These conventions of social interaction are very much connected with the idea of skills. People who are good at communicating really know the rules, whether they realize it or not. Skilled use of conventions would also be another way of defining appropriate or effective communication.

One of the main forms of interpersonal communication is a conversation between two people. Such conversations take place in all types of social situations listed in section 2.6 above. Different situations will affect the use of conventions. But all conversations have similar processes.

British Telecom (BT) introduced a project in 1997 called TalkWorks which was about speaking and listening skills. As part of this research they asked hundreds of people how they recognized a good conversation. From these comments, TalkWorks identified four key things about a good conversation:

(a) It feels like a genuine two-way experience, with both of you equally involved and interested.

(b) You both feel you're being heard and understood. There's a willingness on both sides to be open.

(c) The atmosphere feels comfortable, so even if what you are talking about is difficult, the important things get said.

(d) The conversation makes a difference. Something useful or satisfying happens as a result.

Do we say what we mean?

Hint: when do people try to cover up their true feelings?

When does regulating communication become nothing but manipulation?

Hint: think of ways in which you can try to get what you want or can help other people to feel OK.

---

3 Perception – of ourselves and others

GEORGE'S STORY

George Moorcroft had worked at a precision instruments factory for twenty years. He had graduated through an apprenticeship to assembly work, to building prototypes for new instruments. He was a careful man who took a justified pride in his work. There were three other men of similar age and skills who shared the same workshop with him. Between them, the men had tackled many exacting tasks, from building a miniature control arm that could pick up a human hair, to making a device for measuring the effects of pressure on any piece of material.

George was a perfectionist, with a well-regulated life. He was a neat man and a creature of habit. In fact, the only unpredictable thing in his life was the time he would take to do a job. If his work was going perfectly, George would clock out at 5.30 p.m. on the dot. But if he was not making the progress he had hoped to, or the projects manager was up against a deadline, then he would work all hours to finish the job.

But the management of the company also knew that George and his workmates would not be there for ever, and they wanted to train up some younger staff as replacements. However, George was not pleased when, one day, he was faced with his new trainee, Jill.

For a start, he was suspicious of Jill because she hadn't been through an apprenticeship and she was a woman. In fact, the traditional apprenticeship system had gone anyway. But, worse than this, Jill had a foundation degree qualification and she had only been with the company for two years. George seemed to forget that by the time he was Jill's age – 24 – he had completed his own apprenticeship.

But it was when George actually first saw Jill, one Monday morning, after he had been warned of her arrival, that he decided the girl wouldn't do. And he went straight to Ron Dowling, the projects manager, to tell him so.

'I mean,' said George, 'you give me a girl who doesn't even turn up in proper overalls.'

'Ah,' said Ron. 'But you can't say that yours is exactly a dirty job, George. She doesn't need overalls to do the job.'

'But you know that's not the point. It's a matter of attitude. The girl didn't even look as though she'd ever used a proper machine with her smart clothes and high heels. What do you think I'm to make of that?'

'I don't know. You tell me.'

'I will tell you. It means she's got no idea what to expect here. And another thing, she's a sight too familiar. Calling me George at first meeting. But anyway, it's not just that. It's the little things. She doesn't look strong enough to do what I need. And she was just sitting on the edge of a bench when I came in. And so far, she doesn't seem to be listening to anything I say.'

'But you left her working?'

'Oh yes. I left her with a small calibration job.'

Ron Dowling appeared to lose interest in George's problems, and turned his attention to a small metal component lying on his desk. It was a complex valve, which immediately distracted George too.

'A nice piece, this. Not our work, of course. So it must be the opposition. How did you get hold of it, Ron?'

Ron Dowling looked at George without a smile.

'Jill Lovat made that, George,' he said.

ABOUT GEORGE'S STORY

George's story tells us that we shouldn't judge people by appearances. But we often do. George had a view of the kind of person who should be doing the kind of job that he was. This view was based on himself and his experience. He made assumptions about Jill, what kind of person she was and what she was able to do. And all this from a few signs and traditional perceptions and expectations. And in making this assessment of Jill, George was much influenced by his own view of himself.

When we talk about perception and interpersonal communication, it is all about how we assess ourselves and other people; about why we do this; about the results of this assessment.

Perceiving is very much about communicating, because it affects what we say to other people and how we say it. George perceived Jill mainly through what he heard and what he saw. All signs must come in through our senses.

But the important thing was the meaning that he made from these signs. Especially as he was wrong about Jill.

And you may have noticed that the idea of perception is very much connected with the idea of feedback, which we have just been talking about. It is feedback messages that we perceive when we are talking to other people. And so, of course, it is the non-verbal signs that are extremely important to the way we perceive others, because they are also important in feedback. In each case we need to look at the signs, their meanings and their effects. But where feedback refers to the ways in which a conversation can be regulated and adjusted, perception goes further. We perceive people before a conversation has even started. And we perceive ourselves.

3.1 Perception of self

Perception of self is rather important, because how we see ourselves very much affects how we communicate. For example, if we see ourselves as quiet, shy people, then we aren't likely to be very positive in talking to others. We won't start conversations. We will be especially poor at talking in public situations.

And yet we weren't born as quiet, shy people. There is no law of nature that says we have to be like that. We could learn to communicate in a more positive way and then perhaps get a more positive view of ourselves. And perhaps we could learn to take a more positive view of ourselves, concentrating on what we know and what we are good at, so that then we end up communicating more positively.

There are two main aspects to the way that we perceive ourselves: we have a self-image and we have self-esteem (see figure 14).

Self-image

Self-image is a view of ourselves as we think we are. This always contains a mixture of optimism and pessimism. We may think that we are taller than we really are. But then we will also probably think that some spot or blemish on the face is larger and more noticeable than it really is. This self-image includes, therefore, a notion of our physical selves, but also refers to our personality. Of course, we do not see ourselves as others see us. Again it is probably easier to prove this in the physical sense. Have you looked at yourself in a snapshot lately, or listened to yourself on a recording device? Do not despair! It can be a shock, but once you stop to think about it, what you see and hear is not bad.

This self-image is developed through our relationships with others. Other people's attitudes towards us may affect our self-image. For example, a child in a lower-stream class at school might have a rather negative self-image, caused by seeing other people's attitudes towards 'lower-stream children' as being rather negative.

In many ways it is the personality aspect that is more important. The kind of character that we think we have, and the kinds of qualities and abilities which we think we have, must obviously affect how we get on with others. If we see ourselves as being good at a particular sport, or as knowing quite a lot about that sport, then it is likely that we will talk well when it comes up as a subject.

In very general terms one can also talk about having a positive or a negative self-image. Those people who see their skills and qualities in a positive light are likely to be more positive about talking and listening.

We also have an ideal self-image. This is an image of ourselves as we would like to be, and as we would like others to see us. Some people try to make their self-image match up to this idea by behaving in certain ways. It can be a good thing to try to be a 'better person'. But it can also be a bad thing

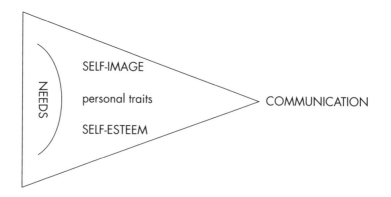

FIGURE 14   We communicate out of who we are, who we think we are, how 'good' we think we are

to have ideas that are impossible to achieve. Failure to match up to ideals can be destructive to the personality. Parents may expect a lot from their children at school. A child can build these expectations into their ideal self-image, but then there may be a problem if, for example, the child fails examinations.

Self-esteem

In effect, we have already referred to self-esteem. Esteem is about the good or poor opinion one has of something – in this case, ourselves. Whatever picture we have of ourselves, it is esteem that affects our interpretation of that self-image. For example, we may see ourselves as being bad at passing exams and getting paper qualifications. But we don't necessarily have to have low self-esteem about this. We could shrug it off because we know that we are good at other tasks. Or we might think that it is actually a bad thing to have passed too many exams because that would suggest that we were the kind of person that we don't want to be.

Esteem is about the attitude that we have towards ourselves. By looking at ourselves more objectively, it could be argued that we could improve our self-esteem, and so improve our use of communication.

One could visualize self-image as in figure 15.

In 2005 a new magazine titled *Psychologies* was launched in the United Kingdom. The first edition in October 2005 set out its aims:

> Welcome to *Psychologies*, the first women's magazine that's about what we're like, not just what we look like. If you're interested in the ways we think, behave, communicate and connect, then this is for you.
>
> Whether you want to develop your own potential, or become a better parent, partner or friend, we'll bring you the ideas, insight and inspiration to help you do it.

It is noteworthy that this magazine is aimed at women, but, like other women's magazines, no doubt it is widely read by men too. Why in our culture is it still considered that the psychology of communication and relationships is more interesting to women than to men?

One of the launch posters for this magazine simply asked the question:

Would you
like you
if YOU
met you?

It targets a key aspect of self-image and self-esteem: do we have a view of ourselves that is positive or negative?

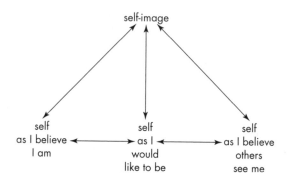

FIGURE 15 Elements of self-image

3.2 Perception of others

We assess other people by looking at and listening to them. This happens when we first meet others, and while we are talking with them. Our judgements are mainly about what they are thinking and feeling, and are made mainly on the basis of their non-verbal cues. In this sense, perception is like a series of guesses about the other person, based on our previous knowledge and experience of them, or of people like them. We start weighing up and passing judgement on people as soon as we set eyes on them. So, we cannot help perceiving others. The real question is whether or not we perceive them accurately – quite often we don't.

The longer we are with someone, the more we are likely to find out and notice about them, and so the better our judgements are likely to be. But in fact many of our contacts with other people are quite brief – as in interviews, say – so we are likely to have to make judgements on the basis of limited information. That being so, we should be careful about looking and listening, and then about making our minds up. Too often our judgements are wrong. For example, we are initially inclined to think that because someone is wearing glasses, they must be intelligent. It may take a while to find out otherwise. And by that time we may already have acted on the mistaken impression that we have formed.

What we say to others and how we say it is significantly affected by the way we perceive them. If we see someone else as threatening and dominating, then we may try to back off, or be rather negative in what we say. And the point is that they may not see themselves like that at all. Indeed, they may not be like that – it could be that our perception is faulty because it has been reached carelessly.

So, where other people are involved, we are continually monitoring their non-verbal signs in particular. From things like their tone of voice and their gaze we hope to find out what they really mean when they communicate with us. This is not just to do with what they mean by words that they may be using. It is to do with meanings about themselves and what they may be thinking, especially about us!

One thing that is well evidenced is the way that people try to make very rapid judgements about others. They try to sort out the kind of person that they are dealing with before they know them very well. This is called **impression formation**. An example of the kind of error this can lead one into is given in section 3.4.

We perceive their personality

That is to say, when we meet people we form an opinion on what kind of person we think they are. There has been much discussion about questions such as do we have a fixed personality or have we a variety of personalities? Looking back at the idea of the various personae that we present to other people, it seems that the second idea is more likely to be true. But in any case, one can agree that we usually assess others' personalities in terms of a few major concepts such as friendly or hostile, dominant or submissive. We build a picture of the person we are dealing with and, according to our view of their personality, as well as our perception of ourselves, we decide how to communicate with them.

For example, if a normally quiet and retiring person gets into conversation with someone who they perceive to be very confident and outgoing, then they will probably end up doing more listening than talking.

You should also remember that there are always a variety of factors such as context, or knowledge of the subject of conversation, which should be taken into account when explaining what is happening and why.

We perceive their emotional state

That is to say, we form an opinion as to what people's dominant emotions are at that time.

Again, this matters because it affects how we carry on talking to them. We will decide what strategy to use. We will choose the most appropriate signs. We will use our communication skills.

And it should be remembered that it is a skill to perceive accurately what is going on. The other person might be pretending that they are calm and content, when they are not. We may notice signs like eye blinking, tensing of face muscles and slumped body posture, which suggest that all may not be well.

The other person's emotional state matters because it affects how they communicate with us, as well as how they will receive our communication. We know that. That is why we pay attention to how they are feeling. It probably isn't much good asking an employee to check a book-keeping error if you know that they have just realized that they have a big National Lottery win!

We assess their attitude towards us

That is to say, we try to work out what the other person feels about us. We know that they will form an opinion of us, as we do of them. So, we try to find out what that opinion is. That common phrase 'It's not what you say, it's your attitude' tells us just how important attitude is in our dealings with others. Perceiving is an active, searching process, so we look for attitudes in others. We need to evaluate their position in relation to ourselves before we feel confident about talking with them. But, as with the other instances discussed, it is very possible to make mistakes. For example, signs of emotional state can easily be misread as signs of attitude. Someone who is tired and drained emotionally can easily be thought of as being negative in attitude.

We should also beware of reading our own attitudes and emotions into others. For example, if we are feeling pleased and happy about something that we have achieved, then we are likely to see others as having a more friendly attitude towards us than may in fact be the case. If we show a friendly and caring attitude towards the other person and they return that attitude towards us, then there will be a good flow of communication. There will be sharing and understanding.

We make assumptions about attributes of the other person

That is to say, we make guesses about who they are, about their background and about their lifestyle. We do this from their appearance in particular. We like to be able to place other people in a role or a job. We like to be able to define them in various ways so that we can fit them into our scheme of things. So, we would guess their age from their clothes, hair, face. We would guess their job from their clothes, or perhaps from possessions that they have about them. Uniforms are actually meant to define people's jobs to others.

We would certainly want to guess the other person's sex, from things like clothes and hairstyle. Some fashions of the young, at the moment, confuse the traditional signs of sex (or gender). For example, make-up is no longer the exclusive sign of being female that it once was. This can be confusing and threatening to some people because it breaks the conventions, or rules. It also shows that the meaning of signs is not fixed.

We would try to guess someone's status. This could be in terms of the class that we suppose they belong to, or in terms of their rank within the type of job we think they do. For example, we might assign someone to a certain slot in society if they were wearing expensive clothes, or drove a Rolls-Royce car, or were addressed as 'my lord' by another person.

We would guess the other person's role in a given situation. For example, a female who appears to be between the ages of 18 and 45 and who is seen pushing a pram is likely to be placed in the role of 'mum' in the minds of onlookers. She could be the aunt of the child in the pram; she might be childless. But still, she will be seen as a mother.

All this tells us that perception is not only about recognizing signs and making assessments of others. It is also about placing other people in categories. We need to define the kind of person they are so that we can decide what is the best way to communicate with them. Unfortunately, we are often too hasty in placing people in categories because we are too hasty and careless about reading the signs.

This placing in categories has its plus and minus points. It is useful to be able to organize our understanding of the world. Such categories in our heads are called **perceptual sets**. If we have a 'set' such as creatures with claws, then this can be useful in learning to avoid creatures with claws if they have proved dangerous in the past. Equally, there is a danger that we will put everything we know in 'boxes' in our heads, and not make connections between the categories.

Stereotyping is another kind of categorizing. Here too it is quite useful to organize our understanding of people in our heads in terms of types and characteristics (see figure 16), but it can lead to a damaging and limiting prejudice about people. It is a mental function that can increase the probability of our sorting out the attitudes of others towards us quite quickly. If you like, this is another example of communication coming from survival mechanisms. Older short female with smile is likely to seem less threatening to a child (to anyone?) than is older tall male with frown.

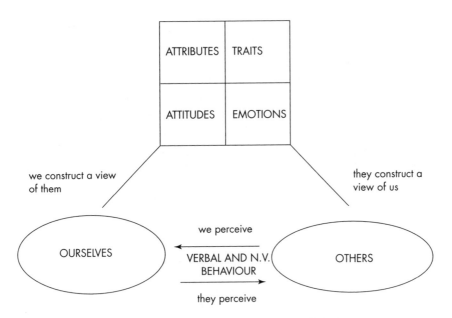

FIGURE 16   We construct in our heads a view of ourselves and of others

Attribution and motivation

One approach to perception is known as **attribution theory**. There is much research in this area, which is in effect about perception, as we are describing it. However, one major aspect of it has not yet been properly brought out. That is to do with how, when perceiving people, **we attribute motives to them**.

We make guesses as to why they are doing or saying what they are. These guesses will come from our close observation of how they act and talk, as well as from our observation of the consequences of their behaviour. We want to understand people's motivation because we want to work out what are their real attitudes towards us, and perhaps towards others.

For example, if you see someone lose their temper, shout at someone else and cause that person to cry, then not only will you want to work out why they did this, but you will also think rather carefully about how they might treat you.

3.3 The basis of assessment

So, perception is about 'reading' signs and seeking the meaning of those signs. Our judgements are based on those signs and our ability to notice them and then to make sense of them. The way we make sense of them is itself based on our previous knowledge and experience. People can become nervous in strange social situations precisely because they don't have previous knowledge and experience. They don't know 'how to behave'. That is to say, they don't know what signs to look out for and what the rules are for making sense of them. To take another situation, this is why some magazines can continue publishing successful articles on the subject of 'what to do on your first date'.

It is also important to realize that our assessment of others is based on all the information available. That is to say, our judgements are based on all the signs operating, verbal or non-verbal. Or at least they are based on a number of signs. And the information that we have could include a relationship with the other, or things that we have already heard about the other.

Perception is a continuous process. The more we interact with another person, the more information we have to go on, and so the more accurate our judgements are likely to be.

3.4 Problems with perception

Projecting our wishes on to our view of others

To some extent we see what we want to see in other people. For example, if we think that other people like us and we like them, then we are inclined to think that they have the same sort of views and opinions that we have. This isn't necessarily true.

Making assumptions about others

When we make assumptions about others, it is as if we fill in missing information. We would assume that someone carrying a sports bag and a hockey stick was a hockey player. We assume that someone who 'looks us in the eye' is sincere. We have learnt probable meanings of signs, and tend to assume that these probabilities will always hold true.

Making categories of people and the signs associated with them

In one sense, it is a useful skill to be able to put labels on things. But it is dangerous to do this too quickly. The fact that a man is wearing a straight white collar round his neck does not prove he is a priest, and it certainly doesn't prove that he is sweet-tempered and forgiving.

The worst kind of categorizing is called stereotyping. This is when we (or the media) use a very few familiar signs to place people in jobs or roles in an uncritical and simplistic manner. And when we have placed a person in such a slot, then we assume that they have all kinds of qualities or attributes. Usually the key signs of stereotyping are those to do with appearance. For example, someone wearing a suit is usually assumed to have status and some kind of white-collar professional job. Assumptions may also be made about this person's character and lifestyle.

Allowing first impressions of others to influence us

In particular, we tend to pick on one or two characteristics of the other person and let these influence our opinion of that person. This is called the 'halo effect'.

For example, at a business meeting one could be unduly influenced by the fact that the other person was wearing expensive clothes and an expensive watch, and using an expensive pen. We might assume that they were rich, successful and worth listening to. That might be what they wanted us to think, so we shouldn't be too influenced by these first impressions. Nor should we jump to conclusions taken from a few details. Indeed, usually the halo effect fades away as one gets to know the other person better, gets more information about them. But we still need to beware, because it isn't always possible to get to know that much about someone else.

Do you think we underestimate ourselves as communicators?

Hint: think of times when you have surprised yourself by what you have said.

Figure 17 illustrates key elements in the process of perception.

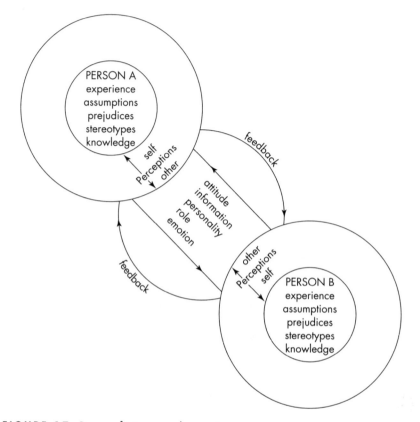

FIGURE 17   Process of interpersonal perception

4 Barriers to communication

ANGELA'S STORY

Angela didn't like the early morning turn with the patients. It was hard work if you took it at the end of a long night. It was hard work if it was the first thing that faced you at the beginning of a day. It was especially hard with the old people. Many of them were so lively at six o'clock in the morning. That wasn't always a good thing.

There was old Mr Cummings in the bed at the far end. For a start, he wore a deaf aid. It was so old-fashioned that it looked like a sea shell stuck in his ear. No wonder he couldn't hear anything. Besides, she suspected he turned it down deliberately. After he had shouted 'What?' a couple of times, Angela would lean over him to yell into his ear. That was when he came up with his favourite line, 'Give us a kiss, love.' In one week, Mr Cummings had got more kisses out of the nurses than the doctors had in two _years. It was all a laugh, really. Just irritating at six o'clock in the morning. With that wonky deaf aid, you never knew if you had got through to him or not._

Of course Angela felt sorry for him as well. It was no joke having an artificial hip joint put in you at the age of 71. But then it was no joke looking after someone like Cummings. People had this idea that old folk grew light like sparrows, but Cummings was still a big man and it took two of them and a lot of effort to shift him around for bed changes.

When Eric Cummings opened his eyes he knew it must be six o'clock. He always woke up at that time – a habit from years of having to get up and out to beat the factory clock. The dull ache in his side was still there. He wished that he hadn't woken up. There wasn't much fun left in life nowadays. In fact, there wasn't much life left. But he didn't like to think of that, even though this hip business had given him a shock.

The nurses were a starchy lot. Rather stuck-up young misses, he thought. The girls in the factory had been different. Always larking around and not minding the occasional cuddle. Times had changed. He blamed it all on this women's liberation stuff. These nurses all took themselves too seriously. They wouldn't even call him by his first name. It was all Mr that, and Mrs this. He liked to feel comfortable with people. And he didn't feel comfortable here. The doctors were the worst. They would come round, look at their sheets of paper. Whisper about you with the nurses. And then when you asked what was happening, you got a mouthful of long words. Talking about . . . whatever it was . . . micturition or something like that. If they meant a Jimmy Riddle, why didn't they say so?

Anyway, it was terrible, being surrounded by all these old people. Eric sighed, jiggled his deaf aid to stop the buzzing, and tried calling for the nurse.

Angela sighed. There he was again. Probably wanted another pan or something. Her feet ached as she set off down the ward. Silly old devil, she thought. He probably didn't need her at all. Just wanted to chat. And she didn't feel like it now, especially after last night. That was the trouble with some of the old people. They didn't seem to think you were human, had a life of your own. After all, she did have a job to do.

ABOUT ANGELA'S STORY

This story tells us about some of the things that get in the way when we communicate with other people. If interpersonal communication is meant to be about understanding between people, then it seems that Angela and Eric Cummings didn't entirely understand one another. The problem is that there are many things that can get in the way of saying what we really want to say to others, of putting over our feelings. Because, of course, there is more to interpersonal communication than just exchanging messages of fact. And even the facts of his condition were not being put across clearly to Cummings by the doctors.

The factors that get in the way of free and full communication between people are generally called 'barriers'. A more accurate word is 'filters', because there are rarely total barriers to understanding. You may also come across words such as 'noise' or 'interference' in some older texts on communication. It all adds up to the same idea of obstruction. And often the most important barriers are in the mind. For example, it is clear that Angela and Mr Cummings had different attitudes towards one another, coming out of their different experiences. This also meant that they had rather different beliefs and values, partly to do with their ages and partly to do with their backgrounds. We need to recognize such barriers and filters for what they are before we can do something about them. Then we may improve our communication with others.

4.1 Perception and filters

We have already discussed how poor perception filters communication (in section 3.4, 'Problems with perception'). The types of problem are also types of filter.

You should also make a link with the idea of psychological barriers, because the filters are in the mind. And it is in the mind that the coding and decoding aspects of communication take place. This is where we make sense of the information about the other person that we see and hear. So, we may filter before we say something or after we have heard something.

The basis of this filtering is in the assumptions that we make about other people. In one sense it is a useful skill to be able to make intelligent guesses about another person's character or behaviour. We want to know how to deal with them. But on the other hand, it isn't much of a skill if we simply jump to conclusions. It is important to learn to perceive accurately and thought-fully. Consider the following examples. As a general instance, what about those occasions when adults talk about children in front of them, as if they are not there? Somewhere there is a filter operating that cuts out awareness of children as people and as part of the same world as the adults.

A rather more particular example of a filter could be to do with reactions to accent. It has been known for people to think that users of regional accents have less credibility and authority than those who use so-called middle-class accents. People are put through perceptual filters, and in this case the regional accent users could come off worse. At one time the BBC demonstrated the existence of this filter and the belief behind it in their reluctance to allow regional accents in newsreaders, presenters and correspondents. This is a useful example because it also suggests that the media play some part in constructing our beliefs and values. These beliefs and values in turn become filters through which we perceive the world. We shall discuss more of this in chapter 5.

4.2 Mechanical barriers

Communication may be blocked or filtered by physical factors in the communication process.

Noise around those talking can create a filter within the context of communication. A physical problem like deafness could block the reception of communication. A physical problem such as a lisp could impede the production of communication. Any breakdowns in equipment involved with communication would also count as mechanical barriers.

4.3 Semantic barriers

Communication may be filtered by the careless use of words. Semantics is to do with the meanings of words. If words aren't used appropriately, they can't produce meanings which are likely to be understood. This comes back to the idea of codes and conventions. If we break the agreed rules of grammar or spelling or use of individual words, then we are likely to set up a semantic barrier.

'Dot cre wot yuo is ezier when fergetting' is more or less gibberish. It breaks the conventions agreed by the users of the English language code. The meaning is filtered or blocked.

Of course, the meaning depends entirely on the code, its conventions and other factors such as the context within which the code is used. For example, 'drop-out' means something particular and technical to a video user or engineer. It is part of a secondary code of language to do with that technology. More generally, we use it as a piece of idiom to describe a certain kind of person.

So, another definition of this kind of barrier is useful.

Communication is blocked when we cannot attach meanings to words used because the conventions of the code are broken or because we don't know the code and its conventions in the first place. If someone talks to you in Italian, and you don't 'know' Italian, then there is a semantic barrier.

As we suggested in the first chapter, **words are only signs to which meanings are attached. Meanings exist in the mind, not in the words themselves. So, if we can't attach a meaning to a sign, even if we know it is a sign, then there must be a barrier to communication.**

4.4 Psychological barriers

Communications may be filtered or blocked by attitudes, beliefs and values.

Attitudes are particular views of people, situations and events. They are based on beliefs.

These are the most common cause of difficulties with interpersonal communication. These filters shape what we say before we say it and affect how we interpret what others say to us.

Since it is inevitable that we have beliefs and opinions of some sort, some kind of selection and interpretation within the process of communication is also inevitable. But the question is, how conscious are we of what we are doing to messages when we talk to other people and listen to them? We shouldn't jump to conclusions about what other people mean by what they are saying. We should think about what we are trying to say before we speak. If we don't do these things, then once more we are making assumptions. We are not perceiving ourselves and others clearly.

The effect of these barriers in the mind rather depends on who is talking to whom about what, and with what intention. But obviously, these fixed assumptions that we call prejudices need to be taken seriously. And these prejudices lurk just below the surface of the mind in many of us. There has been much talk about racial prejudice in recent years. Clearly, it matters a great deal to an applicant for a job if that person is black and the interviewer has a subconscious prejudice that black people are unreliable or bad timekeepers.

It isn't the most blatant examples of prejudice that necessarily cause the most problems. It probably wasn't rigid male chauvinism that kept females out of newsreading jobs in broadcasting for many years. Rather, it was a kind of ill-considered prejudice which suggested to the controllers of broadcasting that a woman reading the news wouldn't be 'quite right'. And there was evidence that quite a few people in the audience felt the same way! More recently, there has been the case of two French owners of a British company coming to terms with national prejudice. In fact, they took on the mildly prejudiced jokes about 'Frogs' and were sensible enough not to take them as deep insults to their nationality and eating habits. They made a point of getting to know their workforce personally and built a good relationship with them, which proves the point that effective communication can create mutual understanding and banish assumptions and prejudices.

Some books on communication refer to factors such as religion or culture as separate types of barrier. We don't, because in the end it is the beliefs and values in the minds of people involved that set up barriers when, for example, culture is a factor in a given situation. Again, the barrier is psychological. If a Sikh suffers abuse to do with his wearing a turban, or an Australian is the butt of jokes about kangaroos and beer, then it is no good blaming the turban or the kangaroo. The barrier to free and friendly communication is in the mind of the person offering the abuse or making the joke. Once more it may be seen that meanings are in the mind, not in the sign.

Comment

It is useful to visualize how these three types of barriers, or filters, affect the communication process (figure 18). Mechanical barriers in particular exist in the context and the coding processes; semantic barriers in the formulation and

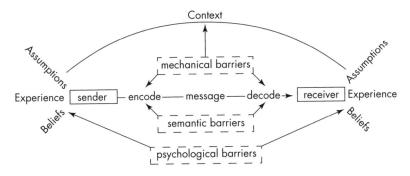

FIGURE 18   Barriers to communication

interpretation of the message; and psychological barriers in people's emotional processes.

How open is your mind?

Hint: be honest about times when you put up barriers against other people and their ideas, or even say things just to please other people.

---

5 Interpersonal skills

Communication skills used between people depend on recognition of and good use of verbal and non-verbal communication. When people are talking to one another they are not just talking. They are using body language, among other kinds of non-verbal communication. They are also in some kind of social relationship: friends, employer and employee, parent and child. For this reason you will also hear the phrase 'social interaction' used by people interested in communication. So too, the phrase 'social skills' is often used instead of 'interpersonal skills'. These social skills of communication can be described, learnt, and used successfully.

5.1 Social skills

Social skills are used to make communication with other people effective and satisfying to those involved in the interaction. For example, if you are talking with a friend about holidays that you both have had, then the conversation will be enjoyable and both of you will feel happy with it if you show that you are listening to each other and that you like each other. This listening and liking is something that you both learn to communicate.

When you communicate such attitudes and feelings, you are making a response. Your response is based on how you assess the other person – in other words, it is about perception. **It is a skill to notice aspects of someone else's behaviour and to judge these accurately**. But one also has to do something about what one has noticed. We call the reactions that we notice and assess 'feedback' (see figure 19). We have said that the idea of feedback includes our reactions to feedback. Our reactions should include an adjustment in our own communication. When we adjust and give out our own feedback, we are doing something positive. This positive response can take different forms. For example, if you are talking to someone about their work and that person shows signs of unhappiness, you might then respond by steering away from the subject or by trying to find out what is wrong. Such responses depend on exactly who is involved and on what the situation is. Either way, the feedback has been noticed and some kind of positive response has been made.

It is a skill to recognize feedback and to make a positive response to this feedback.

Interaction with others goes well if they feel that we have noticed what they are trying to say about us and what we are saying. It doesn't mean that one has to agree with everything that someone else says. But it does mean that the other person has to feel that basically we are paying attention and that we like them. Feedback in interpersonal communication means that each person is recognizing the other person. People like to be liked.

If someone comes along with a personal problem – say, they have quarrelled with a friend – then there isn't going to be much real communication if they feel that you aren't listening or aren't interested. You don't even have to approve of their quarrel in order to recognize the problem and to talk it over.

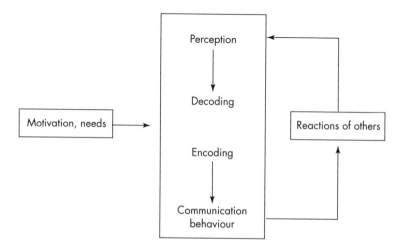

FIGURE 19   Social skills model, after M. Argyle (*The Psychology of Interpersonal Behaviour*)

To show signs of recognition is part of communication. To do it well is a skill. So one can also say that:

It is a skill to be able to give signs of recognition and approval to others.

Getting on with people isn't just a matter of talking and acting in a socially correct manner. It is also a matter of using feelings and intelligence in order to try to understand them. When dealing with other people it is important to be able to 'put oneself in the other person's shoes'. This involves a sympathetic understanding of the other person's views and of their experiences and of their place in the situation in which you are both involved. This understanding and ability to take the view of another is called *empathy*. The act of understanding in this way is called *empathizing*.

It is a skill to be able to empathize with others.

In order to achieve this empathy, one also has to pay close attention to the other person, to their apparent needs, to making sense of those needs. This attention that we pay to others when talking to them is in fact listening. It is surprising how often people do not listen to others. These are the conversations where someone's response to a comment leads away from what the speaker is talking about. Or it might be a response that starts talking about personal experiences and 'ignoring' what the speaker has been trying to talk about. In these conversations an exchange of words is taking place, but there isn't much listening going on. It is also worth pointing out that there are actually two broad types of listening experience. The one we are talking about here has to do with everyday conversation. There is also the listening that one does in a lecture or classroom. We will say more about this in the final chapter, and more about 'social listening' in section 5.2 of this chapter. But either way, one has to make a positive effort to listen. The proper receiving of information (listening, reading, and the like), which involves decoding, is as important as effective creation of communication.

It is a skill to be able to listen to others.

Of course, all these ideas about communication and skills are linked together. For example, if one shows that one is listening, then one is also giving feedback to the other person. In the same way it is possible to say that such listening and feedback are also part of self-presentation. We have already explained what this is. What is worth emphasizing is that effective presentation is something that we can learn to do. As with listening, it is possible to say that there are two broad types of presentation. The more formal kind, involving presentation to a group, will be discussed in chapter 6. But the kind of presentation that we make in everyday life, which includes strategies, is the one that we are now interested in.

Some performances are more conscious than others. If you are working in a shop at the end of a hot Saturday and are tired, then you may make a deliberate effort to keep up a polite and interested performance for a customer.

You will use your skills to do this. On the other hand, if you are trying to talk to a friend about something that you have decided to do, then your performance may be fairly unconscious. Still, the point is that you want them to see you in a certain light, to see you perhaps as a decisive and cheerful person. It will take skills to do this. It takes control of those skills to do it successfully.

One particular expression of listening is the skill of what is called reflective listening. Quite simply, one shows that one is listening by asking follow-up questions. The best kind of questioning is that which picks up on the word or phrase of the topic that you want to know more about, and uses it in the form of a question:

> '. . . and the coach stopped at this really weird place on the way back.'
> 'Oh? So what was weird about it?'

As well as showing that you are paying attention to people who are talking to you (and not just thinking about what you want to say!), this is a good way of getting people to talk, of getting to know them.

It is a skill to be able to offer self-disclosure in a manner appropriate to the occasion.

In this case the skill is about you being able to talk about yourself – but not endlessly! In fact, it is rather more about revealing something of yourself. If you are having – or trying to start – a conversation with someone, then it helps to tell them something about your background. If you are prepared to 'give something away', then others will feel that you are more trustworthy. Anyway, it is likely to provide a starting point for more conversation. This is not about telling the story of your life as soon as you meet someone. But it could be about revealing some of your likes or dislikes – places you like to go, favourite things to eat, and so on. It sounds trivial, but once people feel OK about sharing small secrets, then they may (but only may) want to share bigger ones.

This idea of having 'hidden' information about yourself has been expressed through a diagram called the Johari Window (see figure 20). The diagram has its explanation attached, but you will notice that it is not just about things you know about yourself, but choose to keep to yourself. It is also about things that you do not know, or see, in yourself, though others do see them. Obviously this idea is both about our self and about our ability to communicate effectively.

It is a skill to control self-presentation, with a sense of what is appropriate to the situation.

We have also talked in this chapter about perception and about the problems and barriers that relate to this in particular. We will say a little more about these in section 5.3. However, it is important to realize that such perceptual skills are part of social skills and are used in everyday life. We learn to make judgements about other people. We ought to be careful about how we do this. It can take an effort to avoid the kinds of problem referred to in section 3 of this

OPEN PANE What I know about me which is what others know about me	**BLIND PANE** What others know about me, but which I don't see
HIDDEN PANE What I know about me, but which I am keeping a secret from others	**UNKNOWN PANE** What no one knows, not even me, but which I may discover about myself one day

FIGURE 20   The Johari Window describes the hidden and known self, which affects how we talk to others and they to us

chapter. And it is worth remembering that perception is about the communication we make after the judgement as well as about making the judgement itself.

It is a skill to perceive carefully.

Finally, there is one social skill that one might say is the basis of all good interpersonal communication. That is the effective use of verbal and non-verbal communication. It can be said that all the other skills depend on this. Ultimately, interaction between people depends on verbal and non-verbal signs, how we make sense of them and how we use them. This is not to say that things like judgement and feelings are not important. But the fact is that we guess their existence from our words and deeds. We express our ideas and feelings through external signs of communication. The quality of our expression will define what other people think of us and how well we get on with them in conversation and in all situations. When we try to say what we mean or to say the 'right thing', we are trying to control our communication so that we do just that.

It is a skill to control and use non-verbal behaviour effectively.

5.2 Listening skills

It follows that effective listening is tied up with effective use of verbal and non-verbal communication. The latter is especially important because it is often not noticed, and because we have already seen that messages about feelings and attitudes are largely carried through this channel.

When we are talking to someone, they 'know' we are listening because of signs such as the head tilted to one side slightly, direct gaze, a certain amount of nodding and even some noises that we make to punctuate what they are saying. The importance of this is perhaps shown by the trouble that television producers go to when shooting the 'noddies' showing an interviewer apparently responding to what the interviewee is saying (these listening signs are recorded after the interview is over!).

Just try a conversation in which you deliberately make no response at all to your friend and watch how they dry up and ask you what is wrong! These responses show them that you acknowledge that they are there and talking, that you are keeping up with the main points that they are making and usually that you go along with what they are saying – that you approve. Like all the other skills, you have learnt to do this. Some people have not learnt to do it very well – and so may not get on with others. But again, one can still learn such listening skills and improve them. Of course, one should not be too deliberate. If one ends up looking like a nodding toy dog with a daft smile on one's face, then this is as disconcerting as showing nothing at all. So, of course, skills have to be tried and practised and adjusted to the person and the situation concerned.

It is a listening skill to acknowledge the person who is talking.

It is a listening skill to help keep the conversation going.

It is a listening skill to show some approval of the other person and what they are saying.

It is a listening skill to be able to feed back to the other person what they said and intended rather than what you selected from what they said.

Most of us can think of conversations we have had recently in which we have failed to listen properly to what the other person has said. We allowed our attention to wander or interpreted what they said to suit ourselves. Even in close relationships, one person can say to the other, 'You never listen to what I have to say.'

Listening with an open mind that does not filter out what is said to fit your own requirements or perceptions requires you to listen from the other person's point of view rather than your own. When we are listening, it is tempting to judge what we're hearing from our own perspective. Listening with an open mind, you do not hear the words and see the non-verbal cues simply to jump to your own conclusions, making snap decisions or anticipating what you are going to hear and think. How many times have you made up your mind about the other person's point before he or she has even made it?

5.3 Perceptual skills

It is also useful to elaborate on perceptual skills. We have seen that essentially there are three phases to perception. There is the first stage, where one actually notices the appearance, behaviour and words of the other person. The second stage happens in the mind, where one makes judgements about the other person, perhaps using previous knowledge of that person, or knowledge of people and situations which we believe are similar to the situation that we are in. There are internal decisions made from those judgements about how to carry on the conversation. Then the third stage is where we actually talk back, respond and give feedback.

It is possible to say that perceptual skills are also to do with avoiding the kinds of perceptual errors which we have described. One can summarize key perceptual skills as follows.

It is a perceptual skill to make accurate observation of the other person's words and behaviour.

It is a perceptual skill to avoid jumping to conclusions about the other person.

It is a perceptual skill to make careful judgements about the other person.

It is a perceptual skill to make an appropriate response to what they have to say.

How skilled are you as a communicator, and in what ways?

Hint: ask your friends and listen carefully to their feedback!

Review

This is to help you check on the main points of this chapter, 'Interpersonal communication'.

First we said that interpersonal communication is about communication between people, usually face to face. It is about making contact with others and about how and why we do this.

1 MEANS OF CONTACT

1.1   Non-verbal communication is one channel that carries messages to and from other people. It includes three codes, called body language, paralanguage and dress.

1.2   Speech is the other main channel of communication between people. It is a code, composed of signs. It includes secondary codes. The signs can be used selectively, as when we choose a register. Our verbal and non-verbal signs are special to our culture.

1.3   Contact is for exchanging messages and meanings.

2   DEALING WITH OTHERS

Dealing with others is about how we use the means of contact that we have.

2.1   We use strategies when choosing our words and non-verbal signs in order to achieve some purpose through communicating. Some strategies are used so often that they become habits, even rituals.

2.2   Games are strategies for manipulating other people.

2.3   We present ourselves through a persona when we deal with other people. We stage a performance. We have different personae for different situations.

2.4   We can learn a variety of communication skills, some interpersonal, some requiring use of a range of media. Interpersonal skills help us make contact with others. Skills help create and confirm various kinds of relationship.

2.5   Relationships are defined by the ways that we use communication, for better or for worse.

2.6   There are various categories of social situation, and these affect how communication is carried on.

2.7   We regulate our contact with others by giving and receiving feedback. This comes through non-verbal signs in particular.

2.8   Communication with others is affected in many ways by gender. There are discourses of male and female, which include meanings about maleness and femaleness.

2.9   The way we talk is affected by our culture and its beliefs.

2.10 The way we talk is affected by our sense of class, and expresses our ideas of class.

2.11 There are conventions of social interaction which we use unconsciously to manage how we deal with others.

3   PERCEPTION – OF OURSELVES AND OTHERS

Perception is about noticing signs that tell us about ourselves and another person, and then making sense of them.

3.1   There are two main elements in the self that we perceive: the self-image and self-esteem. What we think of our self will affect how we communicate.

3.2   When we perceive others, we make an assessment of them. This assessment is concerned with personality, emotional state and attitude. We also make assumptions about attributes of the other person: job, sex, status, role, age. We attribute (suggest) motives to people when we perceive them.

3.3   We base our perception on what we see and what we hear, especially on non-verbal signs.

3.4   But we perceive others imperfectly because of certain problems:

- We may project our wishes on to our view of the other person.
- We may categorize people too readily and too simply.
- We may make assumptions too easily.
- We are inclined to be influenced by first impressions.

4 BARRIERS TO COMMUNICATION

When we communicate with others, there may be factors that filter our messages when we are putting them together, or that cause us to filter the messages of others when we are making sense of them.

4.1   In the process of perception, the most common kind of filtering happens because we make inaccurate assumptions.

4.2   Mechanical barriers are to do with physical obstructions to communication.

4.3   Semantic barriers are to do with problems in conveying, receiving and agreeing about meaning.

4.4   Psychological barriers are to do with assumptions and prejudices that cause the message to be filtered. They affect encoding when communication is given and decoding when it is received.

5 INTERPERSONAL SKILLS

Interpersonal communication skills are also social skills that are used in various social relationships.

5.1   Social skills can make communication with others effective and satisfying. It is a skill to make sense of others' feedback and to make appropriate responses.

Key social skills are: to show approval to others; to empathize with others; to listen effectively; to present oneself appropriately; to perceive oneself and others accurately; to control verbal and non-verbal behaviour to good effect.

5.2   Listening skills use non-verbal communication.

Key listening skills in social situations are: to acknowledge the person who is talking; to maintain the conversation effectively; to show approval of the other person.

5.3   Perceptual skills are present in the three stages of perception, recognizing, reflecting and acting.

Key perceptual skills are: to make accurate observations of the other person; to avoid jumping to conclusions; to make careful judgements; to make appropriate responses to what is perceived about the person.

Debates

Is it true that females are more socially skilled than males? If so, why?

- One issue raised is to do with exactly what we mean by social skills.
- Another issue is to do with why this might be so. Here you need to look at socialization and upbringing, at what girls do that boys don't do, at what is valued in female behaviour.
- You'll probably want to question the relevant view held by some that females are somehow naturally better at dealing with others, at caring, even at getting their own way!
- One other issue related to this debate is whether or not it matters anyway.

WHAT DO YOU THINK?

Why do some people seem to be better at communicating than others?

- One point is to decide what you mean by 'better'.
- Another point is that it is often easy to confuse how much a person says, or how freely they speak, with 'good' communication.
- Another point is that people's communication performance often varies from situation to situation and from audience to audience.

WHAT DO YOU THINK?

Assignments

Assignment 1

Draw up a grid with the categories of body posture, body proximity, touch, gesture, gaze, down the left, and with two wide columns for situations 1 and 2 along the top. Then fill in the grid boxes in note form to explain how you would:

Situation 1 – express disapproval of an elderly man who is jumping a queue that you are in.

Situation 2 – express approval to a 5-year-old child for a drawing that she is showing you.

Assignment 2

Through either discussion or role-play, work out and write down strategies for the following tasks:

(a)   making an excuse to a friend for not meeting them;
(b)   encouraging someone who is shy to come out with you and your friends;
(c)   persuading the boss where you work part-time to give you extra hours' work.

Your description should cover verbal, paralinguistic and body language signs.

Assignment 3

Arrange to observe someone whom you don't know for about five to ten minutes, by inviting them into your group to talk with you, perhaps about their job.

Use a grid which you have previously copied (see figure 21) for people in your group to fill in two copies – one after one minute, one at the end. The grid rates a person in terms of attitude and personality, on a scale of points. You could add other opposed pairs of qualities to the grid if you want to.

At the end of the exercise, add up points or check ticks, and compare your scores. See if there are any changes from the first to the second assessment. Discuss what you may learn about perception both from these changes and from whatever overall agreements or differences there are.

	6 very	5 fairly	4 not very	3 not very	2 fairly	1 very	
hostile							friendly
dominant							submissive
extrovert							introvert
unsympathetic							sympathetic

FIGURE 21   Personality assessment grid

Suggested reading

Burton, G. and Dimbleby, R., *Between Ourselves: an introduction to interpersonal communication* [3rd ed.], London: Hodder Arnold, 2006.
Hartley, P., *Interpersonal Communication* [2nd ed.], London: Routledge, 1999.

See also the resources list at the end of this book.

Chapter 3

Communication in groups

Definite advantages come to those who learn to be successful and skilful group participants. At the personal level, if you develop your skills in groups you stand to gain enormous benefits, ranging from monetary and position-enhancement rewards, to your own self-actualisation. The better you are in group contexts, the more likely you are to accomplish your own goals and projects. The more of your goals and projects you accomplish, the better you feel about yourself.

(Wilson and Hanna, *Leadership and Participation in Small Groups*, 1993)

This chapter deals with some aspects of communication in and between groups. We provide insights into why people form and join groups and how people behave in groups. Such knowledge can help us to express ourselves more effectively in social situations.

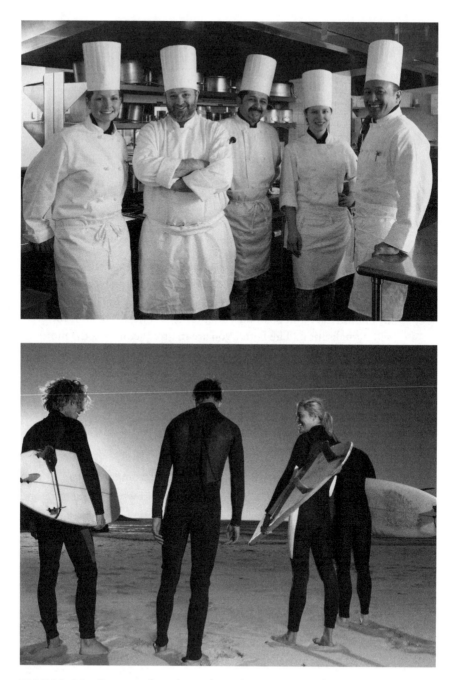

FIGURE 22 Groups are formed at work or at leisure. Courtesy of Getty Images

1 What is a group?

TRACEY'S STORY

Tracey looked round the snug room she inhabited, frowned, and threw herself on the bed. She could hear Sonje's TV bubbling through from next door. Sonje claimed she had to watch a lot of TV to help improve her English. She came from Denmark. Tracey thought that Sonje's English was better than that of some of the British students, even though she occasionally asked for help with her essays. She certainly doesn't need any help with pulling boys, thought Tracey. Sonje was tall, and with a figure to die for. We couldn't be more different, thought Tracey, with a tinge of self-pity.

Still, you had to like Sonje. She was a moving force in their small group of flat-mates. She cheered you up. She organized great parties. And she was, sadly, going home for Christmas.

Tracey sighed, and looked at the posters that she had stuck on the ceiling – against uni. rules, of course. She was thinking about going home for Christmas herself. She sort of looked forward to it, yet didn't want to go. In the flat they all had an amazing time together. She didn't want to leave the late-night chats, the shared crises over assignment deadlines, and of course the partying. It was strange to think that only about three months ago she and her Mum had had a little cry together about her going off to uni. Tracey had been homesick for two weeks, until they all got to know one another.

Now, home seemed further away than the hundred and fifty mile train ride. Her former college mates were not forgotten, but were now part of another life. She had kept up with a couple of them by phone, but everything had moved on so fast. She had been amazed to find herself joining a netball team – one of the other girls in the flat was dead keen. And Tracey enjoyed it, after the initial shock of finding out how unfit she was. She hadn't played since she was 14. But she had been quite good then, which had helped. It was a laugh. And she got on fine with the other girls on the team, even though she didn't feel that close to them.

But now she had to face making that call. Mum would be disappointed. But Tracey wasn't going home until she had to. Other people had knocked off after handing in their final assignment. And the flat was going to have one last party. Besides, Tracey wanted to earn as much as she could from her work in the union café/bar. She needed the money. 'What do you buy two horrible little 14-year-old brothers for Christmas?' she wondered.

ABOUT TRACEY'S STORY

This story is partly about the kinds of group that we belong to. Tracey is part of a family group, a social group, a sports group and a part-time work group. She is also a student, and no doubt felt herself to be part of her year group, not to mention her subject seminar groups. The story also suggests that we have to 'keep up' our group membership for it to be live and meaningful. Her group of friends from college and A-level days had reached the end of its 'natural' life. This indicates that we do move on and change in our lives. We change the groups that we belong to. Education, work, social opportunities, all mean that we find new groups and change our roles and relationships within (and with) those groups that we do stay with – especially family.

1.1 Groups we belong to

Each of us inevitably belongs to a variety of groups. You could list those groups you joined from your own choice, for example a sports club or a music group. You could also list those groups you joined without a free choice, for example your family or your school or college. There are many different sorts of groups with different sorts of purposes. They cater for our different needs. These needs may be short term (a Saturday night party) or long term (a swimming club). It is interesting to consider why we join and form our various groupings (see figure 23). Groups are often about doing things (task dimensions), and/or about being together (social dimensions). Some commentators describe groups as *primary* or *secondary*, according to how often we carry on face-to-face communication with group members.

The word 'group' can carry many different meanings and associations. **It is helpful to describe different types of groups according to their functions and qualities**. We have just noted that some are short-lived gatherings of people and others are more permanent gatherings. Some are formal, others informal. Some are small (say, five people), others are large (say, several hundred). Some are local, others international. Some are mainly social, some are work based; many have a mixture of socialising and work-type activities. Some are very goal oriented – trying to achieve specific ends. Others are more socially oriented – the satisfaction in one another's company. People in a group have some interest or purpose in common that brings them together. Having come together, they will have some influence on each other. This influence will persist even when they are not with group members.

Although **individuals in a group share common interests**, these people may not always share all of themselves. Having agreed on some purposes, people may disagree fiercely about how these purposes should be achieved. They might disagree on how the group should be organized. Some members may want all members to be equal, but other members may prefer to have a designated leader for others to follow. When people gather together there is usually some sort of struggle for power.

Relationships and patterns of communication have to be developed for the group to function. **If there is a lack of interaction between individuals, then a group cannot be formed or maintained**. A college or school class is a collection of individuals; it rarely becomes one group, but usually consists of several sub-groups.

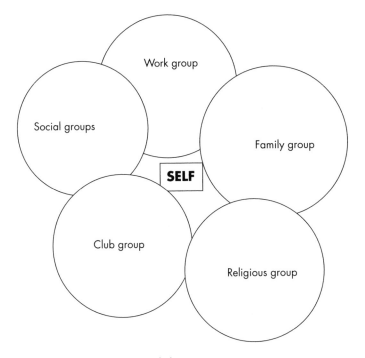

FIGURE 23   Our self and groups we belong to

Family groups

The first group that most people join is the family group. As babies we have no choice about this, since we are born into a particular situation and depend on those around us for physical and emotional support. Domestic groups, whatever the family set-up, serve to provide security and an environment in which people can develop and grow. A vital part of developing and growing is learning how to use the languages of human communication.

The first relationships we form are often with our blood relatives – a phrase that indicates the importance of these contacts. Our needs as growing individuals must be met by these people close to us who form our *primary group*.

Informal friendship groups

Informal friendship groups satisfy important needs for belonging. Everyone recognizes that children develop through playing with other children and with adults. But people of all ages continue to benefit from relaxed contact with others. An atmosphere in which we can communicate ourselves freely and share with others comes from a secure friendship group.

Such groups are often called *peer groups* because the relationships of these groups are between equals. These groups are most evident among adolescents at a time in our lives when we especially need to be with other people we like. We are often seeking to redefine our individual identity, to seek our own concept of what we are like and what we want to become. We therefore tend to seek out others who we believe are similar to ourselves. As we change, so we change our group memberships. Our family relationships often undergo strains as we experience and make these changes.

Formal organized groups

Formal organized groups are an element of all societies. For you, they may include school or college groups, or voluntary organizations such as Brownies, Guides, youth clubs, church groups, sports clubs and places of work.

These organizations have stated aims and structures. We are compelled to join groups such as a school (though not the activity groups within a school). Membership of groups helps each of us to develop his or her individual characteristics. We also develop our relationships with other people and the society in which we live. This process of development is often called *socialization*. This term describes the progress of becoming an active, participating member of the society into which we are born. Being a member of many groups is necessary to develop as a person who is able to relate to and communicate with other people.

The obvious functions of an organized work group may be to produce goods, produce a service or to make some sort of profit. An organized group of human beings will also inevitably fulfil other functions for its members, for example functions such as developing relationships, developing images of the self and personal identity, and enabling or preventing fulfilment of people's potential talents.

More will be said about communication in organizations in chapter 4.

1.2 The nature of groups

So far we have tried to get you to think about yourself and the different sorts of groups you encounter.

The rest of this chapter will concentrate on the ways groups operate and on the individual's behaviour within them. Before we go on to this, however, we wish to focus our previous comments by drawing up **a list of qualities that define what a group is**:

(a)   To become a group, the individual members must exist in some sort of **relationship** together. There must be some form of communication between them as the group develops so that it stays together. Not all the members of the group may like each other, and they may not always find it easy to co-operate, but these tensions would not be enough to break up the group.

(b)   Group members must share **common goals, purposes or interests** and recognize these. A crowd at a bus stop share the goal of hoping to catch a bus, but they may not interact together at all, and therefore do not form a group.

(c)   Groups 'set themselves' **tasks** that help them achieve these goals. If your goal is to raise money for charity, then your tasks may be to organize and carry out various money-raising events. Tasks don't have to be about material achievement. Organizing social events, or just a night out, might not be seen as a task as in 'work task'. But it is still 'work' within the group, and with the goal of maintaining and improving the social dimensions of the group.

(d)   Members of a group accept a system of **common values or norms of behaviour**. Some groups, such as the Guides or schools, indicate such norms (and membership) by requiring obedience to a set of rules and the wearing of a uniform. Within other groups, the pressure for group conformity is less obvious (see also section 3.3 of this chapter). Depending on the group, norms can be documented (written down), explicit (actually said) or implicit (suggested through behaviours).

(e)   Members of a group develop **set roles of behaviour** in a particular situation. These roles can be assigned, as for example in a committee when one person is elected as chairperson, one is secretary and so on. Alternatively, in a specific group one person may become the silent one, one becomes the joker, one the show-off, and so on. But that same person in another group may adopt a quite different set of behaviours.

With a family group and other groups that exist over a long time, these set roles may change. A lifetime may take the same person from being the baby of the family to an independent child and then an adult who takes responsibility for other members of the family.

(f)   This **conformity to norms of behaviour does not mean that everyone in a group behaves in exactly the same way**. Not all relate to each other in the same way. The stability of a group usually depends on people accepting different roles, and sometimes there can be a clear identification of status in which one person is openly the leader and others are followers.

(g)   Members of a group have an **identity** that may be represented through their dress and pattern of behaviour.

Which groups do you *choose* to belong to?

Hint: think of groups that you could choose to walk away from or to change.

2 Why do people join groups?

> Not only do they [groups] variously make it easier for us to do
> our job, they provide companionship, support and even a sense of
> identity.

(O. Hargie and D. Dickson, Skilled
Interpersonal Communication, 2004)

2.1 Reasons for forming and joining groups

In most societies there are three main reasons for people wishing to join
themselves into a group:

(a)   to achieve a shared goal;
(b)   to oppose a common threat;
(c)   to have a sense of belonging and security.

(a) To achieve a shared goal

On your own you may not be able to wield much influence, but if you can
persuade others to join you, then the influence of the group can be greater than
the separate efforts of lots of individuals. There are countless examples of
pressure groups formed to lobby decision makers to make or change a decision
in their favour. Can you think of some local and national pressure groups? They
could be concerned with environmental issues or the rights of a particular
section of society.

For the group to perform effectively it has to achieve the group qualities
that were listed in the previous section.

- What sort of uniting relationship can be built?
- How will the group ensure that its supporters really do pull together?
- Will everyone want the leading roles?
- Will no one actually want to do the donkey work?
- Can such a group work informally or does it need a stated structure, for
  example chairperson, secretary, treasurer, publicity representative?

A group of people that is formed to achieve a set task assumes at least one
common interest in its members, but there may be many more differences
between the individual members which will make their relationship and communication difficult.

In such circumstances, group members normally seek a formal structure
that all are required to agree to. Aims have to be agreed. Responsibilities have
to be assigned. The group must present a united front.

At the heart of these issues is the need for group problem solving. An
individual can weigh up the evidence, formulate alternative courses of action

and then select the most desirable one. However, for a group to follow this problem-solving process is less easy. One dominating individual may be seen to wield excessive influence, or the opposite may happen and the majority, who may be looking for the easy way, dominate the discussion. The communication skills outlined in chapter 2 – of using non-verbal communication; of careful listening; of taking note of barriers to communication – are all needed to influence a group in coming to the appropriate universally supported view.

We have concentrated on a 'pressure group' example. But these ideas are appropriate to the workings of committees, working parties set up to perform a specific task, and, indeed, to a total organization or association.

People in all these sorts of group may have only one thing in common. They would not 'naturally' join together – as a result of similar backgrounds, or because of closeness of age, or some other factor.

(b) To resist a common threat

This second reason is mixed up with the other two. It may be seen as one of the group's goals to pull together against some external threat – real or perceived. The pulling together will also give group members a sense of belonging, as well as helping them feel more secure in the face of that threat. On a grand scale that idea of threat can be illustrated by the way in which whole societies pool internal differences and work together in the face of the threat of war from some outside power. On a more immediate level, you can think of sports teams, and how some will raise their game in the face of the threat of losing a game to their opponents.

(c) To have a sense of belonging and security

In this case there may not be any particular task you wish to achieve, but you simply enjoy being part of the group. You may enjoy dressing and behaving like other people to show you identify with them. In saying this people might think of goths or chavs, who are obviously groups of people who have some things in common. But then the same comments could be made about company executives, who adopt certain patterns of dress and behaviour at work and in their social lives.

Simply wearing a certain sort of tie or a particular badge can show group solidarity. The use of communication skills to form relationships has been noted in chapter 1, section 2.1 as one of the main functions of communicating.

Many groups form almost accidentally; people with like interests gathering together. The purposes of such groups may not be formally stated, but the members simply enjoy being together and enjoy the social contact the group provides. After-work groups of drinkers at the pub satisfy these sorts of group needs.

Many people recognize in themselves and in others a desire to be 'sociable'. They want to be able to speak to and mix with other people they identify with. **We create our own personal identity through membership of groups and through displaying that group's identity**. We define ourselves by a list of 'I am . . .' statements.

We feel secure in the knowledge that we share values, attitudes and beliefs with others, so that to say 'I am a member of Friends of the Earth . . . a hip-hop fan . . . a student . . . I play football . . . I live in . . .' gives us a feeling of security, even if the security of the group may seem to be in opposition to that of other groups that other people belong to. Such statements will lead others to react in different ways: some favourably and some unfavourably. If membership of a group is important to the social identity of members, then they tend to stay with it; the group is cohesive.

For each of us, shared values can provide an important reference point for what we are and how we see ourselves. As children, our reference group will be primarily our family group, but as we mature we choose other groups to align ourselves with. We are prepared to give up some individual freedoms and accept some imposed norms of behaviour because such conformity gives advantages. One of the main advantages is ease of communication with like-minded members of the groups to which we belong.

The opposite of this, of course, is that a person who shares the norms of the local Conservative Club may well not find it easy to communicate with and share the norms of someone who belongs to a thrash rock group, and vice versa. Their attitudes, values, beliefs and perceptions of each other will strongly affect how each interprets what the other says and does.

Membership of groups is very much concerned with how we perceive ourselves and other people. We assign status to various groups, although there may not be universal agreement on which groups confer which status. One person wears with pride a uniform that another person 'wouldn't be seen dead in'.

Groups can give us a sense of status. Mixing within a group can give us self-knowledge.

An alternative view

You may also find it useful to consider another model as to why people join groups, based on the idea of needs, referred to in Chapter 1.

- material needs – e.g. wanting to make business contacts;
- interpersonal needs – e.g. needing to establish a sense of identity;
- information needs – e.g. wanting to find out about and join in a social world.

This overlaps with what we have outlined above.

Comment

In this book we are seeking to make processes of communication more conscious. Being aware that our opinions, our attitudes and our beliefs have been learned from the reference groups to which we belong can help us to see why we hold such beliefs. We tend to join with people who confirm our existing beliefs or offer us beliefs we wish to develop. We tend to reject ideas from people who challenge our beliefs.

Labelling people with group identities can prevent communication happening. Angela's story in chapter 2 (pages 78–9) illustrated some of the barriers that labelling and placing people into stereotypes can produce. Stereotypes often result from our perceptions, even if false and prejudiced perceptions, of group memberships and identities.

We need to be aware of what group membership does to us and to other people's perceptions of us. In the final sections of this chapter we are going to look at how people communicate in groups.

Are you a group kind of person?

Hint: have you said or done things to 'stay in with the crowd'?

---

3 Features of groups

PHIL'S STORY

Phil Jenkins wondered how he had got into this. It seemed to be mainly his little brother's fault. Tom had picked up the skateboard craze from Phil. Then he and his mates had got into trouble for boarding down at the shopping precinct. The layout down the overpass end made it a great place to roll. Phil had been there himself. But the complaints had got so the coppers had decided to do something about it.

Phil walked through the bar, stopping to talk to a couple of girls he knew. Then it was through into the back room which Griff the landlord had let them use for free. He was mates with the community warden, who had brought them all together in the first place.

So, the meeting got started, and there was the usual clamour from the younger kids wanting to tell their stories of being moved on and being hard done by.

'Now just shut up!' said Phil. 'I'm running this meeting, and I've got something you want to hear. No – be quiet, Mikey – you'll get your turn to speak when we get to "reports". I want to raise something that comes out of my record of the last meeting. It's major.'

Everyone on the skateboard park development committee looked interested. They were mostly young. Only Ferdy, the community warden, was really old, and he had roped Phil into this project. He was clever at sitting on the sidelines, knowing that Phil had credibility with the younger kids.

'Well,' said Phil, 'it's like this. Since last fortnight's meeting, I've had a reply from the Council at last.'

The atmosphere in the room grew tense.

'You know that previously a few of us met the recreation man at the council, and talked about sites and our plans and our budgets. Well, the council has had its meeting, and it's agreed to support us.'

Cheers broke out.

'Apparently they've earmarked the Builth Road site, and set aside five thousand towards the work.'

Ferdy whistled softly.

'But we have to raise the rest. So what do you think?'

'We've made a good start already,' said red-headed Ricky.

'Let's go back over the plans and go down the site again,' said Mary. She was taller than most of the lads there.

'I reckon we should go back over the budget and plan more fund raising,' said Nick Jones.

'Funny you should say that,' said Phil . . .

ABOUT PHIL'S STORY

Phil had a semi-formal role to play in the group. He took it seriously enough to call a meeting to order, to introduce items, to communicate for the group to the local council. He wasn't like this in social or family groups; taking such a role would have been inappropriate.

He is also involved in a typical group process of decision making. He knows that he is not supposed to jump in first in a discussion. In fact, Phil has previously worked out that it is possible to get some of what you want through a group by letting others make suggestions, by listening and maybe then steering things. What people in groups have to do is be prepared to compromise, to suppress individual wishes sometimes in favour of the collective feelings of the group. Equally, individual personalities, people's relationships, their social status, also affect interaction and decision making.

3.1 Roles

We adopt roles in our lives which help us to form relationships with other people. **A role is a way of behaving that is considered to be suitable for a particular situation**. From an early age we learn to play parts according to unwritten scripts in our heads – provided by parents, brothers, sisters, teachers, friends, and so on. There are times of course when we prefer not to play the role that others try to assign to us.

We accept to a greater or lesser extent the goals and expected behaviour patterns of a group to which we belong. There are often tensions between individual wishes and group pressures. Hence we join and leave many groupings during our lifetime. We join or form groups to serve our needs; in return for this, we may have to be prepared to sacrifice some individual freedom of action.

It is helpful to identify the roles we play as communicators. A great deal of our education and our socialization consists of our learning what are considered to be patterns of appropriate behaviour in different situations.

The greater part of our lives is spent with groups of people, and we learn how to behave in those groups. If we attend an orchestral concert at a venue such as the Barbican Centre in London, we are expected to sit still and quiet and listen. If we attend a pop concert at the Birmingham Arena, then we are not expected to sit still and quiet and listen in silence. If we attend a BBC Promenade Concert at the Albert Hall in London we are, by tradition, allowed to sing and dance at particular moments. If we attend an event like the Global Gathering, then the freedom of movement, of sound, of eating, and so on is again quite different. In each case we are part of an audience listening to music, but in each case we accept the role of a different sort of audience in which the patterns of behaviour are quite different.

This concept of role in communication is difficult to define, but it is useful to help explain why people behave as they do. At one extreme it may seem that we are playing a series of roles, or merely taking on ourselves a number of dramatic characterizations. You might ask, where is the 'real me', the real person and personality within these different roles? To reconcile this apparent contradiction it is important to realize that a role is an expected pattern of behaviour, but that each person will bring to it their own personality, attitudes and experience. Within the broad framework of a role there is a lot of room for individual interpretation.

For example, if we were to compare two formal committees they would both have a chairperson and a secretary. Each of these roles is defined; however, each person that fulfils these roles will fulfil them differently. One person may be a firm, authoritarian chairperson, while a second person may be content to let the committee discuss issues in an open way with each committee member's views being equally valued.

Another example might be to observe young children. Especially at the pre-school age from 3 to 5 years, children are often trying out roles. Their play will include being mother and father, or maybe playing at being a farmer, a policeman/woman, a shopkeeper, or some other occupational role that they have encountered. It is through trying these out and interpreting them for ourselves that we develop our own self-identity and our own personal approach to the roles we shall play.

FIGURE 24 We all have core roles to do with family, work and leisure. Some roles are assigned – daughter. Other roles may be adopted – mother.

In order to manage the many relationships that we enter into and to communicate with other people, we have to assume some predictability of behaviour. Hence, we tend to predict that people will behave in certain ways according to categories of roles. The following list of types of roles is one that we often consciously, or less consciously use. There is an example of these for a man in figure 25.

Professional roles

If someone is labelled a farmer, a social worker or a teacher, you have certain expectations of them. You would allow a doctor or nurse to do things to you that you would allow other people to do only if they were very intimate with you. A nurse or a doctor in a hospital wears a uniform to signal their role and to decrease their human individuality and personality.

Age roles

Different sorts of behaviour are considered appropriate to particular stages of your life. You can get away with things, for example a display of tantrum, when you are a young child. A 40-year-old throwing a tantrum would be viewed differently.

Gender roles

Even though the differentiation of sexual stereotypes is rightly being challenged, there still presently remain some expectations about appropriate

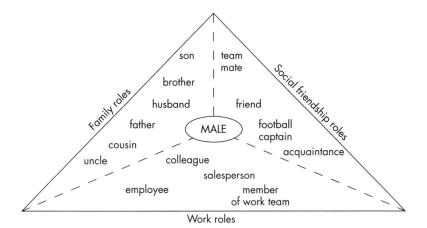

FIGURE 25 Types of roles in groups

behaviour for men and women. If you see a man crying, do you react differently from how you behave when you see a woman crying?

Class roles

Again, class roles are changing. The idea of class is quite subtle – compounded of elements such as wealth, birth and communication style. Dominantly it is about status and power. In many people's perceptions, whether they are acknowledged or not, there still remain expectations about upper-, middle- or lower-class behaviour. To label another person as middle-class or working-class or 'posh' can have quite different meanings according to the perceptions and the tone of the person who says it.

While these four categories of role – professional, age, gender and class – can be helpful in understanding other people's behaviour, they are not in any way fixed, and we are free to choose the way we play our roles. Although we may not be able to change our gender and age, we can change out of the expected behaviour patterns of a 50-year-old male. Do you have expectations of a 50-year-old male who is a solicitor from a middle-class background? What sort of person do you expect him to be? You might like to try to describe your expectation of what he looks like, the people he mixes with, the way he spends his time and the way he behaves.

3.2 Groups, teams and roles

When one looks at how people behave in either social groups or work groups (sometimes referred to as teams), it is noticeable that they will fall into various **role types**. Descriptions of these types are almost like personality labels. The words used say a lot about how any one group member contributes to the group. This contribution may be to do with helping the atmosphere and mood of the group – jokers and peacemakers. It may be to do with getting things done – ideas-person or organizer. It may be to do with supportiveness – compromiser and conciliator. You should cross-refer these ideas to the next chapter, on organizations, where it is important that people in work teams should be able to contribute to the task(s), as well as to the happy maintenance of the group.

Of course people do not always help a group. Some can destroy it – at work or in our social lives. The backbiters and the complainers are destructive. Those who help groups are said to have *functional roles*. Those who damage groups have *dysfunctional roles*.

Role titles and role types can help us distinguish between the various functions of group members: chair or secretary, leader or finisher.

3.3 Norms

In a group to which we belong we must be prepared to accept the norms of behaviour that the group has developed.

These norms can sometimes be stated as formal rules – laws in a society, or rules and regulations for a school or college. Such norms are imposed quite clearly.

Other norms can be left unstated and informal. For example, it may be expected that people in a group at a café will be noisy, joking, fast-talking, interrupting each other, and that each person will be treated on equal easy-going terms. However, the same people transferred to their home situations may accept that at the dining table only one person talks at a time, and conversation is conducted slowly, politely and quietly. Such norms are developed by the groups themselves, not externally imposed. This development of norms usually results from the processes that have formed the group into a stable entity.

3.4 Stages of group development

It has been suggested by B.W. Tuckman and repeated by Michael Argyle (*Social Interaction*, London: Methuen, 1969) that groups usually go through four clear stages in their development:

(a)   **forming** – anxiety, dependence on leader (if any); members find out about the task, rules and nature of the situation;

(b)   **rebellion** – conflict between individuals and sub-groups, rebellion against leader, resistance to rules and demands of task;

(c)   **norming** – development of stable group structure, with social norms; conflicts are resolved, cohesiveness develops;

(d)   **co-operation** – interpersonal problems are solved, the group turns to the constructive solution of the problem, energy is directed to the task.

The third stage of development is significant and the point at which the individual members are prepared to forgo some of their own personal demands in favour of the solidarity of the group. This solidarity may be considered desirable in order to fulfil the task that the group has been set or has set itself, or in order to fulfil the social processes of the group in supporting each other.

Another version of group development stages is proposed by B.A. Fisher and D.G. Ellis (*Small Group Decision Making* [3rd ed.], New York, McGraw-Hill, 1990), which can be paraphrased as follows:

•   **orientation phase** – in which people sort out who is who and why they think they have come together;

•   **conflict phase** – in which differences of ideas, of relations, about decision making are argued through;

- **management phase** – in which the group resolves those differences;
- **productive phase** – in which the group gets things done;
- **leave-taking phase** – in which a group breaks itself up, having achieved goals. (Of course, with many groups this does not happen.)

3.5 Group conformity

If an outsider enters the group, he or she will feel the pressure to conform to norms. A famous study of this pressure to conform was carried out by an American researcher named Asch. He put together a group of people in a room, some of whom had agreed with Asch to deceive the others. These others in the group were shown several lines such as those in figure 26.

The members of the group were told to give an obviously wrong answer about whether the standard line was the same length as line number 1, 2 or 3. The outsiders were therefore faced with a conflict between what their eyes were telling them and what they heard from a majority of those they thought were their fellow group members. Were they to believe what they thought they saw or were they to believe what they thought the other people must be seeing? The results showed that 37 per cent of the outsiders conformed to the judgement of the inner group and were thus in error. In other words, quite a significant proportion of the outsiders were prepared to conform to the group pressure rather than rely on their own observation and judgement.

You might like to try a version of this experiment among some of your friends. In order for it to work, there must be an amount of trust among those taking part. The group must be prepared to keep together. Such group thinking does, of course, show that there are dangers if we completely subdue our individual judgements in favour of conformity to the group. The Asch experiment indicates how group norms can lead to conformity. But it doesn't have to be like that. Here is a quotation from Peter Hartley (*Interpersonal Communication*, London: Routledge, 1993):

FIGURE 26   Comparisons of lines

On the one hand a group can develop norms which restrict its members' behaviour and communication: on the other hand a group can provide support and understanding for its members and allow them to express themselves in ways that they otherwise would not have done.

The protection afforded by groups can either stifle you or support you. Families can do this as much as work groups. The kind of family that imposes expectations on its young members in terms of their careers can be stifling: the family that gives them space to discover their abilities and convictions is supportive.

3.6 Groupthink and negative features of groups

Excessive pressure towards group conformity and obeying group norms has been described as *groupthink*. In this state, the minds of the group become closed to new ideas and outside influences. The group collectively achieves a kind of arrogance in which it overestimates its powers, and perhaps the moral force and justice of beliefs that it holds.

Such a group – like a street gang – might well have bonded strongly in the face of outside pressures: other gangs, social disapproval, and the like. But things can get to the point where the group thinks it is invulnerable, that anything it does is OK. Group members tend to subscribe to stereotypical views – pro-Nazi gangs. Pressure is put on anyone who doubts the group view or who questions group behaviour. Some group members adopt the role of 'guards', making sure that no one steps out of line. Perceptions and judgements are distorted in the cause of conformity.

Another negative feature of groups can be what is called *de-individuation*: losing one's sense of being an individual person, with responsibilities for thinking things through for oneself. We can see this most obviously in the behaviour of crowds or mobs. Members of these groups lose a sense of accountability, and can become violent and destructive. Their logic is that everything is down to the group, and whatever happens is nothing to do with them personally. They feel anonymous. Social ties and obligations – moral codes – can go out of the window.

In terms of groups carrying out tasks, there is a negative behaviour called *social loafing*. This matters especially in the workplace. It comes down to the fact that in some groups one finds lazy people. They loaf around and let others do the work. It's a way of thinking that says, it doesn't matter if I don't do much, the rest of them will get the job done. If you have ever been in a situation where a group of people are singing – or have watched singing taking place – you have probably been aware that some people just open and close their mouths, but don't sing properly. This social loafing is quite common, and more common the bigger the group. Conversely, in smaller groups, where members are more 'exposed', they are less likely to avoid pulling their weight. This is also a cultural phenomenon. In cultures where there is more belief in collectivism and co-operation – in Asia, for example – researchers find far less of this 'loafing'.

3.7 Leadership

> In the Chinese book of wisdom Tao Te King, dating from 600 BC, it was written that most leaders are despised, some leaders are feared, few leaders are praised, and the very good leader is never noticed.
>
> (O. Hargie and D. Dickson, *Skilled Interpersonal Communication*, 2004)

The final aspect of behaviour in human groups that we wish to note in this section is the question of what is often called leadership. The example of Orwell's novel *Nineteen Eighty-four* indicates a leadership principle that is totally dominating, totally controlling and totally autocratic.

There are, however, other styles of leadership. In societies that believe in being democratic, the autocratic style, whether adopted in families, in friendship groups or in work groups, would be frowned upon. In groups with hopes of being democratic or equal, decisions are not imposed by one member. It is worth remembering that leadership is a quality: being a leader is just a role – which has to be acted out in one way or another.

Effective leaders are good at communicating with others. They are adaptable in the way that they communicate – reacting to the needs of the group, and to individuals within the group. They know what they are talking about. They help give the group direction in setting and achieving goals. They help it achieve a structure, a kind of organization, especially in respect of carrying out tasks.

Four major styles of group leadership are usually described as autocratic, laissez-faire, democratic and collective.

Autocratic

Here one person imposes his or her will on the rest. Often, hostility and lack of personal commitment among the other members of the group are the result. However, in groups with formally stated hierarchies, like the uniformed services, such a style is accepted as the norm.

Laissez-faire

Here no one person or sub-group takes responsibility for decisions. In consequence, little is usually achieved and there is a general state of confusion.

Democratic

Here the group welcomes initiatives from all members and no one person dominates the group. Usually there are more united common efforts, and group members consider themselves to be 'we'; that is, decisions are perceived to be group decisions, shared by all. There may be an 'elected' leader, or the role of leader may be rotated.

Collective

Here the group seeks to avoid the concept of a leader and operates as a team of equals. Each person is assigned equal status and power. Actions and decisions require the agreement and support of all, hence there is need for lengthy group discussion and persuasive communication skills. 'Collectives' can be slow to decide and act, but they can create a very solid and committed group.

Can you apply these broad categories of leadership to groups you know? Are you a member of an organization that seems to be autocratic or laissez-faire or democratic or collective?

The autocratic style is sometimes seen as being the most efficient. Decisions are often taken fast and implemented fast. The comparative loss of personal freedom and satisfaction may be accepted for the good of the group.

Research suggests that women tend to lead more democratically than men. Equally, how female leaders operate can be affected by how they are perceived. For example, there is evidence that some men react negatively to female leaders, especially if the latter are assertive. It is also the case that effectiveness of leadership does depend on context – what the group is trying to do, under what conditions.

More will be said about groups working as organizations in chapter 4.

To conclude chapter 3 we shall explore specific examples of how communication operates in small groups.

Are you a team player?

Hint: think of how often you work with others and how often you get impatient with other people.

4 Communicating in groups

4.1 Observing group communication

We hope that from reading this chapter you now have a clear notion of how human groups exist on two levels: (a) the goal, task or purpose which brought the group of people together; and (b) the social, communicating processes that enable the group to work as a group. In this respect, groups can have task cohesion (working together) or social cohesion (bonding together). A given group may not be strong in both areas.

In the case of Phil's story, if we recorded such a meeting we could observe a good deal of non-verbal communication, for example tone of voice, nodding of heads, facial expressions, gestures, body posture. These signs of non-verbal communication would indicate what feedback each speaker was giving and what attitudes towards the topic and towards each other the speakers wished to show, or indeed what each was showing unintentionally. Without speaking, each committee member would be likely to express a reaction to each proposal. Maybe some members were not very interested at all in what others had to say, only thinking of their own ideas.

It is possible to observe communication in groups, which is often called group dynamics, in two ways.

4.2 Participation and interaction patterns

We can observe the participation and interaction of people in the groups. We can see who talks most and least. We can also see who talks to whom.

Participation in a group

You can record levels of participation by drawing a circle to represent each member of the group and placing a mark in the circle for each time the person speaks.

For example, in a group of five people, labelled A–E, we could record the participation of each person, as in figure 27. In this figure we can see that person A spoke five times, person B spoke ten times, and so on.

Interaction in a group

To record the interaction between people in the group you can draw the same circles with the same labels and then indicate who talks to whom by linking the circles by lines with arrows indicating the direction of speaking. This sort of diagram is called a *sociogram*. For example, the discussion which we recorded in figure 27 might have indicated interactions such as those in figure 28.

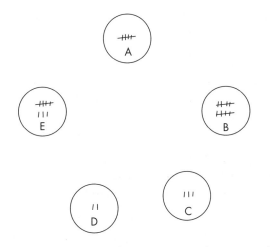

FIGURE 27 Participation in a group – how many times each person speaks

In figure 28 we can see that person A spoke generally to the whole group twice, spoke to person B once and to person E twice. Person B, on the other hand, spoke generally to the group four times, spoke twice to person A, once to person C, twice to person D and once to person E. The patterns of speaking and interaction between these people can thus be recorded. If one observes a group discussion and records the interactions in this way, it can often be seen that the discussion can centre on one or more people, with others remaining very much outside.

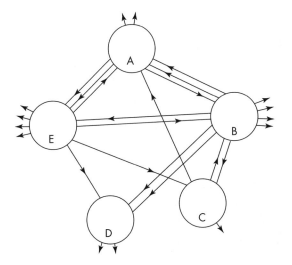

FIGURE 28 Interaction in a group – who speaks to whom

4.3 Group communication: tasks, relationships, individual needs

Thus, by drawing circles to indicate group members we can record the levels of participation and interaction. These sorts of diagrams, however, do not really indicate what the content of these communications is. In order to do this, a different method of recording the group processes is needed. We can draw up a grid as in figure 29, which records whether the group members are:

• contributing to the task of the group; and/or
• contributing to the maintenance of the group relationships; and/or
• only concerned with their self-centred needs.

By using headings for different sorts of communication, some of which are concerned with the task of the group, some of which are concerned with the members of the group contributing to the group, and some of which are more concerned with the individuals working as individuals, we can build a picture of what each person is contributing to the actual discussion or meeting that is being observed.

Types of group communication		People				
		A	B	C	D	E
	TASKS					
1	giving information					
2	questioning/seeking information					
3	organizing ideas					
4	clarifying ideas					
5	summarizing					
6	evaluating					
7	deciding					
	RELATIONSHIPS					
8	encouraging					
9	harmonizing					
10	sharing/gatekeeping					
11	listening					
12	relieving tension/compromising					
	INDIVIDUAL NEEDS					
13	blocking					
14	seeking attention					
15	dominating					
16	not involving					

FIGURE 29 Analysis grid for observing group communication according to contribution to the tasks of the group, to the maintenance of relationships in the group and to individual needs

We have not entered any details for the various people on this analysis sheet, but suggest that you use a sheet like this in order to observe a group discussion. You can of course change the headings for the different tasks, relationships and individual behaviours. The headings that we have given provide a range of the types of contributions that people often make to group communication.

From our own experience of taking part in such observation exercises we can say that these methods of observing group communication often reveal that how we behave and communicate in groups is quite different from how we thought we had. I may sit in a group discussion and feel that I am making very positive contributions by giving information, summarizing, encouraging other people, listening and relieving tension. However, another observer recording an analysis of the group may have perceived my contributions quite differently. An outsider's view of my contribution may be quite different from the self-image that I have of my group behaviour. We recommend you try some of these observation exercises with groups that you know.

4.4 Becoming an effective group member

At various points in this book we use the phrase 'effective communication'. By this we mean the ability to express your ideas, to understand other people and to build satisfying relationships with other people, whether in pairs, in small groups or with larger social groupings.

This chapter has tried to provide some insight into aspects of social psychology in order to understand the communication processes that occur within groups. Membership of groups is a fundamental human need. We define ourselves, both for ourselves and for other people, by our group contacts and relationships. We often have unchallenged prejudices and stereotypes arising from our perception of people's membership of groups.

To understand how to become an effective group member, you need to take notice of the following points:

- what motivates people to join groups;
- the expectations of roles within groups;
- the relationships between group members;
- the skills of verbal and non-verbal communication;
- the ways that groups develop from a collection of individuals to a cohesive force with their own norms of behaviour;
- the significance of group identities and the labelling of people according to group memberships and roles.

4.5 Communication skills in groups

Members of a group can use certain communication skills in order to make that group satisfied with group relationships and effective in carrying out group tasks. These skills – ways of using verbal and non-verbal communication – often draw on interpersonal skills. For example, we have said that good one-to-one relationships depend on signs that recognize the worth and importance of the other person – giving them rewards. The same thing is true for group members. The person who scores the goal in a team sport enjoys praise given by group members. The giving and receiving of this praise also adds to the good feelings about being a member of the team. And if the main task of the group in this example is to score goals, then one can say that the rewarding skill actually helps the group in achieving its tasks. There are certain skills that relate especially to group members as people in a relationship, and others that relate to these people as problem solvers and decision makers. Some are personal, some are more practical.

On the personal side, phrases such as 'well done' or 'that's a good idea' offer reward to the group member and help the group.

It is a skill to be able to offer praise to group members for ideas or actions.

Another personal aspect of group activity that may be underestimated can be described as fooling around or as casual chat. Again, the sense of group solidarity can be reinforced by behaviour such as making jokes. If someone does this, then they can help the group member to relax, which will then help them to get on with the group's main activity. Obviously, too much joking actually becomes destructive – it gets in the way of the business of the meeting or of the play rehearsal – but, as with praising others, a certain amount can create group harmony. You may have noticed that news reports of high-level political meetings judge that things have gone well if there are pictures and accounts of smiles and joking, as well as of the serious business.

It is a skill to be able to relax group members without distracting them.

One kind of behaviour that works both on a personal level and on a practical task level is that which shows agreement. If a group is going to work positively, then there has to be a fair measure of agreement anyway. Music groups are notorious for splitting up and re-forming because there is dis-agreement about musical direction. If a group member positively expresses agreement with some decision or action or idea expressed, then this helps the group work together. To say something like 'I'll go along with that' or 'OK, and I'll help with the stalls' (a fund-raising group) is a positive contribution. Opinion and attitude have been expressed.

It is a skill to be able to show agreement with group ideas, actions, decisions.

It may be noticed that all these group skills require positive action. This is not to say that a quiet group member cannot be effective. Equally, a compulsive chatterer can actually impede a group. But someone who communicates nothing gives nothing to the group. This is true of the more practically oriented examples of skills which we will now look at.

People in groups commonly make plans, solve problems, make decisions. This is true whether one is talking about a formal group such as a council finance committee, or an informal one such as a group of friends deciding what they want to do for the day. To carry out such tasks it is necessary for group members to make suggestions or to give information: 'we could do this or that' – 'why don't we go to that place?'

It is a group skill to be able to offer information and ideas to the group.

But decisions are also well made on the basis of group discussion. So, another skill for any group member is to be able to weigh up suggestions, to evaluate what is being said. Someone might say, 'But would that work if . . .?' or 'What's wrong with the idea of going into town?'

It is a group skill to be able to evaluate ideas and information offered.

A good group member is also aware that groups are by definition co-operative. So, communication which encourages that co-operation must be a good thing. In various kinds of discussion – and groups do a lot of talking – certain phrases accompanied by appropriate non-verbal behaviour can encourage involvement and make people feel valued at the same time. Someone might make comments such as 'What do you think, Sue?' or 'How do you feel about going there?'

It is a group skill to invite opinions and involvement from other group members.

It may be that group leaders are identifiable as people whose opinions are valued. They are the people who are often asked what they think or want to do by other group members. But usually group leaders are also active and positive in their communication. The following two points may relate to any group member, but put together they are also likely to pinpoint a leader. One point about group communication has to do with bringing things together. If there are various ideas under discussion, even if there is disagreement, it is a positive move to help the group to try to reach agreement: 'So how do we all feel about doing this or that?' – 'Could we agree on Beth's suggestion for a place and time first?' – and so on.

It is a group skill to bring together ideas and opinions.

This sort of communication is obviously important in bringing any type of group to make decisions. But decisions also have to be turned into action. Group discussion, and argument, is often about the actions which may be the result of making certain decisions. Again, it can be group leaders who suggest courses of action. They try to wrap up the task and arrive at the goal. In sports teams the captain is the appointed leader and no one argues very much if that person actually gives orders during the game. But in most groups it is more subtle. The positive group member who may be a leader will say something like 'Let's do this or that' or 'Why don't we make up a list of things to do and share them out?'

It is a group skill to suggest actions involving the group.

You will notice that we have just emphasized the importance of group involvement. An effective group member talks with the group in mind and always tries to bring in other group members. Someone who says things like 'I don't know about you lot but I'm going to do this or that' is actually saying that they are going their way, not a group way. Group skills are used for the group, not for the individual. Sometimes group members will agree to things that privately they actually disagree with, to a greater or lesser extent. They do it for the group.

What's your favourite group?

Hint: there may be differences between whom you feel comfortable with and whom you most enjoy being with.

Review

This is to help you check on the main points of this chapter, 'Communication in groups'.

1 WHAT IS A GROUP?

1.1   It is a collection of people who have some shared interest or aim. We each belong to many different groups, such as:

- family groups;
- friendship groups;
- work/organized groups.

1.2   Groups:

- depend on relationships;
- have common interests, goals and tasks;
- expect norms of behaviour;
- develop set roles for members.

2   WHY DO PEOPLE JOIN GROUPS?

2.1   There are several reasons for forming groups:

- to achieve a shared goal;
- to resist some kind of threat to group members;
- to develop social contact and personal identity;
- to satisfy different kinds of need, both material and psychological.

3   HOW DO PEOPLE BEHAVE IN GROUPS?

3.1   Each of us plays different roles according to group expectations and our individual personality. Roles are influenced by professions, ages, gender, class and status.

3.2   There are various role types in groups, which affect the success of the group in completing its tasks.

3.3   We follow group-imposed norms of behaviour.

3.4   There are recognized stages in group development, which are all about getting together and getting things done.

3.5   Groups tend to create conformity among members, which can affect individual judgement.

3.6   Negative features of groups are seen in groupthink, de-individuation and social loafing.

3.7   Group leaders may adopt any of four different styles of behaviour.

4   COMMUNICATING IN GROUPS

4.1   Observing group communication for achieving the task of the group and for maintaining the group relationships.

4.2   Participation and interaction patterns.

4.3   Individual functions in achieving group purposes.

4.4   Understanding ourselves and our relationships with others in the groups we belong to.

4.5   Group members can use skills to make the group happy and effective. Key communication skills in a group are: offering praise; helping the group relax; showing agreement; offering ideas and information; evaluating ideas and information; inviting opinions; summarizing ideas and information; suggesting action.

Debates

How can groups influence people's communication?

- The first point to sort out is whether those receiving the communication are outside the group concerned, or part of it, or part of another group (see types of group and group roles).
- The next point would be to sort out what kind of group one is talking about, operating in what kind of situation.
- Another point to weigh up would be how far that influence is deliberate and how far it is a matter of how the individual sees the group rather than how the group treats the individual (see group behaviour and group norms).
- Finally, one might consider whether that influence, if it exists, is for better or for worse. Groups can give individuals the sense of security that encourages them to be unpleasant, but groups can also moderate the behaviour of individuals who 'go too far'.

WHAT DO YOU THINK?

We are told one way and another both to 'be yourself' and to 'learn to get on with others'. Is there a contradiction here between individualism and groupness?

- One point here is to decide what 'yourself' is (see self-image).
- Another point is to decide what 'getting on with others' means (see group co-operation and cohesion).
- Another idea in the debate would be to look at common words and phrases that seem to fit in with individualism or groupness: team spirit, the winner (see ideology).

WHAT DO YOU THINK?

Assignments

Assignment 1

To separate non-verbal signals from words, video-record a televised discussion or chat show. Then replay it with the sound turned down. If you have slow tracking, use this to pick out signs. See how many different signs you can identify. Try to work out what they are doing, both in relation to speech and in terms of managing the interaction between members of the group.

Assignment 2

(a)   Make a list of all the groups that you belong to, beginning with family. Write some accompanying notes in answer to these questions:

- Why do you belong to these groups?
- Are they task or social groups?
- What patterns of leadership do they have?
- How high a level of conformity does each expect?

(b)   Imitating the diagram for roles in figure 25, make a similar chart for yourself. This should indicate the sorts of role which you believe that you adopt in family, work, social groups.

Assignment 3

This is a role-play involving conflict – and resolution, we hope! You need quite a few people to play this out. And you will need to be imaginative in developing roles. We can't put extra and 'secret' details on the page of a book that all the players will read. But you can. So work on and develop the scenario which follows.

The situation is one where there is a demonstration going on against scientific experiments using animals (vivisection) outside Ardmore Laboratories.

One group of you are the demonstrators, with placards, shouting, stopping vehicles from going in or out, determined to stop work going on by one means or another.

Another group of you are the scientists inside, who are cross at being targeted, some angry at being trapped, some even a little frightened. Some of you are half-sympathetic to the demonstrators, but others firmly disagree with their views and irritated by what you see as scientific ignorance.

A third group of you will play the police, who are watching the demo to make sure it doesn't get out of hand, but who are also protecting the right to peaceful public protest. What you would like to do is to negotiate a peaceful solution and an end to the demo.

If you like, you can add a separate character – a reporter. This person is of course interested in getting a good story, in which conflict is a central ingredient.

So, talk through your handling of the situation separately. Then come together and improvise the role-play to see how your groups behave, both within themselves and with relation to others. In your debriefing, see whether you can recognize some of the points that we have made in this chapter.

Assignment 4

Take an example of a TV show in which groups of people are put under some pressure. Current examples might be *Big Brother* or *I'm a Celebrity, Get Me Out of Here*.

Examine a recording of one such show to see how group members shape up with relation to ideas such as leadership or co-operation. Talk about whether or not you recognized stages of group formation or the emergence of group roles.

Suggested reading

Burton, G., and Dimbleby, R. (2006): *Between Ourselves: an introduction to interpersonal communication* [3rd ed.], London: Hodder Arnold (see the chapter on groups).
Schneider, M., and Corey, G. (2002): *Groups: process and practice* [6th ed.], Pacific Grove, CA: Thomson Learning/Brooks, Cole.

Chapter 4

Communication in organizations

It seems that if you have an organization with more than about seven people then lines of communication can become extended and messages can be confused.

> (Michael Broadbent, Director of Group Corporate Affairs, HSBC Holdings plc, quoted in Theobald and Cooper, *Shut Up and Listen: the truth about how to communicate at work*, 2004)

This chapter looks at a particular sort of social group: organizations. We analyse formal and informal methods of communication used by people in organizations. Our focus is on people and their working relationships.

FIGURE 30 Dilbert, by Scott Adams. © United Feature Syndicate, Inc., 1993

1 How do organizations operate?

JANE'S STORY

Jane Foskett was a determined person. She wanted to go to see the new Romeo and Juliet *film because the play was part of their course. In fact, she wanted the whole class to go, because it would mean some time off school, and anyway that was what she had decided. The only trouble was that Mr Denham, he of the stained tie and an inability to pronounce his Rs, didn't seem to be that bothered.*

'It's a nice idea, Jane,' he said. 'But the organizing is so much trouble in this place. There are forms for everything. Really it would be easier if you lot went to see it on your own.'

'That's all very well, sir. But you know what people are like. Most of them won't do it. My older sister says it's really good. And I think that we should see it.'

'You do, do you? Well, I'll tell you what, Jane, if you do the organizing, I'll sign the forms and stick them in the right place, and then we can go. But you'll have to get people to sign up, and pay deposits, and book the coach and all the usual things. I'm afraid that you'll find it hard to get pupils to make that sort of commitment, let alone cough up for the coach as well.'

He obviously thought that she would be put off. He had underestimated her. This was a young woman who belonged to a largely male Venture Scout troop, had the lads eating out of her hand, and who organized most of their activities. So, she was not going to find the school system much of a problem. Jane set about organizing things in her usual pleasant but persistent way. Within twenty-four hours she had chatted up the secretary about the forms and clearances they needed, and had persuaded the cinema manager that if she could get more than fifty people into an afternoon showing then he would give them a group price on the tickets.

'That's easy,' thought Jane. 'All we need is two classes, and we can have a big coachful.'

Her trip folder grew fat with clearance forms, insurance forms, booking forms, lists of names with ticks, and letters to and from the cinema and the coach company.

To be fair to him, Mr Denham didn't make any more excuses. In fact, he backed her up, and put through all the paperwork that she wouldn't have been allowed to. He did check things before he signed them. And she did begin to see why he hadn't rushed to organize the trip himself. They had been handing in a lot of course work.

And even though the paperwork was necessary, it really was quite a business getting it all together. Strictly speaking, her Dad also helped her a bit. He was a teacher at another school.

'A school may not be a business,' he said, 'but we have to run it like a business. It won't do you any harm to find out what goes on behind the scenes. I think your Mr Denham has been quite clever in getting you to do all this.'

ABOUT JANE'S STORY

It is clear that organizations require systems and a range of means of communication in order to go about their business successfully. The people who work in organizations have to know the systems to be able to operate them. They have to be able to plan. Teachers have to plan their year's work, or plan trips. Schools have to plan their finances, manage their resources, obey health and safety regulations, just like businesses and organizations.

Organizing the trip to the film showing needed a lot of communication. Apart from what has already been mentioned, Jane had to make telephone calls, conduct negotiations, fill out forms, make lists. She had to do all this in some kind of order, so that she working her way towards her objective. These activities, this order, can be mapped out on paper. Jane made lists of things to do. But she could have made a flow chart of activities needed. An algorithm is a kind of flow chart. There is a version of one for Jane's trip in figure 31, showing a sequence of decisions and actions.

1.1 What is an organization?

This chapter is about communicating in organizations and also about organizing for communication. The word 'organization' can refer to a particular institution such as a school, factory, office, bank; it can also refer to the process of organizing as in a phrase like 'It took a lot of organization.'

In the title of this chapter **we are using 'organization' to mean a collection of individuals who have been brought together to carry out tasks to achieve set aims**. In this sense an organization is of course a sort of group. When we discussed groups in chapter 3 we generally referred to small groups, although we made some reference to formally organized groups. An organization is a group that has certain specific characteristics, as follows.

It is **deliberately established** at a certain time by an individual or group of people; for example, it is possible to point to the date when an organization was set up – 'established in 1922'.

It develops **formally structured relationships** and interdependence between people.

It has **set objectives** that the people in the organization are seeking to achieve, in the case of a business company, the objective would be to produce goods or services to be sold at a profit; in the case of a school, it would be to enable pupils to learn about themselves and the world in which they live. There may also be 'hidden' objectives that are different from the stated ones; for example, in terms of health care for the whole population the medical system in the United States may be inefficient, but in terms of making profits it is highly effective.

It **divides the work to be done between individuals and groups**. There are systems and sub-systems. For example, in a national service industry some

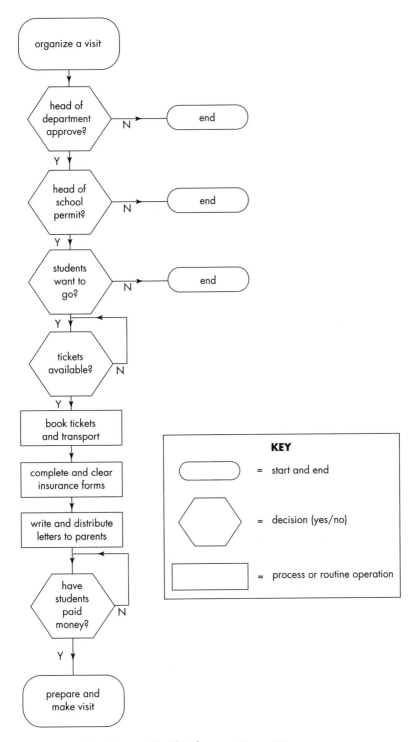

FIGURE 31 Flow diagram (algorithm) for organizing a visit

have the task of laying pipes, some installing appliances, some obtaining the equipment the organization needs, some selling the services, some dealing with accounts, some coping with taxes, insurance, staffing, health and safety, and so on.

All the various people and their tasks require co-ordinating into a unified effort to accomplish the tasks and objectives.

It **manages resources**, both physical (equipment, materials, money) and human (work, ideas, skills). To achieve efficient and effective use of these resources is another aim of all organizations. For example, if two people are setting up a small company to make and sell computer software, how much of their time and money must be devoted to advertising and selling their products instead of actually designing and reproducing new programs?

Finally, effective communication between the individuals and groups is essential if the various activities, processes and resources are to fulfil the aims of the organization. This communication takes place both within an organization and between that organization and many other organizations. For example, if the organization is a manufacturing company, then it must deal with suppliers of various materials and also with many potential customers. It also has to deal with other agencies concerned with things like taxes, insurance, property and employment.

It is the purpose of this chapter to concentrate on the last of these characteristics. The ability to organize, whether an enormous multinational company or a two-person outfit, depends on effective communication between people.

Small organizations can rely on informal and face-to-face communication for much of what they do. But even a small organization, if it is a business, must also have some formal systems, for example to keep accounts, to make tax returns and to employ people.

Large global organizations clearly need elaborate formal systems for communicating within and outside the organization. There will be many small organizations within the overall organization. Imagine Rupert Murdoch's international News Corporation, which employs 46,723 people around the world to produce a large number of media products such as publications, broadcasts and new media. Maintaining effective communication in such organizations demands complex formal and informal systems.

At its simplest, communication as a part of organizing can be illustrated by a basic organizational task: two persons working together can lift an object that neither of them could lift on their own. But to lift that object, the two people must establish a communicating relationship, agree on the objective ('Where's it got to go?'), divide the work ('I'll take this end'), and co-ordinate and manage their resources ('Lift when I say go').

Our concern here is not with such small organizational groups but rather with larger-scale business organizations. We are dealing with organizations in the everyday sense of the word, meaning schools, offices, banks, churches, factories, shops, and so on.

We relate to small and large organizations in various ways, for example as shareholders who own a stake in the organization, as employees who work for there, as service users or customers. We tend to think of organizations in various ways that can range from fondness to hostility. We also tend to use metaphors to describe our ways of thinking about different organizations.

In his book *Image of Organizations* (London: Sage, 1986), Gareth Morgan suggested there are eight popular metaphors that we use to characterize organizations:

- as a machine – designed and operated as machinery and indeed making humans conform to their needs
- as organism – a live adaptable mechanism like our bodies
- as brains – rational, problem solving, self-critical and innovative
- as culture – a set of shared values, principles, attitudes, and beliefs about what is important and how the world works
- as political systems – an institution with set power, authority, responsibility, order; about control and influence
- as psychic prisons – a collection of myths and fantasies that are confined by their own representation of themselves to the outside world
- as flux and transformation – a generative system that develops, grows, and regenerates
- as vehicle for domination – a mechanism to impose their will on others by domination and control.

Many large organizations can be perceived as a mixture of these metaphors.

How do you view the organizations that you know?

List small and large organizations that you are part of or have contact with. Make some notes about how you feel towards them using the list of metaphors above as a way of thinking about them.

1.2 Relationships and structures in organizations

The traditional shape of organization structures is that of a pyramid which shows lines of authority and responsibility. A typical example applied to a school might look like figure 32.

The head of the school is given authority by his or her terms of employment to make requirements of the staff 'below'. In turn, he or she is responsible to higher authorities and involved with other agencies outside the school. The local education authority (LEA) provides the majority of resources, including the largest single budget item, salaries, for a state-maintained school. The LEA appoints and pays the staff – a process in which governors and inspectors are usually involved alongside school staff. The governing body, a group of local politicians, interested people, parents and teachers, is ultimately responsible for the work of the school.

In a 'foundation school' a much greater proportion of money comes directly from the government. Also, the governors have powers to set budgets and appoint staff, including the head. This type of school is set up more like a business, with a board of directors.

The head and other school staff also have regular contact with outside agencies such as awarding bodies who provide the external qualifications, publishers, equipment suppliers, professional associations and trade unions, parents, and so on. The staff of the school are responsible to the head but also are responsible to other senior staff, who may act as intermediaries.

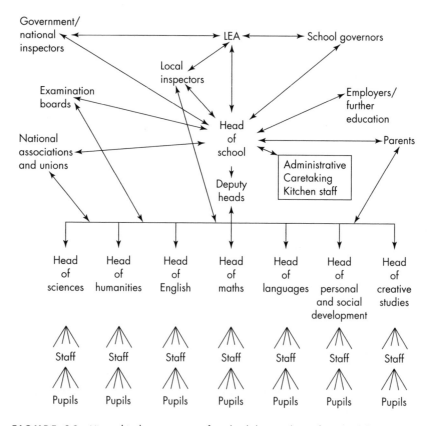

FIGURE 32 Hierarchical organization of a school showing lines of responsibility and agencies outside the school

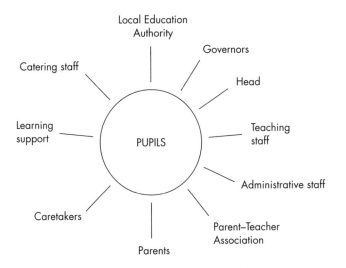

FIGURE 33 An alternative model for school organization showing various groups in support of pupils and their learning

There are different ways of representing the structure of organizations. For example, figure 33 shows a student-centred model. Our pupil Jane might feel better about this one. These diagrams not only can represent lines of communication, but also reveal something about how the organization sees itself. Hierarchical models are more concerned with status, power and control. They can also reveal that there is too much distance between those at the top and those at the bottom. Effective organizations look for lateral lines of communication as well as vertical lines.

We have concentrated on schools so far in this chapter largely because we can assume that all readers have some sort of direct experience of them. However, in terms of structures and networks of relationships, other sorts of organizations are often represented in the same way. The divisions of work into units and sub-systems of people will obviously vary according to the size of the organization, the tasks it has to complete and its aims. A manufacturing organization will need to find ways of dealing with tasks like research and development of new and existing products; purchasing of supplies; production of goods; marketing of products; sales; distribution to customers; finance and accounting; personnel recruitment; training and welfare of staff; and co-ordination and administration of all these tasks.

As a comparison with school structures and labels, we indicate in figure 34 how a manufacturing and retailing company might be structured. Within this hierarchical structure we can focus on one department, such as Marketing. To show how that department is structured and how it relates to other parts of the company we shall use a spider web diagram (figure 35). A spider diagram

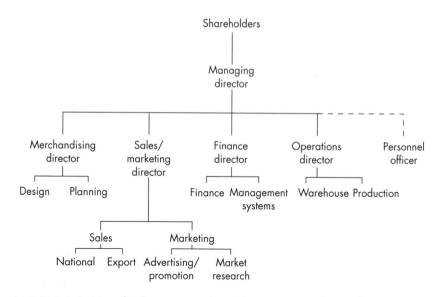

FIGURE 34 Hierarchical organization chart of the management of a manufacturing and retailing company

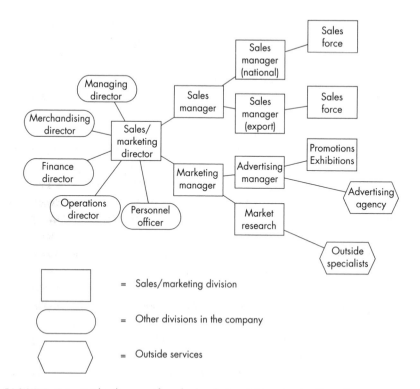

FIGURE 35 Spider diagram of a sales/marketing division showing lines of communication in and out of the company

focuses on the working relationships rather than the status relationships and lines of responsibility of a hierarchical model.

There are lines of communication not only up and down in an organization, but also sideways and diagonally. People will generally speak more freely about their work and themselves and feel more able to initiate contacts with those who are perceived as being of the same status. They will be more cautious in approaching people higher in the hierarchy.

A further point to make is that there are networks of friendship and social contact that can to some extent cut across these matters of status. At lunchtimes, tea breaks or at gatherings like those at churches or sports clubs, people from all levels and sectors of an organization may have personal communication. A criticism of some industries has been the separation of canteen and other facilities according to status within the company. The development of group norms and loyalties, which were discussed in chapter 3, is also a strong influence in these matters of open or limited communication: in some companies, if you were known to be friendly with 'the Boss', people would be careful about what they told you.

Organizations develop their own norms like any other group of people. An employee who moves jobs from one organization to another within the same industry is often surprised by how different the conduct of relationships between colleagues can be.

There are alternatives to designing organizations as hierarchical structures. One alternative is to design a co-operative structure in which all are working together, with a division of labour but without notions of superior and inferior status and power. Especially in a small organization, it is possible for people to complete the necessary tasks without rigid specialization of functions; jobs can be shared or rotated, communication relationships can be open and equal.

These relationships will be affected by the fact that organizations are very much composed of groups, which are themselves all about relationships. The formal structure creates teams with various jobs to carry out. The informal structure (see 'The grapevine', pages 147–8) is affected by the nature of informal groups.

1.3 Networks of communication

Whatever structure an organization takes, networks of communication and contact will develop between the people in it. In the spider web diagrams of the previous section we have in fact drawn a network of communication showing the channels by which formal messages flow. In the final section of chapter 3, figure 28 shows a group of five people where all channels are open; that is, everyone can speak to everyone else.

If we use the same example of five people (labelled A, B, C, D, E) or imagine that these five could represent departments or units in a larger system,

FIGURE 36 Chain network

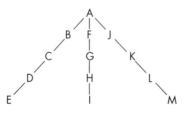

FIGURE 37 Pyramid network

we can describe other network shapes in which not all channels are open. A network might be set up in which one person or unit has the key position to channel or withhold information.

There are several network shapes for a network of five in addition to all channels open to all five.

Figure 36 illustrates a very constrained network in which C has an important position, because if a message is to be conveyed from A or B to D or E it must go via C. If a strictly hierarchical chain of command were the structure in an organization, then the formal network of communication would look like this. If A were the boss, he or she might occupy a position at the end of several chains (figure 37).

Rarely does the network remain so constrained because, as we noted in the previous section, some sideways and diagonal communication will take place. However, figure 37 could reflect a managing director at Head Office (A) giving and receiving information from regional, area and branch offices.

In a circle network (figure 38), no person or unit holds the dominant position but each can communicate only with two others.

In the wheel network (figure 39), A clearly has the dominant position and is best able to co-ordinate the whole system. A's position at the centre of the network makes all the others dependent on A.

FIGURE 38 Circle network

FIGURE 39 Wheel network

FIGURE 40 Y network

In the Y shape (figure 40), A occupies a key position as filter and focus for communication. This shape of network could reflect the information flow between managing director (A) channelling information from shareholders (B) and board of directors (C) to company managers (D) and supervisors (E).

In outlining these possible networks of communication we have not indicated whether the flow of information is one-way or two-way. It can of course be either, depending on the situation. We suggest you try to apply these network patterns to actual situations. With a group of four other people you could experiment by sending messages orally according to different network patterns to see what effects the patterns have on the messages and the people. If during holidays you wanted to organize yourself and four friends living in separate towns to meet for lunch one day, what network would represent the communication tasks?

As we indicated at the start of this chapter, organizations need to have some sort of formal structure that indicates lines of communication and responsibility. The network diagrams (figures 36–40) show how these structures may work. With increased access to electronic communication via emails and the Internet, it could be argued that formal lines of communication are becoming less important. For example, even in a global organization such as News Corporation it is possible for one person to email the same message at the same moment to every single employee of the 46,000.

Emails are changing the ways organizations communicate internally and externally. You may receive daily junk emails which indicate that lots of organizations seek to communicate with you whether you want them to or not. Within an organization you may receive copies of emails that you feel are unnecessary, or receive emails when you would prefer the other person to meet you face to face or to telephone you.

Like any new means of communication, it needs to be used effectively and sensitively, taking into account the purposes, the needs and the contexts of sender and receivers. Nicky Stanton in her book *Mastering Communication* (4th edition, 2004) lists some advantages and disadvantages of emails:

Advantages of email

- It is very cheap, normally only the cost of a local telephone, even when the message is sent to international recipients.
- You can send a message to several people at a time for the same cost as one message.
- It is very quick provided that the recipient is online.
- The messages are sent normally in plain text, so you don't have to worry too much about layout, typefaces and other metacommunication, but can just concentrate on wording the message.
- Its simplicity, convenience and independence of time zones is tending to make it more popular than telephoning.
- In the early days of email, Tom Peters quoted William Esrey, head of United Telecom, who recommended email 'for opening a "dialogue" with employees at all levels all over the firm. They feel that they are dealing directly with me', he said, 'and speak differently than if the communications were screened by staffers'.
- Although an email can be simple and informal, it is possible to insert or attach a more complicated document in another format – a letter, report, or even photo or graphic material previously sent by fax.

Disadvantages of email

- Because of its advantages cited above, it has become almost too popular: some people report getting literally hundreds of emails a day! And, because some people take the informality to extremes, many emails have so many misspellings and missed out words, that they become incomprehensible and reflect badly on the writer.
- Email does not allow you to show tones of voice and so on; misunderstandings can arise and emails can come over as blunt and aggressive, even unintentionally. So courtesy is at least as important as in face to face communication.
- Although it is a form of written communication, it encourages people to behave very impulsively and thoughtlessly, resulting in sending into the ether things that cause regret or embarrassment – but by then it is too late!

- Its ease and convenience mean that notes, memos and letters are seeing a rebirth, and telephoning and face to face communication are dying. Anyone who is not an addict may be irritated by this and certainly regretful.

As I was writing this page, a pop-up came on my screen to let me know that I had received a new email! Emails have become the dominant form of communication for day-to-day communication in and between organizations, and between friends. You may think of other advantages and disadvantages to add to this list.

Similarly, mobile phone texting has become a daily means of communicating for organizations when a short, instant message is needed.

For both emails and mobile phones, people are careful about who they give their email addresses and phone numbers to. Twenty-four-hour and seven-day working may be necessary for some organizations, but the people within them may not want to be available 24/7. Additionally, for many people a 'junk filter' on their email has become an essential to filter out unwanted emails.

Teams and networks

The networks of communication described above can be applied to many situations, not only in organizations, but also in social groupings. For example, in an extremely tense family situation it may be that some members of the family will not speak to others so that a wheel or Y network may develop, with one person being the mediator. Difficult negotiations may be carried on in the same way.

Additionally, such networks show that controlling the channels of communication confers power. In chapter 5 we shall consider the way in which the mass media act as gatekeepers – selecting, filtering and representing the information they receive. The Y network provides a model of this process, in which the editor (A) gets information from sources (B and C) and channels it to audience (D), who in turn may discuss it with groups of friends (E).

At first it might seem that the open, all-channel network is the most desirable. But for the purpose of conveying simple information it might be wasteful to have all available people discussing it with everyone else when it could simply be sent out, as in the wheel.

Email networks have an impact here too: in many organizations it has become necessary to have an email protocol to prevent everyone receiving copies of everything whether they need to know it or not. If you are receiving hundreds of daily emails, it leaves no time for anything but dealing with them!

Which networks would you use for the following tasks?

(a) A marketing director has four managers for whom she is responsible, and she wishes to decide marketing strategy with them for the following year.

Which network would be most appropriate? If the director is A, should she use Y, chain, circle, wheel or open?

(b)   The same marketing director has to decide the date of a sales conference that is held annually. Which network would be most appropriate?

There is not a single correct answer, but we suggest that in (a) the director should seek an open exchange of ideas where all of them can speak and listen to each other. If when the director called the meeting for (a) she was also in a position to decide the date for the conference, she could do it there. But if when she needs to decide the date the managers are scattered around the country in their own offices, she could use the wheel network: obtain from each separately the convenient dates, decide which is most convenient for all and then inform them.

1.4 Teams and roles and leadership

You should refer back to chapter 3 for much of what is relevant in the idea of role. But it is worth reminding yourself now that work teams are a type of group. They are groups formed by the organization, not voluntarily. People's functional roles (job descriptions) within these groups are also assigned to them. This already provides the potential for conflict (see section 1.6 of this chapter) because of differences of opinion about status, for example.

For instance, one common type of organizational group is a quality circle group, formed to get together people who would not normally meet much. The idea is that they discuss at regular intervals the quality of what is done in one broad area of the organization, perhaps in respect of how the public or customers are dealt with. This circle may well have members of different status within it, but that is irrelevant to the work of this team. So, the question is whether some members can forget their roles or status, or whether the ways that they communicate are affected by these factors. In this example the receptionist is as important as the personnel manager.

You might also remember the distinction between specific job roles in the team, and performance or personality roles. The sales manager could be a poor chair for progress meetings if they tend to be a Dominator and won't let others speak enough. On the other hand, an accounts assistant might be a positive team member at such a meeting if they are strong as an Organizer.

In terms of effective communication within organizations, one often has to look at the performance of individuals when assessing the capability of teams. And when looking at individuals, one often has to look at possible tensions between the requirements of role and the actual skills of the individual both in and out of role. Putting job labels on people does not make them able to do that job. Sticking people together in teams does not make them good team members.

In *Management Teams* (Oxford: Butterworth-Heinemann, 1996), R.M. Belbin describes research that identified an interesting description of team roles complementing one another in a successful group. These may be summarized as:

- chairperson: good at co-ordinating and working with others;
- team worker: good at putting the team first, at co-operating and being supportive of others;
- shaper: dominant and very involved with the task in hand;
- company worker: good on matters of practical organization;
- monitor/evaluator: good at analysing ideas and tasks, quite critical;
- investigator: good on research, making contacts and getting along with others;
- plant: good at producing ideas, but not necessarily good with others;
- finisher: good at details and deadlines.

A combination of such people should produce an effective team that is good at these things: generating ideas; being clear about tasks and goals; generating free communication and trust between group members; problem solving; helping each other; generating constructive criticism; reaching agreement.

The notion of team working is fundamental to how organizations operate and develop. Much time and resource is put into forming teams of people to perform permanent or temporary functions to meet the needs of the organization. One of the prime purposes of any organization is to assemble people together to achieve things they couldn't achieve alone.

Being able to work in teams is a requirement of any employee. There are many books and manuals about effective team working. Ciara Woods in her book *Everything You Need to Know at Work* (2003) naturally has a section called 'Working in a team', which sets out seven traits of effective and high-performing teams:

(a) Shared goals

- Everyone is working towards a common goal.
- People do not have hidden agendas.

(b) Productivity

- The team doesn't waste time and gets the work done. Deadlines are met.

(c) Division of roles

- There are clear divisions of labour, and everyone knows what their roles and responsibilities are.
- People work outside their role when necessary to get things done.

(d) Clear communication

- There is an open channel of communication where all ideas are considered and problems discussed and resolved.
- Everyone gets a chance to speak, and when someone speaks, everyone listens.

(e) Personal growth and recognition

- People are individually praised both within the team and publicly for the work they do.
- People have mentors and are given opportunities for growth.

(f) Team spirit and respect for one another

- There is a good relationship between all members. All members support and are sympathetic to one another. Working with one another is enjoyable.

(g) Openness to people outside the team

- The team never becomes a clique that refuses outside input, influence and criticism.

This list presents the characteristics of an ideal team: when any one of these characteristics is not operating, the team will not perform effectively as a team. Competition between individual members within the team is a key cause of difficulties, as is failure to reach the agreed aims.

Think of any teams, either at work, in college/school or in sport, that you have been a member of. Was it a satisfying experience for you and other team members? Did you achieve as a team? If so (or if not), make some notes to identify why, using the characteristics above.

In a sport context, teams have captains. In an organization context, not all teams have designated leaders. But the ways in which teams manage themselves is significant for the individuals in the team, for the team as whole, and for achieving the tasks set by or for the team.

Issues of leadership styles and what makes a great leader have interested students of communication and social psychologists and management theorists for generations. There are books on the topic from the ancient Greek and ancient Chinese civilizations. Many people even now will use the word 'Machiavellian' to describe a ruthless and scheming leader who seems to follow the advice written for rulers – or leaders or managers – by Niccolò Machiavelli in *The Prince* in 1513!

In previous generations the preferred theory of leadership was a function of personality. A leader had something called charisma that somehow made other people follow him – it was traditionally a him! If we were to try to unpack what charisma means, it would include ability to communicate and relate to other people as well as to have the knowledge to achieve the set objectives. Personality is not a fixed quality; we can acquire attitudes, behaviours and skills that can develop our 'natural' personality.

Chris Brewster, Professor of International Human Resource Management at South Bank University, London, reflects this sceptical view of charisma as the key factor in leadership:

> I am extremely personally suspicious of words like charisma, first of all because I don't know what it means and secondly, because you might look at someone and say they've got charisma, and I'd say they look really boring, so unless we can have more certainty about judgement I think the whole concept is flawed. I don't dismiss the importance of other traits, like 'empathy' and a kind of understanding of where your audience is coming from.
>
> (quoted in Theobald and Cooper 2004)

A more modern view sees leadership as a function of several variables:

- the composition and function of the group;
- the social context;
- the nature of the task;
- the leader's ability to communicate and mobilize the group and to complete the objectives of the group.

These variables may then require different styles of leadership and management to be successful. For example, if the task for the group is to deal with some sort of emergency, then the style will need to be directive and clear – there is no time for open-ended discussion on what to do and how to do it.

Figure 41 suggests different leadership and management styles. But which do you think is most effective? Is each of these potentially effective in different circumstances? Is the laissez-faire style ever appropriate?

Review the characteristics of effective teams on page 143. What communication techniques and leadership styles are likely to help in creating such a team?

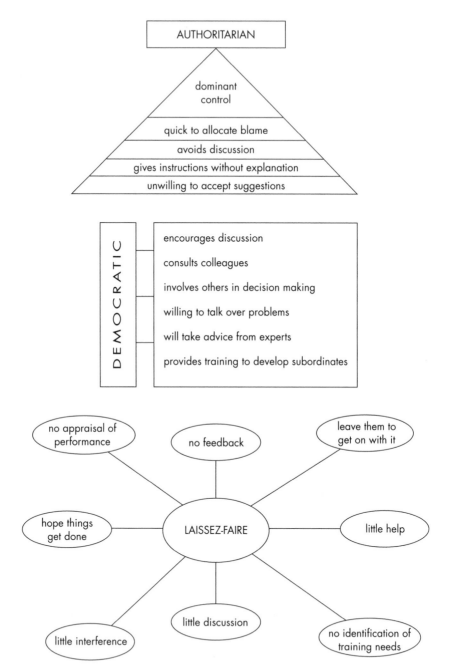

FIGURE 41 Three different management (leadership) styles

The social context or situation also has a significant bearing on what sort of leadership is likely to be most effective.

1.5 Informal channels of communication

People in organizations may carefully lay out a plan of the structure, including networks of communication. They may establish policies for keeping people informed of what is happening through regular meetings, notices or emails. They may establish policies for communication with outside agencies; for example, who is to have responsibility for signing orders and letters to go out. Most organizations do now recognize the need for such communication policies to keep people informed.

However, it is not possible to predict all the informal and personal networks and channels that develop. These informal, to some extent hidden, communication systems are a significant part of the human life of an organization. In a very restricted communication environment, such as an extreme example like a prison, this underworld of communication becomes very active. In a more open communication environment, where people know that there is a systematic way of learning about things that matter from their supervisors and managers, the hidden networks are less active because fear and uncertainty decrease. People have a tendency to consider that secret information is sinister information – 'Why don't they want me to know?'

The grapevine

The most common term to describe the unofficial, informal network of communication in an organization is the grapevine. This communication system, based on hearsay, rumour and speculation, is sometimes highly developed and fast. It is less concerned with information about how to carry out the tasks and objectives of the organization than with gossip. Gossip can perhaps be defined as information about other people, attitudes, opinions, relationships, interpretations, predictions, values. The grapevine fosters and spreads rumours, and is often full of prejudice and partial truth ('Well, they say there's no smoke without a fire . . .'). Rumours spread fast, especially on issues where people are uncertain or anxious. It's often said that on the grapevine the outcome of decisions is known before the decisions are taken.

The effects of the grapevine are usually seen as harmful to the smooth working of an organization, but it does not always pass on malevolent gossip. It can convey good news fast as well, and may serve to boost morale through creating interest in developments and innovations.

Grapevines are based on opportunities for communication, probably verbal but possibly written. Common examples of opportunities are before and after meetings, in the canteen, on shared journeys to work, even in the toilets. Also, internal email systems provide the opportunity for gossip. So, sometimes opportunities are linked to formal communication situations. But they can also come out of informal situations, such as when workers play a particular sport together, or even when they have relationships that cross over the lines of official company structures.

It is generally agreed that an active grapevine is present when people are kept ill-informed through official channels of communication. But another aspect of these informal channels is simply personal relationships between people. People have lives outside the organization in which they work. And it is natural to talk about work sometimes when you meet socially.

It is beyond the scope of this book to discuss at length the topics of industrial relations, consultation procedures or methods of employee partic-ipation in high-level decision making and formation of policies for companies. However, from a communication perspective it does seem that if people are kept well informed and involved in the issues and changes facing an organization, then there is less distrust and conflict between 'us' and 'them'.

Many companies and other organizations make great efforts to keep everyone informed about what concerns them through methods such as regular newsletters or team briefings in which every supervisor at every level in an organization is required to brief the team he or she is responsible for.

1.6 Conflict

It is sometimes mistakenly thought that all problems and conflicts between individuals and groups can be resolved through effective com-munication. Very often the phrase 'a breakdown in communication' is used to describe the cause of conflict. This certainly does happen, and misunder-standings and mistrust can develop simply because people have failed to talk to each other. Hostile attitudes can be eased by openly discussing the attitudes and their origins.

However, it must be acknowledged that conflicts do also arise because there are real differences of interest, differences of attitudes, beliefs and values. Certainly, open discussion of these can enable all sides to understand and face the conflicts as problems to be solved together.

As we said in chapter 1, communication can have the purpose of changing attitudes and behaviour.

Origins of conflict can usually be placed under three headings:

First, *personal* – within an individual there are conflicting ideas and desires and values; frustrations in achieving one's aims; conflicts of roles between personal inclinations and the expectations of the groups you belong to or the position you occupy.

Second, *interpersonal* – there are differences of experience, perceptions, opinions, values and patterns of behaviour between people; there is often competition for scarce resources, whether for salaries, promotion, new equip-ment; people can fail to agree on how a relationship should be conducted in terms of status, authority or role.

THE ORGANIZATION

CONFLICT OF NEEDS AND VALUES OF THOSE INVOLVED

FIGURE 42 Three kinds of conflict in organizations

Third, *in the organization itself* – potential for conflict exists when differences in status and power in a hierarchy are not mutually accepted; different parts of an organization often perceive their needs and interests in opposite ways (see figure 42).

Facing conflict as a problem that can be tackled is the starting point. If two people or two sides in a dispute are only interested in which one is right and which one is to blame, then the conflict can only be worsened. If the sources of conflict can be defined and communicated, then there's a chance that the problem can be 'managed', with both sides winning.

Ability to face conflict issues does certainly relate to communication abilities and skills in relating to and between people. An understanding of how we share meanings, how we use language and non-verbal communication, how we perceive one another and how we behave in groups can help us in our relationships. And, as we have previously suggested, the quality of personal relationships is a key factor in organizations. **Willingness to trust, to listen, to use and accept different communication styles and roles in different situations are all abilities we need for effective communication**. If you treat people with mistrust and are always on the defensive, only listen to your own ideas, always seek to use the same communication style whatever the situation, then you are likely to experience communication breakdowns.

ASHLEY'S STORY

It was time for his progress interview. Ashley Barnes was nervous. He knew that he didn't really have to be. His supervisor in the insurance company was very fair. But she was also the sort of person whom you felt you didn't want to upset. This was the end of his first year, and he had already had two interviews. They always did spend more time on you when you were new.

He had hated his first interview because he hadn't known what to expect. But the second one hadn't been too bad. In fact, because of that he had been moved around to get more experience, so he couldn't really complain. Sue Clarke was all right, really. She had told him exactly what he was there for.

'I want you to talk to me,' she had said. 'I'll ask you some questions. But you have to speak up for yourself, otherwise I may not find out things that will help you enjoy your job more and hopefully make some progress in this company. I get the same thing from my line manager. I find it really useful talking to people like you. It gives me another view of things. It gives us a chance to talk about you and this place, not just the work that you have to do. So tell me for a start, how do you think things have changed for you since the last interview that we had?'

Ashley hoped that he hadn't talked too much. But she had asked him about himself and about how he saw himself in the company, so he had told her. At least you felt that somebody cared. Some of the old hands were rather cynical about the process. It doesn't bring you a pay rise, they would say. But there was more to work than money, thought Ashley, even though it comes in very handy. He wanted to end up being a manager because he didn't want to stay stuck doing the same thing for ever. He should get more money if he was made up, but that wasn't the only point.

He looked at his watch and realized that it was time. He knocked on the door.

ABOUT ASHLEY'S STORY

This story reminds us that organizations are not just about systems and about means of communication. They are actually about people. Companies invest time and money in what is now called human resource management. People are not just cogs in a company machine. They are skilful, useful, communicating beings. Their ability to communicate in one way or another is actually what makes the organization function.

Ashley's progress interview is about recognizing the worth of people in an organization; it is about making people useful to that organization. His story indicates that people may respond to this recognition: that they are not motivated only by money, that they want what is called job satisfaction. Giving them time for talk and self-expression makes it possible to find out what will bring that satisfaction, and helps them work productively.

It is also the case that people at work often have to be part of groups or teams. Again, face-to-face communication skills become very important here, as do group skills. People need to accept roles, to work with others, to co-operate. The game that follows emphasizes these points, as well as the need to be able to communicate clearly and accurately.

2 Applications: case studies and activities

In this section we want to bring together ideas from chapters 3 and 4, through material for discussion and activity.

2.1 Case situation: a progress interview

This is for you to discuss in terms of why we often feel negative about interviews, and what would have made you feel more positive about interviews that you have had at school, college or work – even those that have been concerned with matters of discipline!

2.2 A model-building game

This section takes the form of a game designed to investigate the ways in which channels of communication might operate in a chain network. Such a three-level chain network could be the pattern in a small hierarchy. This game will also teach you something about roles and leadership styles.

If you cannot get a group of people together to play the game, you can probably try something similar with just three other people. Ideally you need at least ten people and an organizer to set it up and build the original model. You need some Lego bricks or other materials with which you can make something. One version is to give each group a fixed quantity of paper or card, paper clips, etc., as used for the original construction. You need a room, preferably with tables and chairs. You need another private area that only some of the players have access to.

How to play the game

(a) Groups with at least five people in each group must be formed. We suggest that nine is the maximum number for one group. If there are fifteen people and you have sufficient model-making materials, then it is advisable to form three groups of five each.

(b) Each group organizes itself into the following roles:

- *builder* – two or more people
- *supervisor/instructor* – one or more
- *manager/planner* – one or more
- *observer* – one or more

Builders will attempt to construct a model that is a duplicate of the original model built by the game organizer. Builders must not see the model until the game is over.

Supervisor/instructors take instructions from the managers to tell the builders how to construct the model. They can ask the managers questions. They act as intermediaries between the managers and the builders. Supervisors must not see the original model until the game is over.

Manager/planners go to the private area with the game organizer to look at the original model that is to be copied. The manager's task is to describe the model to the supervisors, who will then tell the builders how to construct it. Managers must not let the supervisors see the model, nor let the builders hear the manager's instructions.

Observers observe the whole process between managers and supervisors and between supervisors and builders. They can see the original model at the start. They must not communicate with any of the players. Observers are required to write notes about what is happening which are to be used for later discussion in debriefing after the game for all participants. The notes could include comments on things such as how roles were allotted by the groups at the start; whether leaders emerged; whether too much or too little information was given by anyone; whether the managers' instructions were changed when they were passed on to the builders; what problems or conflicts arose and what their causes were; whether there were frustrations, what they were and why they arose; how they could be resolved.

The game

During the course of the game, each group has to build a model that is a duplicate of an original. This original can only be seen by managers and observers. There is a time limit set for completion of the game. This must depend on the nature of the model, but about fifteen to twenty minutes is suggested. Nothing must be drawn or written down except by the observers for their own use. Only builders can take part in the construction.

The debriefing after the game

When the time is up, all participants come together to discuss questions such as:

- How did they feel about their assigned roles?
- Were the channels and techniques of communication effective?
- If not, how could they be improved?
- Did the observers' views of things differ from the players'?
- Did they learn anything from the game about communicating between people?

This game has been adapted with permission from 'Communication in the organization – a simulation', which is published in M.T. Myers and G.E. Myers, *Managing by Communication* (New York: McGraw-Hill, 1982). The Laboratory Manual in the book provides many other activities, simulations, case studies and assignments related to communication in organizations.

2.3 Case study: I heard it on the grapevine

Rumours spreading on a grapevine flourish when people are hungry for information or believe that they are being kept in the dark. Even if you are at school or college, this case study is relevant, because all organizations have grapevines. There are questions for you to answer. In any case, you could discuss how your grapevine works, what kinds of rumour travel along it, where they come from, what effects they have.

Here we present a case of an office grapevine on which there is currently a strong rumour.

AN OFFICE IN THE CITY

Brian presently works as a clerk in an insurance office in the City of London. He has been there for seven years and intends to stay because the people are friendly, the work is interesting – dealing with different sorts of claims – and the company gives attractive fringe benefits like cheap loans and mortgages. Brian enjoys working in the City, with easy access to shops, concerts, plays and art galleries. His office is a short walk from the station, so he can get from home to office desk in forty minutes.

Since it's an open-plan office with a relaxed but busy atmosphere there is a good deal of contact between the staff. They talk about the work but they pretty well all talk about their interests outside the office as well. Brian thought there wasn't much going on that he didn't know about.

So, it came as a jolt to hear a rumour that the company was thinking about closing its City office and opening a new office in the west of England. The person who told Brian said that he'd heard it from someone upstairs who said she'd heard it from a cleaner who overheard a phone conversation one evening.

The story went round the office like wildfire. When a few of them talked about it in the pub at lunchtime there were mixed reactions. Some of them said they would love to get away from London to the country and if the company offered the right terms they'd jump at it. Others certainly didn't want to move and they hoped there was nothing in the story.

Arising from this situation, consider the following questions:

(a) Is there anything Brian should do after hearing this rumour?

(b) Imagine you are the office manager and you hear about the story going round the office. You have been told nothing about any such idea and it bothers you that such a story is circulating. It is certainly affecting your staff at the moment. What action (if any) would you take?

(c) Alternatively, imagine you are the office manager in this situation but you have been told confidentially that there is a proposal to move the office out of London. The decision has not been taken yet. What action (if any) would you take?

> **How does our communication change when we are at work?**
>
> Hint: look back at ideas about context, audience, purpose in chapter 1.

Review

This is to help you check on the main points of this chapter, 'Communication in organizations'.

1.1   HOW DO ORGANIZATIONS OPERATE?

We made an overview of organizations and listed characteristics that help us to understand how they work:

- They are created for a purpose.
- They have structured relationships within them.
- They set goals.
- They divide up the work tasks.
- They co-ordinate the separate parts.
- They manage resources.
- They communicate within themselves and with the outside environment.

1.2   RELATIONSHIPS AND STRUCTURES IN ORGANIZATIONS

We looked at the formal and official perception of structures. These are often expressed in diagram form as pyramidal or web-shaped. Questions of hierarchy and status arise. Alternatively, there can be co-operative equal status.

1.3   NETWORKS OF COMMUNICATION

Information flows in several ways, and networks are a way of visualizing this. An open access to and exchange of information may be desirable. Or it may be preferable, or more efficient, to restrict the flow.

1.4   TEAMS AND ROLES

Work team members have various job roles and personality roles. A successful team contains a particular combination of role types. Teams also require some sort of leadership and management to work effectively. There are various styles of leadership.

1.5 INFORMAL CHANNELS OF COMMUNICATION

Alongside or outside the formal structures and networks, people develop their own information flows and channels for communication. The grapevine and social relationships are features of this.

1.6 CONFLICT

Effective communication takes account of the differences between individuals and groups. People can learn to see the sources of their conflict. These may be:

- within the individual;
- between individuals or groups;
- a result of tensions in the organization.

If conflicts are faced, they may not disappear but they can be managed as problems to be jointly solved.

2 APPLICATIONS: CASE STUDIES AND ACTIVITIES

Finally, we focused the general account of organizational communication with three case studies based on problems and issues:

- a progress interview;
- channels of communication;
- I heard it on the grapevine.

Debates

Why is it so common to hear people talk of 'communication problems' when an organization or company is in some kind of difficulty?

- One point to discuss has to do with organizational culture, which can put a lot of emphasis on systems and finance, above anything else.
- Another point to sort out is what kind of communication and what kind of problem one might be talking about.
- Another point may have to do with communication within the organization in general, within work teams in particular, or with communication from the organization to others.

WHAT DO YOU THINK?

How is it that communication means different things to different people within organizations?

- One problem is that different people have different roles in an organization.

- Another problem is that different organizations place a different emphasis on different kinds of communication. You need to discuss different examples of such organizations.
- Another problem is to do with the ways that people think about communication and ways in which we use the word in our society. You need to discuss the differences between communication as system, as technology, as something that people do.

WHAT DO YOU THINK?

Assignments

Assignment 1

Make an investigation of an organization that you know about or are part of. We are not telling you exactly how to carry out this investigation, but if you work it out from the tasks below, then you will have to do some interviewing and talking to people. It would be good communication practice to present your findings in the form of a report. You could also present them orally to a group, using audio-visual aids. In the list of tasks below, we have assumed terms relevant to a school. But you can easily add topics or adapt the tasks slightly, according to the organization that you are dealing with.

(a)   Draw an organization chart, with labels for departments and people's titles. The chart should show the whole structure and lines of responsibility.

(b)   List the outside agencies that the school has contact with. You may use general headings such as 'suppliers' rather than going into great detail.

(c)   Explain what regular meetings are held and why. Include those that are for staff and pupils within the school as well as those that include outsiders.

(d)   Explain what systems exist for keeping people at all levels informed of what is happening in the school. Refer to examples of the types of written and oral communication that do this.

(e)   Describe what publicity brochures are produced. Describe what has been the most recent publicity in a local newspaper.

(f)   Is there a school newsletter or magazine? What is its purpose, readership, content, style? How often does it appear? Who contributes to it?

(g)   Describe the contents of three noticeboards in the school. Where are they located? Who are they for? What topics are on them? Are they kept up to date? How well are the notices written and designed? Do people take notice?

Assignment 2

Arrange an interview with someone who works in an organization that you don't know about. Write up a summary of what you find out. Your topics could include the following: means of communication used by the organization; time spent by the interviewee on communicating; what forms of communication the interviewee uses; public relations.

You should prepare your questions in advance, let the interviewee know what they are about, and ask them if you can record the interview. If they have time you would find it very useful to discuss your summary of what you found out with the interviewee at another meeting.

Assignment 3: Case study

For this assignment, refer to the photo of Sophie Sanderson and to the newspaper article about her.

Extract from article in local newspaper

You are a member of the Local Education Authority Schools Service that is responding to complaints made by Sophie's father, as well as to the increasing public outcry about the case. You already have some knowledge of the school

15-year-old Sophie has caused an uproar at the school by writing a letter about the staffing situation, which we published in last week's edition of the Post. Now she has been suspended from school by the Head, Patrick Benson, for 'bringing the school into disrepute'.

Chair of Governors, Mrs Molly Bergreen, has backed the Head saying that the matter could have been dealt with internally. But Sophie's father, David Sanderson, disagrees. He has already involved the local education authority, who have told us that they are actively investigating the case.

Mr Sanderson claims that he has previously tried to talk to the Head about the problems with teachers missing from classes and having supply cover, but without success.

'Sophie has as much right to freedom of speech as anyone else,' he said. 'The school has a problem which they are not admitting to.'

Sophie told us that she still believes that lack of proper teaching is going to affect her exam results this summer. The L.E.A. has promised to make a statement in the near future. Mr Sanderson claims that the Parent–Teacher Association is backing his daughter's claims.

involved. As part of your preparation for bringing people together to resolve the conflict, you carry out a number of tasks, among them the following.

(a)   List the people in the school who you think should have been dealing with Sophie's concerns about the quality of her education.

(b)   List those people who you think should now be dealt with in discussing the situation as it is.

(c)   Draw a small group network model covering the people involved in the discussion, which you think would help deal with the situation most effectively.

(d)   Describe how you think the complaints should have been dealt with by the school system.

(e)   Draw a network diagram for the school organization which you think would make sure that such a situation would be dealt with in the future before parents or pupils go public with complaints.

Suggested reading

Stanton, N., *Mastering Communication*, [4th ed.], Basingstoke: Palgrave Macmillan, 2004.
Theobald, T., and Cooper, C., *Shut Up and Listen: the truth about how to communicate at work*, London: Kogan Page, 2004.
Woods, C., *Everything You Need to Know at Work: a complete manual of workplace skills*, London: Pearson, 2003.
See also the resources list at the end of the book.

Chapter 5

Mass communication

The media . . . tell most of the stories most of the time to most of the people, in both fiction non-fiction genres. They begin to socialise children almost at the same time as family influences are activated, taking over that basic master-narrative role once occupied by other cultural institutions and wells of identity – religion, nationality, family, the workplace. The influence of all these has declined in proportion to the growing power of the media and the leisure industry.

(Farrel Corcoran, in Eoin Devereux, *Understanding the Media*, 2004)

This chapter concentrates on the mass media and takes examples from the press, radio and television. The institutions, processes and products of mass communication are the focus. The chapter considers what it is like to live in our mass-media society, and refers to the influence and effects of the mass media. Advertising, news and visual images are discussed in particular. There is reference to current developments in communication techniques.

Go to: [Guardian Unlimited home ▼] (Go)

Guardian Unlimited

Best daily newspaper on the world wide web
Read today's paper · Jobs

Search: [   ] (Go)
⦿ Guardian Unlimited ◯ Web

MediaGuardian.co.uk

| Home | Press & publishing | Greenslade | Advertising | Television | Radio | Marketing & PR | City |
| Monkey | Organ Grinder | | New media | This week | The Tenner | Ratings | Special reports | Jobs |

Comment is free
John Prescott gets blogged down

Radio Festival
Catch up with all the news from Cambridge

Advertising
Dermot O'Leary stars in cancer awareness ad

Thursday July 06 2006

Search Media
[   ] (Go)

WEB | FEED
How to use our RSS feeds.
Registration is required for Media Guardian feed.

Register for Media Guardian.co.uk today

greenslade
News and comment ›

Desktop alerts
Breaking news direct to your PC

Regulars
Greenslade
Monday's MediaGuardian section
Media Text Alerts
Audio: Media Talk
The Tenner
Media Briefing
Creative Lounge
Columnists
Student Media Awards
Help
Contact us

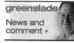
Add Media Guardian to your PDA

BBC revamp: decision imminent
BBC staff are braced for the announcement later this month of a major reorganisation ahead of the implementation of Mark Thompson's Creative Future strategy. By **Ben Dowell** and **Jason Deans**.
Willis steps down

Irish privacy law provokes anger
A top media lawyer has described Ireland's proposed privacy law as a threat to press freedom on both sides of the Irish Sea. By **Lisa O'Carroll**.
Ireland to reform libel laws

Heroes welcome
StuntWatch: When famous names rebrand, there's a danger of losing core values in the search for cool, writes **Mark Borkowski**.

Latest news

Dermot O'Leary stars in cancer campaign
Dermot O'Leary has followed in the footsteps of Rachel Stevens and Robbie Williams by featuring in a cancer ad campaign. By **Mark Sweney**.
Watch the ad

Love Island: the cast arrives ...
Natalka Znak, executive producer of ITV's Love Island, will be blogging for MediaGuardian.co.uk throughout the show. Here she unveils the lineup.

French Connection and Beattie part company
French Connection and Trevor Beattie, the ad man behind FCUK, have parted company after a decade-long relationship. By **Mark Sweney**.

France-Portugal semi pulls in 12m
TV overnights: A peak audience of almost 12m tuned into BBC1 to watch the France v Portugal World Cup semi-final and see Christiano Ronaldo blub. By **Julia Day**.
TV overnights: ratings for the past month

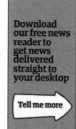
FIGURE 43 The changing face of the media: Media Guardian screenshot, Guardian Unlimited, 6 July 2006

1 A mass-communication society

AISHAH'S STORY

Aishah was in a hurry. She had a lot to do before going out to meet her friends that evening. It was still only Thursday night, and her mum would go on at her about not going out during the week. But there was this wicked bar with live music on a Thursday – and they had all agreed to be there. Her thumb jerked over the mobile keypad as she returned a text to one of the girls. Besides, she thought virtuously, I won't be drinking alcohol. The truth was that she knew it would upset her Dad, and she thought a lot of him. He seemed not to notice what was going on, what with his IT consultancy and everything. But Aishah had a feeling that he noticed more than he let on.

She was into the newsagent's like a small whirlwind to buy her copy of More. *But she wasn't so stupid as to buy it from their local shop. People talked round where they lived. She suspected that Mum would have half a heart attack if she saw some of the advice articles in the magazine. But that was the trouble with parents. So old-fashioned. And they always suspected the worst. As if. Aishah adjusted the headphones on her iPod. She wasn't stupid. She had bought a separate set of black ones to listen to her music. She knew that people had been mugged by those who could spot the white original phones at a hundred metres.*

When she got home she greeted Mum and Granny dutifully, and endured the grumbling while she interrupted television viewing briefly to set the box to record a programme off a satellite channel – for her homework, she said.

Then it was up to the room and on to the computer. She hid the magazine in one of her work files. She had probably picked up her tidiness and organization from her Dad. The first thing she did was to download a music file – it was a track that one of her friends had played for her. Then she searched for coach times to see if she could get a cheap seat to get to Leeds for a concert in a month's time. Others had already booked. Of course there would be an argument about that. But Aishah was trading on the fact that her school results were good, and that her parents thought that the friends they had met were a good influence. If only they knew! She switched to playing with Google Earth. It really was for a Geography project. Then she could hear Mum puffing up the stairs. I haven't got the time, thought Aishah, calculating how long it would take to chat to Mum, do some homework and endure being moaned at because she wouldn't eat half the huge tea that Mum would put out. Then she felt guilty.

'Hi, Mum,' she said brightly. 'I'm just going to mail Aunty in Toronto like you asked. What would you like to say to her?'

ABOUT AISHAH'S STORY

The story tells us something about the ways in which our lives, in work and leisure time, have come to depend on means of mass communication. The very reality of our everyday experience is partly an experience of a made-up world invented by the media.

Aishah's lifestyle and common experience are ones in which she uses mass-produced communication objects, in which she can receive communication broadcast on a mass scale and in which she can communicate with others via communication systems operating on a mass scale. In other words, the mobile phone, satellite television, MP3 players are taken for granted by her. So are the more high-tech items such as her PC computer, with access to the Web and to email, as well as online booking.

Our work and leisure experience are changing rapidly. It is the systems and products of mass communication that are responsible for the greatest part of this change.

1.1 What do we mean by 'mass'?

We could be talking about a *system* or *product*, or *audience*. We can define 'mass' mainly in terms of volume, scale and speed.

The system is the organization that does the communicating, such as the postal service or the radio broadcasting network. We can say that such systems are mass because they operate on a large scale and carry so many messages so widely. When people talk about systems of communication, they are often at the same time talking about *media institutions*. So, if there is a process of news gathering via systems such as telecommunications, then one finds oneself also talking about institutions such as Reuters.

The product is the object produced or carried by the system. It could be something physical like a newspaper, or something that is experienced, like a television programme. The use of the word 'product' will be discussed later on. But the point is that these products are manufactured. Whether we are talking about thousands of copies of a magazine or a best-selling disk, the point is that we are concerned with massive numbers from a mass-production system. The product is also often the same thing as what is meant by the term *text*. This can be a photograph, as much as a magazine article (see section 2.1 of this chapter).

The audience may also number thousands or millions. It may be composed of people who have much in common – or little except the fact that they are all listening to the same programme. But still, the numbers are sufficient that they become significant in any analysis or explanation of the communication process. They affect how and why communication takes place. This communication can be happening on a massive scale (e.g. telephone), and very fast, and in great quantities.

1.2 Mass – so what is the significance?

Mass production of messages also means mass repetition of messages.

The main feature of mass communication when compared with other categories is that it does operate on such a large scale. Before we look at our media society and the operation of the media in more detail, it is worth grasping the basic fact that we need to look critically at them because they say the same sort of thing in the same sort of way so often.

And, apart from this repetition of messages, there is also the matter of penetration. Radio messages can penetrate right into the home or a car or even some remote holiday spot. Leaflets, letters and newspapers are pushed through our doors. And with these objects, and through these systems, come the ideas and beliefs that they can carry. The messages get right to us, again and again. So, it should be clear that we need to look carefully at what the messages are, who is sending them, why and with what possible effect.

The sheer scale of the operation that we are describing means that it is likely to have some effect on things which everyone thinks are important – our relationships with others, what we believe in, how we describe and understand the world around us.

Mass communication is also part of that world. We suggest that there are particular aspects of our mass-communication society which are worth looking at in more detail, as follows.

1.3 Systems – availability, but no control

Our society has been greatly changed as systems of mass communication have become available to more and more of the population. We are more aware of what is going on in the world at large through media such as television and radio, which also use satellite and cable systems. We can keep in touch with people over great distances through a telephone network that allows us to dial direct to the other side of the world, or through the Internet, which allows us global emailing. We can buy examples of a range of technologies that can entertain us through eye and ear. There is much available to us that can make our lives more fun, keep us in touch with others and keep us well informed about events and issues of the day. Systems are available for us to use, even if at a price that cuts out the poorer members of the population. But this view of a society playing and working with readily available mass-communication systems must also be corrected in another way.

We don't have much control of these systems, as individuals. If we don't like the way our television service is run, there isn't much we can do. If we switch off in sufficient numbers, a given programme may be dropped. But that is about all.

These remarks are intended to raise issues about the process of mass communication. The issue of whether or not the system is satisfactory as it now stands is raised when one describes the operation of the system – that is, how communication is taking place. It is our intention to raise issues as a part of communication theory, as we describe briefly these main aspects of mass-communication society.

1.4 Information – a contained explosion

Our society has been greatly changed by our ability to move information around very fast, over wide distances. It is the various means of mass communication that have made this possible.

Government and commerce have always depended on their ability to handle information. The sheer volume of information to be processed for an ever-increasing population has encouraged the development of new technology. Local government could not manage without computer files to store information. Banks and other businesses could not manage without cable-linked computers connecting branches with their main offices. Our holiday bookings depend on the ability of airlines and travel agents to exchange information about flights and passenger bookings via similar systems. The list of examples is endless. Our society could not be administered without mass communication.

But the population in general is also able to obtain and exchange information on a scale unequalled in the history of humankind. Broadcasting and print media are sources of information about many things, including other places and other peoples. The World Wide Web has become a major resource. (You should be clear that the term 'Internet' refers to the overall system that links computers around the world, while the term 'Web' refers to the particular use of the Net by individuals and organizations, especially to set up and access websites.)

Mass communication has made all this possible. As a society, we are now used to the idea of giving, getting and using information on a mass scale.

But we should also realize that **there are certain limits to this new information-based society**. These are mainly limits of access, limits of control and limits of cost. Sometimes this raises very important issues. For example, powerful institutions such as credit-control agencies or the police store information about us. Speed cameras can record car number plates as well as speed, cause a check with a database, cause a summons to be issued to the driver. Police can check car ownership on the spot, and make links with another database to check whether or not the car is insured.

Major issues raised through such uses of mass communication are to do with who has the right to say what about whom, who controls the system and who has access to the system.

There are both limitations of access to new technology, and notable advances. For the citizen, access requires broadband and being able to afford a computer – though many libraries provide some sort of online access. Indeed, library databases can themselves be accessed from home. Equally, the quality of information posted on the Web is only as good as its source, or as the ability of the source to check its own reliability. The online encyclopedia Wikipedia is an example of this, being generally reliable but having let through some major inaccuracies.

In general, British cities are linked and wired up with fibre optic cable, but there are many towns and country areas that are not. Therefore, people do not have equal access to the information revolution. Shopping has changed with the advent of websites for major stores, as well as online sites such as Amazon, and interactive shopping channels via TV. But again, one has to be able to afford the technology to access these sources, as well as to have the cable distribution technology going to one's home.

There is a huge amount of information placed in the home pages of various websites. Some of this information is original material – e.g. university departments. Some of it is plain illegal – copyright material loaded on to the Web and untraceable from source. File sharing, and the open Web programme BitTorrent, are copyright nightmares for the music industry, which can't keep up with individuals posting copyright material on the Web, to be downloaded by other individuals. On the other hand, there is also legal downloading from sites such as iTunes, where the customer does pay for the goods.

Some websites are commercial – newspapers or film companies wanting to promote themselves by providing some information about their operation, and especially about the latest products. Another commercial example is that of house-selling websites subscribed to by estate agents (e.g. Rightmove.com). There is eBay, a huge online auction site for selling anything at all, much used by ordinary citizens. The Web offers open access both to information – and to disinformation. It is a benefit to free speech and information exchange – but it also benefits commerce.

Another issue is that of Internet security. In spite of protection services such a PayPal, there are still examples occurring of security lapses – or even absences for some sites. This doesn't benefit the consumer, or encourage people to use new services, such as online banking. The double-edged nature of the digital and information revolution is typifed by the impending switch-off from analogue TV to digital. More people than predicted are unprepared for this, especially those who are vulnerable through poverty or geographical isolation. **Technological revolutions tend to benefit those who can afford to pay for the services they bring, but to discriminate against those who cannot** – or indeed may not wish to be part of such change.

1.5 More fun – but less real choice?

We are lucky to have more time and more money to entertain ourselves than previous generations.

It is mass communication that brings us this entertainment. Entertainment has, in fact, become an industry in its own right. Our economy depends on the money spent on entertainment, in the form of things like videotapes, DVDs, television and magazines. These things are mass-produced or mass-broadcast – bought and seen in huge numbers. Often, various means of communication interact to produce examples of entertainment on a broad front. For instance, millions of people have enjoyed the *Lord of the Rings* movies. Many have also enjoyed the book of the film, related comic books and toys, to say nothing of posters and related articles in newspapers and general magazines. They will also enjoy the DVDs of the films, or watch them via broadcast or cable television.

The range of entertainment is considerable. It is part of our lifestyle, our culture and our society. Television serials are part of everyday conversation. Women's magazines influence the spending of millions of pounds each year on clothes, make-up and pop music.

Mass communication brings a vast range of entertainment to our society, and so changes that society. But it is also true that the vast range does not offer the choice we may think it does. There are relatively few organizations producing the entertainment that we enjoy. And the types of entertainment are also quite similar in many cases.

For example, one company (Newscorp) owns three major British newspapers: *The Times*, the *Sun* and the *News of the World*. And the last two are pretty similar in look, content and treatment. Much space is devoted to pictures, sport, gossip and sex.

So, this raises the issue of whether or not we get the kind of entertainment we want. It also raises the question of whether we tend to want the kind of entertainment that we get, because that is all we are used to anyway.

Once more, we can support the idea of our being a mass-communication society by looking at the facts. But then we also need to look at the process of communication in order to understand what kind of messages we are getting and why.

All the concepts described in chapter 1 can be used to examine, for example, a newspaper as a piece of communication. What we are now doing is adding to those ideas. It is, you may remember, basic to the study of communication that one must never take anything for granted, or believe that the way things are is a natural way of communicating.

1.6 Mass communications as extensions of ourselves

We have used the various means of mass communication in order to extend our human powers of communication.

The kind of society we have is a result of this extension. It is, most obviously, a society in which its members can keep in touch with one another in great numbers and over great distances. It is also a society in which we may scan the world via the video camera and the TV screen. These facts support the idea that our world has, in a sense, grown smaller, an idea represented by that much-quoted phrase 'a global village'. To this extent we have tackled the problem of a growing population by using machines to extend our powers of communication in face-to-face contact.

A public address system extends the scope of the human voice so that it can address an audience of hundreds. The telephone system extends the range of the human voice across continents. A magazine page stores words more accurately than human memory. A television image represents non-verbal language across great distances and to millions at a time. And now it can be argued that computers extend our abilities to think and remember and make decisions (activities that are behind all our communication behaviour).

In our society, work activities and social activities depend, to a greater or lesser extent, on systems of mass communication. It could indeed be argued that those who do not have items such as a television and a telephone (and a computer terminal?) are socially disadvantaged. They are not fully in touch with society as a whole. And this raises further issues about what we think is essential to a healthy society in the mass-communication world that we have created.

1.7 The media and social reality

The media are part of the reality of our world. They also help create that reality.

We are a mass-communication society because mass communication is a part of that society and its activities.

We have invented new kinds of communication to do jobs for us, in work and leisure. The driving force behind these inventions is often commercial (profit and economy): to make money out of communicating or to help business perform its internal communication tasks more efficiently and more cheaply. But the effects of mass communication go beyond companies and their achievement of profit.

For a start, communications businesses, including advertising, are worth so many billions of pounds, and keep so many people employed, that our economy would collapse without them. But also the media, in particular, shape society through their ability to mass-produce messages. If we think that we are a 'modern and affluent society', for instance, then that view is partly a result of what the media show us. In this way, the media help invent our view of the world, of ourselves, of our whole society. Just as we partly base our beliefs and opinions on what friends and parents tell us, so also to some extent we base our views on what the media tell us.

To this extent, the media are, for example, part of the political process, whether they like it or not. They can show us political events as they happen. They can raise political issues. So, they also help define what those events and issues are.

This in itself raises further issues about the uses and effects of mass communications. What view of the world do the media represent? How accurate is this view? How is it put together? By whom?

Once more, all of these are questions that are basic to any analysis and explanation of the process of communication.

1.8 The media as institutions

The media are made up of, run by and controlled by organizations that are described as institutions.

In general, any organization like Viacom, which owns the American network CBS and the DVD stores, Blockbuster, is an example of an institution. But it isn't just about owners. United Artists UK owns a cable system, but not TV stations. W.H. Smith owns Waterstones bookshops, but not a publishing house. Ofcom controls commercial television operations in certain respects, through its powers of regulation, but it does not own a TV company. There are lots of media institutions that are not owners, but which are powerful in one area of the media or another.

Such institutions, not least those in advertising, are behind our entire mass-communication systems. They run the means of distributing information and entertainment. They run the production systems; they sell the product. The influence and span of control of these companies is made greater by the fact that many own shares in similar companies, and they own similar institutions in different countries.

The predicted pattern of media ownership is that fewer and fewer institutions will own more and more of the world's media/communication systems. One implication is that powerful institutions will control the ideas contained in their media products. Another is that there will be less and less real competition, and so less and less real choice in the types of magazines, programmes and other products that we have available to us (see also section 2.8 of this chapter, on ownership, finance and control).

1.9 The media: power and influence in society

The media have power and influence because of the extent of their communications operations.

We have also referred to their characteristics of repetition and penetration, which contribute to their power. It is a power to communicate on a scale unequalled in the history of humankind. The precise effects of this power and influence are not to be simply measured. Indeed, this book is not designed to take on the detailed analysis and reference which is available elsewhere.

But the broad thrust of influence is pretty clear. In the last section we noted that the media shape our view of the world. Later, we will also examine the idea that they tend to reinforce a view of the world as it is, rather than looking at alternative views.

In terms of media effects, major issues are often raised about the representation of violence or of political affairs, for example. Any general election is now largely dominated by media presentations, so far as the public is concerned. More specifically, the politician, as a media personality, has come to stand for political beliefs and attitudes. Party politics are represented through party personalities. The influence of such politicians depends, to a great extent, on the influence of the media. The precise effects of such influence are, however, much disputed, even though the notion of the power of the media is still accepted in general.

In the United Kingdom, television has the power to reach about 14 million viewers at peak viewing times (for some soap operas during the week). The two most popular UK newspapers each have the power of around 3 million identical sets of messages (copies sold), every day. And if the precise effects of such power are harder to measure than some communications analysts are prepared to admit, it still remains a quantifiable fact that, for example, television advertising does increase the sales of a given product.

Again, the quality of media power is marked out by the range of media through which messages may be passed at the same time. An election campaign can use posters, radio or mailshots, for example, as pure advertising. And it can orchestrate free publicity through news and magazine programmes. So, the messages are being duplicated and reinforced across the media. This point also reminds us that while it is true that those producing media material have the power of access to huge audiences, other interest groups may have the cash or the influence to be able to use the media to exert power. The power of the media lies in who uses them and to what effect. For example, politicians believe that radio and television can influence the opinions of people. The political parties have a right in law (those Acts of Parliament by which government created commercial and public broadcasting) to put out party political broadcasts. Exactly how such broadcasts affect people's opinions is open to argument. But still one may argue that the power of the media lies in such use by politicians to say what they want to say to millions of people.

There is clearly some kind of power and influence available through the use of these media of communication, and so certain issues obviously appear. These may be expressed in terms of basic questions, such as who should be given control of this power? Who controls the controllers? What should the power be used for?

Conclusion

So, we are indeed a mass-communication society. This means that we use the different kinds of mass communication in various ways to conduct business and leisure in our society. It means that the use and experience of various types of mass communication have today become a normal, everyday occurrence for members of our society.

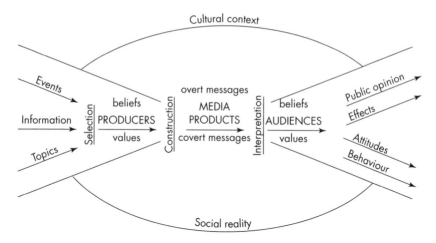

FIGURE 44 Model of mass-communication process

But it also means that the nature of our society has changed significantly in the past fifty years, and it is still changing now.

Mass communication is part of our world, but is also helping to define how we see and understand that world.

Where would you draw the line between information and entertainment when categorizing media material?

Hint: the most interesting examples land on the line!

---

2 Interpreting the media

ALEX'S STORY

Alex was aware that something was wrong as soon as he woke up. But it was nothing he could put his finger on at first. The flat looked the same. The noises of Saturday morning were the same as usual. But there was something disturbing in the air, like the first faint odour of leaking gas that alerts the senses to threat.

He made it down to the front door just as the milk was arriving. That was one custom he had approved of since arriving in England several years ago. Doorstep delivery. But he wasn't prepared for the neat-looking girl who gave him a distinctly inviting grin as she slung the bottles down. Alex adjusted his dressing gown more tightly and wondered what had happened to Whistling Charlie, who usually made the delivery. He switched on the radio while he made breakfast. The news was charting the course of a trade union dispute, and Alex listened absent-mindedly while the offer made to the employers was discussed and a trade unionist was asked whether he thought they could bring management back to the negotiating table.

As Alex was leaving the building for his Saturday shopping round, he was startled to bump into a large and hairy young man wearing motorcycle leathers. As he backed off apprehensively, noting the tattoos and heavy boots, the woman from the downstairs flat came out.

'Hallo, Alex,' she said cheerfully, 'I see you've met Don. He's our baby-sitter. Reg and I came back so late last night we thought he'd better stay.'

'Pleased to meet you,' said Don, as he loomed over Alex.

Alex was happy to be able to get on with his shopping. He prided himself on the speed with which he could get round the supermarket and come away with everything that he really wanted. So, it was rather annoying to be held up in the checkout queue by two children in front of him. They were disputing the price of some item with the cashier. Alex noted with some surprise that they seemed to be in charge of the shopping for a whole family. But they also appeared to be well organized, and the boy won his argument when he told the cashier firmly that, old stock or not, the price on the label was what he was going to pay. Alex frowned. He felt uneasy. He went for his usual cup of coffee, where he often met Steve and the rest of the crowd. At the table next to him a group of young men were laughing together over some magazines, and Alex leaned over to take a look while pretending not to. True Life Romance, *he read on the cover of the magazines. He frowned again.*

'Mandy's very good-looking, but you know girls like that. They're only after one thing,' he heard one of the young men say seriously. Alex paid his bill and left.

Of course he didn't see the car, or he wouldn't have tried to cross the road in the first place. As it was, he found himself lying in the gutter with a severe pain in his right leg. He lay there, very calmly considering, believing that he now knew what it was his seventh sense had been trying to warn him about. In his detachment he even found time to admire the calm efficiency of the female police inspector who had turned up to direct operations. Alex was the only person who was badly hurt. But he had caused three vehicles to crash into one another. It was bedlam. And two male passengers were crying quietly by themselves with no one taking any notice.

'Rotten men drivers!' he heard a bystander say indignantly, before he fainted.

Once in hospital, Alex found that boredom was more of a pain than his leg. The nurses were very pleasant, but they had a job to do. And under the circumstances he hadn't had time to plan for his stay in bed. For some of the day they were able to watch a communal television set, placed at one end of the ward. The trouble was that the programmes weren't much good. Alex watched bemusedly as one drama or comedy after another rolled before his eyes. The only programme he enjoyed was a comedy involving a family with a blind son who had the end of the ward in hysterics with his perceptive remarks about the rest of his family. But at night, there was nothing to amuse Alex, and he couldn't sleep, or suppress an increasing sense of anxiety.

*On one particular night a friendly blond nurse named Michael turned up with
a book for Alex. The trouble was that Alex had nearly got to sleep on this occasion. He
peered blearily at the book's title.* Alex Through the Looking Glass, *he read. Panic
gripped him. All was not right with the world. Alex knew that the only way to deal
with his problem would be to go to sleep. Then he would be safe.*

ABOUT ALEX'S STORY

You will not be surprised to hear that this story was not meant to be taken too
seriously. But it does have a serious point. Much mass-media material, especially
the entertainment side, tends to communicate a rather limited view of people.
It repeats certain types of programme and types of people in these programmes.
This is where the concepts of genre and stereotyping come in. We will say
more of these a little later.

The main thing is to recognize that these limitations are there, and
do mean that our view of the world is, to an extent, limited and distorted.
Recognition of this problem is, in fact, a good way of correcting it. Alex's
alternative experience was one in which men, women, young people did not
behave as they do in the media.

The media represent a world in which nurses are usually angels and
female, and young men are rarely interested in romance and love.

You will recognize other points that the story tries to make. You will
probably not agree with all of them. And certainly the media do not have the
monopoly on generalizations about people and groups. We utter some of them
in our everyday observations and opinions. But then, what we say has a limited
audience. This is certainly not true of the media, whose messages can, we have
noted, reinforce themselves through sheer repetition.

There is more happening than meets the eye, in the process of communication through the media. We must interpret this process, to find out
what is going on. We use certain terms and concepts to do this interpreting.

2.1 Texts

**Any example of media material or media product may be described as a
text.**

So, just as books are texts, so are music tracks, radio programmes, book
covers, and so on. The point of using this formal term is to get into textual
analysis: the decoding of texts to discover their possible meanings. Most people
have been in classes that talk about books, analysing characters or what the
writer is getting at. The same thing can be done for all media texts, visual as well
as verbal.

Any kind of analysis, whether it is about how the story is put together
(see section 2.5 of this chapter), or it deconstructs the image (see section 3.2),

or it talks about the use of camera and editing in films (see section 2.4), is trying to get to the meanings of the text. It is useful to have the understanding and ability to describe the style of a magazine article. But what really matters is how that style contributes to what one thinks is the message of the article; how it contributes to the effect on the reader, intended and otherwise.

So, in a film an unexpected cut to an extreme close-up of a gun firing into camera can be described as just that. But what it is also about is shock, an assault on the viewer, a sense of violence. That is what the text means, rather than how it does it. *Textual reading* is another word for analysis, for getting at the meanings. As audiences for the media we do the reading. It has been suggested that there are three kinds of reading of text.

(a) An **agreed or preferred reading** is one where the audience makes sense of the text pretty much as its creators meant them to. A lot of genre material is like this, very predictable.

(b) A **negotiated reading** is one where the meanings are not so obvious, and one has to think about it. For example, the hero of a story might not be so perfect. We might 'read' them as being a bit of a bully as well as being brave, so we have to negotiate what we think of them.

(c) An **oppositional reading** is one where for whatever reason we as reader take a meaning from the text that is different from the one intended by the producer. For example, the heroine might have been set up as seductive and attractive to a certain kind of male audience, whereas a female viewer might read her as pathetic and foolish.

2.2 Mediation

'Mediation' is a general term used to describe the transformation of original material (scripts, events, etc.) when it is processed through any one of the mass media.

Any form of communication is only a set of signs standing in place of some original event, object, idea, etc., and so a kind of mediation must always take place when communication is happening. A film showing tigers in the wild is only showing tigers. It is not bringing us the real tigers or the original experience.

But the term 'mediation' is usually taken to be about more than just 'standing in place of'. It is about how the original is changed or transformed. We use it with reference to the media because they often actively transform all that they represent.

Again, it is convenient to leave out fictional material in any discussion. It is obvious that fiction does not pretend to present factual experience. Such material may mediate the author's intentions. Or again, one could look at the way in which a television version of a novel like *Mansfield Park* mediates that original novel. But in either case, we are pretty sure that a transformation has taken place.

However, much media material is factual, or purports to be so. It is here that we should look most carefully at the idea of mediation.

This idea should cause us to ask what kind of change has taken place from the original to the media version – and how that change has taken place, why and with what effect. All the points that follow in this second section of the chapter build on the concept of mediation, and confirm the fact that it really does matter that it happens.

For example, sport is mediated in the way that television represents its various events. On a mechanical level, football matches are repackaged by the editing process: they have the illusion of being seen as they happen, but time is compressed until only the drama and the goals remain.

Even when a match is shown live, the football is very much a mediated event. The viewer becomes a god through the mediating power of the camera, which can survey the entire pitch from above, or the details of play as if we are out there on the pitch. Hard disks permit the mediators to control time, giving us an instant flashback of action replay on the goals scored. And the commentator is actually heard as mediator, producing explanations and interpretations of events on the field that might never have occurred to us if we had been at the match itself.

For another example, the events and the very clothes of the fashion world are mediated through magazines. In this instance we note two things: that different media can work together in the mediation process – creating a notion of what is fashionable at any point; and that there can be creation as well as transformation in the mediation process. The idea of what is fashionable for summer wear, for instance, is the result not just of articles on fashion shows or what is available in certain shops, but also of opinions coming from the people who write the articles and take the pictures. The magazines are not just mediating what is 'out there'. The fashion articles become a source of information and ideas in themselves. In this way the media can be an active part of our cultural life. Mediation is an active process.

In this way the media help create culture, as well as our social reality.

2.3 Realism

Within media texts our sense of reality, or their quality of realism, is valued by audiences, but is entirely constructed. **Realism is nothing but a set of conventions**.

Audiences are interested in the quality of realism of a media text for several reasons. One is that we want to believe in the story, at least while we are watching or reading it; it is as if we really are in an American city with exciting things happening. Another may be that we want to believe in the truth of the message behind the story – that true love really does win through every time. Another may be that we want to feel personally involved – have a sense that we really are there in the spaceship. Another is that we expect certain kinds of text to have certain kinds of realism: we don't mind if Bugs Bunny gets blown up but miraculously survives; we do expect documentaries to give a sense of actual events, places and people. All these examples, associated with different reasons for expecting realism, can involve different conventions for producing that particular kind of realism.

You'll remember that conventions are kinds of rules to make sense of codes. So, for instance, to make sense of documentary as just that, there are rules for how the film or video material is handled. You might expect real locations and real people, the use of natural sound and lighting, single camera set-ups, and so on. In fact, there are various types of documentary which use different combinations of convention – you could work these out for yourself. One interesting one is the kind of documentary that is about historical events.

We expect our film to seem real, at least when we are watching it, even if we criticize it afterwards. The fact that we are inclined to criticize material on grounds of realism – 'I don't believe anyone would have been so stupid as to go down into that cellar!' (probability) – is due to Western culture having developed an appetite for realism through the growth of visual arts in particular. Photography, since it started over a hundred years ago, has given the illusion of 'capturing' life on film. Now computer games are having more and more memory devoted to making them seem real – with naturalistic characters and places on screen.

2.4 Media language

Media texts may be described through specialized language, or may use special language, spoken and visual.

It is useful to pick up some of that language, especially as it relates to visual texts. You have already been doing that, in that some special terms have been formally explained – the word 'text' itself. Other terms are assumed to be sufficiently well known – 'close-up'. Others acquire meaning in the context of our explanations – 'double-page spread' (DPS) for a magazine.

It is useful to know what a layout is, or a press release. The final chapter will elaborate some of these points, especially in relation to film and video. Here, it is useful to be able to use language that accurately identifies what you are trying to describe; there is a difference between a pan and a track right.

2.5 Narrative

'Narrative' is a formal term describing the structure and sequence of a text. It is what we call casually 'the story', but is more than that. Certainly narrative is about what is 'told' and the order of its telling. But you need to remember that this does not just apply to fictions. Documentaries and news articles also tell us something in a certain order. What is put first, second and last matters, in fact or fiction. An article on floods in Bangladesh can lead up to what the government agencies are doing about the disaster, just as a story about a murder can lead up to the discovery of the identity of the murderer.

This 'lead-up' is partly about **plot** – what happens in what order – and partly about **drama** – how excitement and reader involvement can be created by that order and by the way the story is told, by the language used. It is argued that many, if not all, narratives are organized around ideas of **conflict and resolution**. The storyline sets up a problem for the characters, develops conflict between some of them, but eventually resolves that conflict in some way – as with 'happily ever after' endings to romances. The drama in such stories works up to a climax of excitement, and then the denouement is where everything is sorted out. Narratives where everything is wrapped up neatly at the end are said to have **closure**.

It is worth remembering that the story is not just 'out there', waiting to be discovered in the pages or on the screen. We actually make the story in our heads from cues that the text gives us. Some texts direct our understanding more than others. Genres are much more what are called **closed texts**, because they are so bound by conventions that they are fairly predictable. If what is happening, and how, is not so obvious, is not so predictable, then the narrative is more open – indeed, one has an **open text**.

The cues referred to are really signs (referred to in chapter 1). Lots of them can come together to help us make the narrative in our heads. For example, think how you could be told that two people in a TV drama are going to fall in love. One obvious way to do this is to cut together medium close-ups of the two apparently looking at one another, and to hold the shots for longer than you would with characters who 'didn't matter' to the story.

Cues can also bring about **narrative positioning** (see also section 2.3 of this chapter). This is all about how you relate to the film or story. This positioning of the reader or viewer is most strong and obvious with fiction. For example, a writer can use the 'I' form to make you think you are being talked to by the person to whom everything really happened. You'll see that this could also be counted as a device of realism. Don't worry about finding overlaps between our sections, especially conventions that seem to apply to different topic areas. They do! And a film-maker can use a moving camera or a particular camera position to make you think that the camera is one of the characters, and that you are that character. This is called **subjective narrative**. You have been positioned – manipulated, in fact – to be part of the story.

2.6 Selection and construction

The content of any programme or newspaper is the result of a process of selection and construction.

Any example of media material is an example of a piece of communication that has been produced from a number of possible sources, and put together from only some of these. What is more, it has been put together in a certain way. What has been left out may be as important as what has been put in.

The way the material has been constructed will depend on a number of assumptions made by the media makers. These assumptions, their working practices, habits, conventions, are all ways of defining what is thought to be the 'normal' or 'proper' way to handle a given subject or a given type of programme, article, etc.

In this book we tend to look at examples from television and newspapers. But the terms used, and the ideas they contain, could be used in any one of the media. For example, a pop single is constructed from a number of tracks laid down in the studio. Some of these are selected from different takes and put together (mixed) to create a number that never existed in this form in the first place. And indeed, there may be several numbers (usually off a CD) that could have been chosen for this single release. Only one is chosen. The studio (and a record company) have selected and constructed this piece of communication because they think it will entertain a mass audience and will sell.

In another example, a typical radio news-magazine programme is constructed from many pieces of material available: live voice, recorded interviews, ads, trails, cable links with foreign places. And all these pieces of material may be on a variety of subjects, treated in a variety of ways. In the end, the programme editor will preside over a selection process that leaves out some material, reworks other pieces, sets up a running order and a time for each item. He or she has made decisions about that piece of communication which we call the programme.

We notice that, in the category of the media especially, it is very obvious that communication is not a 'natural' process. It is an activity that is performed in certain ways for certain reasons. In the end, the media are usually trying to chase audience figures and profits. The ways in which they communicate become more understandable when one remembers these two basic facts.

We may also notice that the media are distinctive in that items of media communication are produced by a group of people, working collaboratively, rather than by individuals. The idea of an individual creator is attractive to us because our culture leads us to believe in individualism – personalities, stars. But the facts are different. For example, this book is the result of collaboration between two authors, an editor, proof-readers, a copy editor, photographers and artists, printers and others. It is constructed by a number of people. It didn't just happen. You are reading these words because we decided that we wanted to communicate about communicating.

2.7 Product

The term 'product' draws attention to the fact that the media manufacture 'goods' that are bought by the audience as 'consumers'. The term is used to point to the fact that most pieces of communication coming through the media have to be promoted and sold in a marketplace. Routledge is not producing this book only because it believes it can be useful. The company also believes that it will make money and enable the company to produce more books.

The concept of product includes the ideas that the communication is produced in quantity and is sold. It is useful to an understanding of how and why communication takes place, because often these facts are obscured.

For example, television series are made on a production line, called a studio, just like a make of car. They will be sold through publicity work, trailers on television, possibly newspaper ads, just like the car. The television company is also trying to please its consumers, called the audience. (Even the BBC must chase the ratings and compete, in order to justify its licence fee.) The consumers in the United Kingdom also pay for the product, through this licence fee or through that proportion of the price of other products which is set aside by advertisers to pay for advertising. To say all this is neither to praise nor to condemn the end result. It simply illustrates the how and why of the communication process. And perhaps it will stop some people from pretending that there is either art or commerce in mass communication, when often the truth lies somewhere between these two ideas.

2.8 Ownership, finance, control

Media messages come from somewhere, and must be paid for by someone.

We can interpret the media and the way they communicate with more understanding if we understand their sources – of ownership as well as finance. It is clear that the cost element, as well as the ability to own all this message-making technology, distinguishes a film, say, from a conversation, or a note put through a friend's door. People see communication in a different light when they have to pay for it.

Other books can give you more factual detail than we are able to offer in the space available to us – but we think it is worth giving the main picture of what is going on.

Our media of mass communication are largely owned and run by business corporations. The BBC is a public service body. It was originally set up by, but is *not* run by, government.) Many of these corporations work on an international (multinational) basis. All of them own pieces of a variety of media industries. The immediate result of this is that they often (but not always) think in terms of large audiences and large profits. And the result of this situation is that they will often produce material which, in order to have a mass appeal, works to a formula. In particular, there is a desire to appeal to the American market, for two reasons. One is that the United States spends more money on communication products (especially entertainment) than any other country in the world. The other is that the Americans have such a well-developed system for distributing and marketing communication (among other products) that it pays to keep in with them. Events such as the Cannes Film Festival or the London VideoCom Fair are used by corporations to sell communications products on an international basis.

For example, Pearson is an international media group, with interests predominantly in education and publishing. Its Penguin group owns such titles as Penguin books, Puffin and Ladybird for children, and Longman books. Through Penguin USA Pearson owns publishers such as the Viking Press and Allyn & Bacon, as well as Addison Wesley and Prentice Hall. Pearson's British and US publishing operations have strong links with a second division of the company, named the Pearson Learning Group. This owns other companies which are concerned with (among other businesses) digital learning and educational measurement. It also owns the British Edexcel assessment business (one of the three remaining examination groups in England). It owns Dorling Kindersley and Scott Foresman educational publications. The third Pearson division is known as the Financial Times Group. This publishes the famous paper of that name, as well as such equivalents as *Financial Times Deutschland* and *Les Echos* (a dominant finance newspaper in France). It also owns 50 per cent of *The Economist* magazine.

Clearly, this network of alliances and of ownership not only typifies the source of communication in the mass media but also says something about their power. It helps us interpret as well as describe. It helps explain why the media sell a lot of entertainment product – it is profitable. As we have said, it helps explain a certain lack of variety in the types of communication product. It helps explain the ability of these owners to market and promote their products as heavily as they do.

Current developments in communication and technology do not change this overall pattern of centralized control and concentration on entertainment formats. New satellite channels across the world are owned or controlled by existing media corporations. This is not least because only they have the cash to finance such developments and perhaps carry the losses involved in starting up such ventures. In British commercial television, when contracts come up for renewal for the existing companies, potential new owners are still dominated by media interests – for example, the Virgin company, which is heavily involved in the music industry. In the American film industry, Japanese household names like JVC and Sony own major corporations such as Columbia. Those same Japanese companies dominate the production of equipment for broadcasting. They are trying to corner the market for the new high-definition television technology.

Public ownership, exemplified by the BBC in Britain, does not change the situation. The BBC does not make a profit, but it does chase audiences and ratings like any commercial organization. If it did not show that it was, in general, pleasing mass audiences, then there is no doubt that the British parliament (which sets the licence fee) would question whether it should go on getting the fees that it does. So, the BBC sells its programmes in world markets, and it sells spin-off products via its hugely successful commercial arm, BBC World. It also retains an enormous power over what we see and therefore what messages are incorporated in programmes. This is because it and the commercial companies still have 80 per cent of the audience. It may be argued that satellite or cable alternatives are no real alternative for the audience, in that they are geared even more to mass appeal: sport, music, films. The bottom line is that any kind of system has to be paid for.

This leads naturally to considerations of finance. Who pays, and how?

One simple answer is that the audience always pays – at the box office, through the cover price, at the counter, through the licence fee, through the goods they buy.

That kind of financing represents no control, other than in the crudest terms, over what is bought. But the immediate financiers may have a powerful control over the communication that we buy. This is why, once more, it is worth describing the situation broadly, so that one can then interpret it in terms of consequences. There are two immediate sources of finance for most examples one can think of.

One is the direct finance that comes from the owning company or its backing bankers. And the cost of media operations is so huge that it is not surprising that the owners have to be what we would call 'big business'. It costs an average of £300,000 to produce one hour of drama for television. Hardly surprising, then, that the BBC obtained American co-production money to finance *Jane Eyre* (2006). And the effect of this is to concentrate power further in the hands of those producers who do have money (and so reinforce their kind of material), and to lock out anyone with ideas about doing something different. Lest our picture looks too desperate, it should be pointed out that, for example, Channel Four in the United Kingdom was set up in such a way as to ensure that smaller companies got some of their productions on to the screen. The Broadcasting Act 1990 reinforced this, across TV media, demanding that at least 25 per cent of production was 'independent', and giving rise to the success of new companies such as Endemol. Similarly, American public service channels also serve minority audiences. They provide some sort of alternative to the mass commercial product.

But then there is the second main source of finance: advertising. Advertisers pay heavily for a special kind of communication, and expect to see results. They may themselves be large companies, with a good deal of financial muscle. And, for example, a magazine advertisement for lipstick sells not only

Books
X value of sales

Reed/Elsevier (e.g. Heinemann)
Holtzbrinck (e.g. Palgrave Macmillan)
Bertelsmann (e.g. Random House)
Newscorp (e.g. HarperCollins)
Pearson (e.g. Longman/Penguin)

Music
X volume and value of sales

Seagram [Universal Music Group] (e.g.
Polygram and Motown)
EMI
Bertelsmann (e.g. Sony)
Warner Music Group (e.g. Atlantic)

**Film production and
distribution**
X investment and returns

Sony (Columbia and Tristar)
Viacom (Paramount)
Newscorp (Twentieth Century Fox)
Disney
Time/Warner/AOL
Seagram (Universal)

Commercial TV
X hours' output/programmes

ITV plc

Magazines
X sales

Emap (e.g. *Elle, Heat*)
United Business Media (e.g. *Music Business*)
National Magazine Company (e.g.
Cosmopolitan, Good Housekeeping, Vogue)
Reed/Elsevier (e.g. *TV Times*)

Daily newspapers
X sales

Newscorp [News International] (e.g. The *Sun*)
Trinity Mirror (*Daily Mirror*)
Northern and Shell (*Daily Express*)
Daily Mail and General Trust

Commercial radio
X listeners

Emap (e.g. Metro, Kiss 100)
GCAP (e.g. Capital FM, Classic FM, GWR)
Chrysalis (e.g. Heart)
SMG (e.g. Virgin)
GMG Radio Holdings (e.g. Jazz FM)

FIGURE 45 Media ownership – with particular reference to the United Kingdom. This chart indicates where in the various media 70 per cent or more of the market, defined as given, is dominated by specific companies. Obviously, a number of 'owners' are in fact multinationals, based outside the United Kingdom. A number appear more than once because of the persuasive skill of the advertisement, but also as a result of the communication in the rest of the magazine. In this case an article that just happened to be about using cosmetics and mentioned certain products, would be described as an *advertorial*. So, one obvious effect of this source of finance is that the magazine producers tend to produce the kind of material that will please the advertisers – material which sells to the target audience that the advertisers are aiming at. No one needs to twist the arms of the magazine owners. If they don't sell copies, then their marketing division cannot prove to the lipstick manufacturers that it is worth paying to advertise in their magazine. No income, no magazine.

So, the matter of who pays for the communication does affect the content and treatment of the communication that we get. Our magazine example is bound to put in feature articles about make-up, which, like the advertisement, suggest that lipstick makes you more attractive. This in itself reinforces a certain way of looking at things, a certain sense of what is 'normal'. And so it would seem that, in our example, the communication is about more than lipsticks and the idea of what is attractive.

2.9 Media and audience

You will see that the word 'audience' appears often in this chapter, not least in relation to advertising.

In the first place, the audience for the various media may be described as those who view, read and listen. It is also common to refer to **mass audience** to make the point that media such as cinema and magazines have viewers and readers whose numbers run into hundreds of thousands a week. However, it is also important to realize that in fact **the media have many audiences**.

Audiences are targeted by the advertising and circulation managers of newspapers, television and all the other media. There is an audience for a magazine on American football, there is an audience for a TV programme such as *Friends*, and so on. All these audiences have slightly different characteristics, measured by the usual markers of age, gender, socio-economic grouping, etc. Audiences with such characteristics can be targeted by producing material that appeals to them. This raises an interesting question as to whether the audience is found or made. Does a TV programmer have an audience in mind and put on material to suit? Or is the material put on, and then finds an audience? Obviously, after many years, radio producers and journalists, for example, do have a fair idea of what their audience is like and what it wants. But still it brings one to another point.

Audiences may be constructed. This idea points to the fact that it is possible to 'find' an audience for a media product and to build it up. For example, *My Family* is a TV comedy which has a pretty broad appeal, but which is still biased towards an older viewer – rueful parents. Then again, something like the soap spoof *The Green Wing* finds a younger audience that can cope with its anarchy and black humour. Or one can look at a British up-market magazine for males such as *GQ*, which again has constructed an audience for its product by appealing to a section of the population through a type of magazine that did not exist several years ago.

Audiences are crucial in any model of the communication process in the media because, after all, they pay for the existence of the media one way or the other: cover price, box office, licence fee, and the like. The response of the audience to media products is carefully checked through continual market research; hundreds of people are interviewed every week by BARB, the broadcasters' research organization. So, we should not look at the audience as a lot of gaping mouths to be fed with whatever pap the media choose to throw in. In fact, this raises another point.

Audiences are active. This means that audiences actively select what they want to read or view. A certain type of audience will actively choose between a range of computer magazines. Another type will choose whether or not to switch on the news. It is still common to hear the mistaken view that the media, especially television, make us passive. This is not true in many ways. First, it takes a great deal of attention activity to watch and understand TV. Then again, there is research evidence to show that people do not sit still and watch TV anyway – they do some surprising things while the set is on. And there are other points about activity, such as the well-evidenced connection between increased participation in certain sports and the amount of exposure they are getting on television. The notion of an active audience also ties in with ideas about how we may or may not be affected by media messages.

The uses and gratification theory of the connection between the audience and the media suggests that we use the media to gratify needs that we have inside us. It suggests that we can be quite active in trying to satisfy those needs. So, we select music to satisfy moods, we select magazines to satisfy interests, we select TV channels and programmes to satisfy whatever we think it is we need at the time: excitement, romance, the need for security, social needs, personal needs and so on.

Audience profile refers to the description of the audience for a particular media product. It isn't very hard to work out the profile for a magazine by looking at the content and style. One can describe the readership in terms of age, gender, occupation, interests and possibly role and location.

Since 2001 the UK government has, for example, defined its population by seven classes, mainly on the basis of types of employment, employment conditions, being paid a salary or a wage, employment benefits. Advertisers are also interested in how much you are paid and how secure your job is.

Class 1	Managerial and professional occupations (e.g. doctors)	8.5%
Class 2	Lower managerial and professional (e.g. lab technicians)	19%
Class 3	Intermediate occupations (e.g. legal secretaries)	9.4%
Class 4	Small employers and own-account workers (e.g. small employers, restaurant managers)	7%
Class 5	Lower supervisory and technical (e.g. plumbers)	7.2%
Class 6	Semi-routine occupations (e.g. hairdressers)	12%
Class 7	Routine occupations (e.g. waiters and couriers)	9.1%

The remaining 29 per cent are counted as unclassifiable, or long-term unemployed, or students.

In all cases, what industry is really interested in is disposable income – how much you have left over to spend after your main costs are covered. The profile that identifies gay people is used to target what is called the pink pound. Gay people generally are not parenting, and have more money to spend than many others.

Audience lifestyle refers to the interests, spending habits, relationships, activities, values of a given audience. This has developed as a refinement of profiling over the past ten years or more. Lifestyle recognizes that some groups of people will spend a lot of money on their lifestyle almost regardless of whether or not they can really afford it. It also recognizes that people generally can be persuaded to consume if it fits with their lifestyle. This affects the media in two ways. Directly it has to do with media products fitting in with lifestyle. So, magazines for specialist music tastes can succeed if they become part of the lifestyle that goes with the music. This kind of specialist media product has found a **market niche**. But second, because the media are generally paid for by advertising income, identification and use of lifestyle also affect the media indirectly. Many television ads clearly represent some way of life that audiences have or would like to have.

Audiences can be primary or secondary. That is to say, the primary audience for a film is the one that first sees it in the cinema. But then there are many in the secondary audience who rent the DVD or even buy it, as well as those who watch the film when it is screened on terrestrial channels or on satellite. This distinction between such audiences applies especially to print media. It is the difference between readership and circulation figures. More people read magazines and newspapers than actually buy them. Market surveys are interested in these 'lost' purchasers – why do they read but not buy?

2.10 Scheduling

A particular method of focusing on audiences is to **schedule your media product so that its timing suits a certain audience**. Usually, scheduling is a term applied to the placing of TV programmes at certain times. So, programmes for young people are scheduled for screening in late afternoon to early evening, to catch the after-school audience. Others are placed on Saturday morning to catch the same audience in its free time. In the United Kingdom, programmes with certain degrees of sex and violence are scheduled for after the 'watershed' – nine o'clock in the evening – in the hope of missing the young audience. The allied concept of programming – choosing types of programme as well as their timing – is seen in the scheduling of sports programmes in the summer. So many people are on holiday or out and about at this time of the year that programmers for the channels will not put out expensive material at these times.

The idea of scheduling obviously applies to radio, for example particular slots for news programmes. In principle it is also what release patterns are about in the cinema. Here, they actually try to release blockbusters that will appeal to children and families in the summer – because they are free and in the mood to go out. The same thing is true of the Christmas slot.

2.11 Overt and covert values

The media often communicate messages about beliefs and opinions.

These stand for values – notions to do with good and bad, for and against, proper and improper, and so on. Newspapers in particular will be open in supporting certain causes or political positions (they are not limited in the way that broadcasting is).

But sometimes the values expressed are not obvious or overt. They may be hidden or covert. Just how hidden is a matter of opinion, depending on a particular piece of communication, and on how perceptive its receivers are. But still the idea of covert values is a useful one for interpreting the media. It should cause us to look more closely at what is really said, and how.

It should also be said that those producing the piece of communication may or may not have intended to conceal certain messages. In the example of an advertisement, it is likely that there is an intention to conceal. Those who construct advertisements are skilled communicators. They are aware that a product can best be sold on the back of an idea, and that that idea should fit in with the audience's existing beliefs and values. But the idea mustn't be too obvious. For instance, a number of advertisements sell food products in association with the idea of health. So far, this is fairly plain: the value of good health is expressed as an overt value, in the case of all those advertisements for items like butter, bread, orange juice and yoghurt. A number of these advertisements also show the product being consumed by families and, even more specifically, being served by the wife or mother. In this case, the covert value and message is that families are OK, and a good family buys and consumes the product. In other cases the ad depicts women, their looks and their lifestyles. The covert messages are about women being worried about their figures (as much as their health) – being worried about being inspected by others, and perhaps found wanting.

To take another example, crime thrillers are always popular because they are presented in an exciting way. So, the first message one may get is that crime and law enforcement are adventurous, whereas the police will tell you that a lot of crime fighting is very boring and bureaucratic. Crime stories may also imply that violence happens but the cop hero will come out OK. This is almost a suggestion that violence is 'safe' – for the hero, at least. This is nonsense. People don't recover easily from even a crack on the head. More bothering still is a suggestion that acts of violence are somehow all right if they are being committed by the police in the cause of law. We, the audience, may be set up to accept this covert message because the violence is being done to the 'baddie', who is a pervert, psychopath or whatever. The overt values may be about the importance of keeping law and order. But covert values can suggest that this is a more exciting activity than it really is; that law-keeping methods are not to be questioned.

We are arguing that such covert messages need to be looked for, debated and condemned if they are 'secretly' presenting values that are unacceptable to ourselves and/or to our society. And in this process of analysis and interpretation we may also come across interesting contradictions in the covert values – and in our society's values in general. For example, we might assume that everyone would say that they believe in the rule of law. This is meant to protect us from the behaviour of unsocial individuals – those we might call criminals. But at the same time, we also believe in the right of individuals to 'do their own thing', and to preserve their own sense of what is right and wrong – a sense of 'natural' justice, perhaps. Crime stories can present a contradiction between natural justice and legal justice, between an individual's needs and the needs of society.

So, there are covert messages in most examples of media communication. These messages are dominantly about values. The values are part of the meaning of the communication. These meanings have more or less significance according to obvious factors like what is said, who says it, who is receiving the message and how many times it is repeated.

2.12 Representations

The media re-present a version of our world to us. They are not a window on the world. They are not a mirror for reality. They reconstruct our world and ideas about it. Even news does this. (Here you should refer back to the section on mediation (2.2), which explains how the media transform what they present.)

The media represent all aspects of our world. So, one can look at how they represent schools or criminality, say, as much as how they represent women or the disabled. However, it is common to look at representations of people by groups or types. The media tend to represent us to ourselves as if we all belong to one group or another. And then they represent those groups as having certain characteristics. What is more, this representation includes value messages about what that group and those characteristics stand for. Common groupings are by age, gender, sexual orientation, job, roles – the same sets indeed as may be used for audience profiling! The value messages are basically about approval or disapproval. Sometimes they seem to be downright contradictory – girls can be either prissy virgins or promiscuous tarts; boys can be either violent yobs or cool and gorgeous.

These kinds of simplistic representation are referred to as stereotypes.

Stereotypes

A stereotype of a person is based on repeated description and ideas. A stereotype stands for a set of people, like women or businessmen. It is supposed to typify that set, and ideas about them.

A stereotype is a simplification. It is not only about appearance, but also to do with relationships and beliefs connected with the type of person. In effect, it adds up to a snap description and an uncritical judgement of that person.

There are many well-known stereotypes of women, such as the so-called dumb blonde. But people are also typed in terms of things like race and religion. Some stereotypes are actually meant to be insulting – the image of the mean Scotsman or Jew. In fact, most stereotypes are insulting in some way, and all are a kind of evasion of the real complexity and interest of complete human beings.

The media use stereotypes of people as a kind of shorthand for getting their messages across. It is easier to represent a stereotype than to describe and build a full character. But while the media are guilty of reinforcing stereotypes, they have not invented them. They use them because it is known that they are used and understood by society in general. They offer an easy point of contact. The worrying thing is that stereotypes are also often a collection of prejudices. In this sense the power of the media becomes destructive, because in repeating stereotypes they are repeating prejudices on a grand scale.

For example, comedy is full of stereotypes. We are certainly not in the business of damning all comedy because of this. But we are saying that much comedy communicates through stereotypes, and that this is not always a good thing. There are arguments about comedy releasing tensions and helping people come together. But some comedy around the stereotype of the mother-in-law is likely to create tension in those ladies, rather than release it. Similarly, if one belongs to the Chinese community, then the exaggerated voices in some radio comedy will no doubt be rather irritating. And on television, if one is male and gay, then the exaggerated limp-wrist style of some comedy stereotypes will also be pretty infuriating.

Stereotypes predominate in fictional material. But they are by no means exclusive to comedy. Boys' comics represent stereotypes of square-jawed war heroes. Horror movies represent swooning female stereotypes in nighties. Romantic novels represent stereotyped heroes. One type, for example, is middle-class, male and masterful. He has the power that comes from his work and social position, and can sweep the female off to exotic places. In short, he represents a fantasy, but a fantasy with a narrow range of ideas.

So, in one sense stereotypes are a device for sketching in a character quickly. In another sense they may be a device for appealing to the audience's existing attitudes and beliefs – and, indeed, prejudices. They certainly do communicate values to the audience and appear to have the effect at least of reinforcing those attitudes and beliefs.

Because they are so recognizable, stereotypes are commercial. They help material become popular and profitable. When Emma Thompson created the title role in the film *Nanny McPhee* (2006) she was drawing on a stereotype of governesses going back a long way through film and literature. Perhaps virtually no one in the film's audience had ever had experience of a governess. But the tradition of *Mary Poppins*, of *The Sound of Music*, of *Peter Pan*, has placed the stereotype in our cultural consciousness. The process of recognition and understanding goes round and round. People's awareness of such stereotypes is reinforced and set up for the next example by the very fact that the media repeat them and have large audiences.

2.13 Genres

This same process of repetition also reinforces the popularity of identifiable forms of media product called genres.

The main idea of genre incorporates a story form in any one of the media, including repeated elements like stock characters and situations. Science fiction stories or cop thrillers are genres. But the idea of genre may also be extended to identify other repetitive types of media product.

For example, television quiz shows may be said to be a genre because they also work to a formula. They are always about competition, often for a prize. They always have the same hero figure – the ever-smiling compère. The backgrounds are frequently the same: garish, theatrical sets. And they even have a kind of repeated storyline that involves the compère as narrator raising the tension until the climax at the end, when a winner is announced and rewarded. A current successful example of this is *Deal or No Deal*.

The word 'genre' helps us to interpret the media because it helps identify a dominant type of media product. It leads us to the repeated elements and then to the messages that are within the stories of genre. For instance, the quiz show's message is something about the importance of competing to get what you want, and about wanting to have material possessions. The media often communicate through the genre formula.

But it is no accident that genres develop. They are popular. And it is not surprising that they also use types and stereotypes in their characterization. Genres are a dominant type of media entertainment because they are popular, and therefore profitable. Stereotypes are part of that popularity.

In the case of either the genre or the stereotype, the point of contact through the communication is immediate and powerful. This is especially true with what are called **icons** of a genre. These are elements of the formula, perhaps the background, more often an object like the tommy-gun for classic gangster films. Decades of films, of publicity, have engraved the image of this ninety-year-old weapon on our cultural consciousness. Even if we have never seen an old gangster movie, we may well recognize this gun – and all it stands for. Any communication sign that can achieve this degree of recognition across such a wide area of the globe must have power. Such power suggests influence as well as popularity.

The significance of the influence of a piece of genre material depends on what one believes its messages to be, as well as on one's point of view. But in particular, genres often represent the main beliefs and values of the culture that makes them at a given time. And in turn the genres also confirm those values as they represent them. The problem is to be objective enough about the communication process to be able to stand back and see what is going on. For example, it is now fairly obvious that those spy, Western and science fiction films of the 1950s that were about invasions and threats to American society were actually about the high degree of anxiety about communism and Russia at the time. Not so many people saw this then. But when we bring together terms like 'genre', 'repetition' and 'covert values' as tools for opening up the meaning of examples of media communication, then we have a better chance of working out what that meaning is.

The unwritten rules of what elements are expected to be in a given genre and of how they are expected to be used are called **conventions**. We have used the same word to describe the rules which bind the use of signs within codes of communication (see figure 46). So, it is a word that is strongly applicable to genre, but not unique to it. What is useful about the term is that it promotes the idea that there are rules. This draws attention to the fact, once more, that we do not make and understand pieces of communication by chance. We can control our production of communication if we choose to. We can also be more precise about understanding the meaning of what is communicated, if we make the effort.

One example of a convention that works on genre material is that which says that the hero must appear within the first five minutes, if not sooner. It is a way of getting the audience to identify and possibly sympathize with the hero

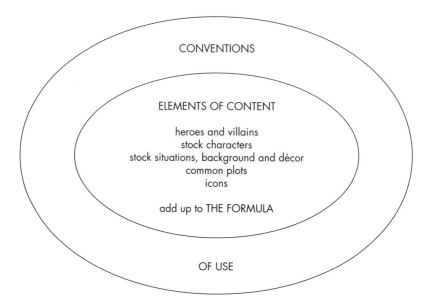

CONVENTIONS

ELEMENTS OF CONTENT

heroes and villains
stock characters
stock situations, background and décor
common plots
icons

add up to THE FORMULA

OF USE

FIGURE 46   The conventions of genre bind its elements together into a formula

at an early stage of the story. But of course it is only a convention. It is not an absolute rule or law of nature. Conventions in genres change and adapt as the genres themselves are used again and again. Try watching a genre thriller serial with the sound down. You should still be able to identify the heroes and villains. Why and how?

2.14 Censorship and control

Mass-media corporations cannot print or broadcast whatever they like. But still it is a matter for great debate as to whether they are or are not controlled enough in terms of what they say and how they say it.

Most censorship of British media is voluntary. What this means is that the content and treatment of newspapers, films and television are monitored by organizations set up by the media corporations themselves: the Press Council, the Advertising Standards Authority, the Video Standards Council, the British Board of Film Certification and television committees, which produce codes of practice for the producers. The media industry decides who will be members of these organizations, which in turn will decide on what is acceptable for young viewers, or on what constitutes excessive sex and violence. Broadcasting is more complicated. Independent Television and the BBC do have their own 'in-house' systems of vetting and perhaps censoring their own output. But one has to bear in mind that members of the BBC Trust are appointed by the government. And commercial television and radio is monitored by Ofcom. This was set up by government, though it is supposed to operate as an independent public body (and is *not* a government department of any kind).

There is sometimes **direct censorship**, or attempts at it. It would happen through direct political intervention – ministers contacting the media in question. It might happen through using the law, or threatening to do so. For example, in the late 1980s the government passed a bill forbidding the voices of organizations described as terrorist (Sinn Féin) to be broadcast at all. (The Act was repealed in 1993.) More recently the Labour government has taken civil servants to court for allegedly leaking confidential documents (the case is not yet resolved).

Indirect censorship can occur if types of legal action are merely threatened. For example, the government can use or threaten to use the Official Secrets Act or the Prevention of Terrorism Act to try to stop material being produced about military matters or about what is happening in Northern Ireland. There is a long list of programmes about Northern Ireland that have been changed or stopped altogether. There are many similar examples relating to the Official Secrets Act. In 2000 a civil servant named David Shaylor fled to France, having released on to the Web details of what he claimed were documents revealing illegal government actions that were against the public interest. He was threatened with prosecution by the government, but his case never came to court. In 2003 he returned to Britain. In 2005 he stood against Tony Blair in the general election.

There is an important media debate here involving the public right to know versus protecting the public interest. There is no easy answer to the questions raised by these debates and examples. Many people do not like the idea of censorship in any form. On the other hand, many people would not want to see hardcore pornography being broadcast at 6 o'clock in the evening when children might be viewing. These are questions and problems that you should discuss when looking at what the media puts out and when considering the nature of media power.

Codes of practice that have been set up and written down by various media organizations could also be regarded in some ways as a form of self-censorship. The Advertising Association, the BBC and Ofcom all have codes of practice regarding what should or should not be shown, to whom, and how. How far you would want to use the word 'censorship' about these rules is another matter. You might well agree that it is fine to have a rule that does not allow advertising aimed at children to ask them to ask their parents to buy them something.

We believe in a 'free press' and freedom of expression, on the one hand. Yet we don't wish any person to have any freedom to say anything.

FIGURE 47 Possible points of censorship of the original material in the stages of making a film

2.15 Effects of the media

Many people believe that the output of the media does affect us in various ways, but this is in fact very hard to prove. The general view would be that the value messages in media material affect us by becoming part of our personal system of values.

There are particular views that, for example, media output has the effect of encouraging violent or antisocial behaviour. Research has been done into this, as it has into the idea that the media affect voting habits at the time of general elections. Other views of particular effects include the idea that media stereotypes encourage sexist attitudes.

If one considers these ideas briefly, it is possible to illustrate **problems with measuring media effects**. In the case of violence it is just as easy to prove that violent scenes in the cinema or on television have the effect of putting people off such behaviour. In the case of voting habits, as with any effects research, it is impossible to separate clearly the influence of the media from the influence of other factors such as the opinions of friends and family. In the case of media stereotypes, the problem, it could be said, is to do with allowing for how the stereotype is handled. A female stereotype in a comic strip is unlikely to affect the audience in the same way as a scene in an action movie. But how does one measure that difference?

This is not at all to dismiss such research. Much work has been done to try to allow for the kinds of problem described. We are learning a lot about factors which influence whether there is an effect or not. It is possible to suggest certain effects under certain conditions. Research has caused people to think more carefully about the types of effect they are looking for.

Common types of effect that have been suggested and investigated include long- or short-term effects, effects on behaviour and effects on attitudes. Generally, media research has moved from an interest in short-term

behavioural effects to an interest in longer-term effects on attitudes. In terms
of violence this is like saying there has been a move from trying to prove that
people go out and commit violent acts after watching violence on TV, to trying
to prove that over many months or years people may come to accept or even
approve of violence.

This view, that one has to be concerned with effects on people's thinking,
fits in with a concern about the media messages which make value statements,
most obviously seen in advertisements or genre material. Examples might be –
put a big value on appearance and spend money on clothes and make-up – or
put a value on being tough and macho as a male and don't be sentimental with
women.

**The repetition and reinforcement of such messages is what, it is
believed, gives the media such power to affect our attitudes and values.**
This is to say, similar ideas are repeated across different media over months
and years: 'increasingly today it is believed that the most significant naturally
occurring influences of television may be long term ones' (Barrie Gunter,
Television and the Fear of Crime, London: John Libbey, 1987). So, the effect of
the media may be made possible through the fact that, for example, messages
about Germans, for some people at least, start with comics and continue
through cinema films and TV comedy. The same messages about what
Germans are supposed to be like, what we are supposed to think of them, are
repeated in different ways. Such messages, perhaps about Germans being
humourless or violent, are remarkably persistent and go back to media views
formed in wars that finished over sixty years ago. This persistence is also part
of the power of the media and their effects. It forms attitudes and values that
become part of the way that we see the world. As recently as 2005 the German
ambassador spoke on British radio about his concerns regarding the persistence
and effects of these representations.

2.16 Ideology and the media

The attitudes and values that we have just talked about affect our view of
everything that we experience. They are part of our beliefs. They apply to our
view of people, and to our views about everything from class to sex, good laws
to bad behaviour (see figure 48). In fact they add up to a **view of the world**,
especially in relation to **ideas about who should or should not have power**
in the world. This is ideology. The main view of the world held by most people
in a given culture is the view that dominates – a **dominant ideology**. Ideology
works in the interests of the few, not for the many.

Media messages are affected by that ideology. The way articles are written
and programmes are shaped partly comes out of that dominant view because
the journalists and programme makers are part of it. But then once the messages
are there, coming through the programmes and articles, they go back into that

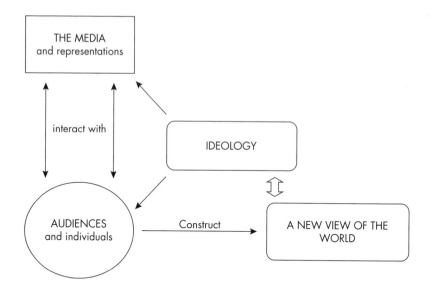

FIGURE 48 Ideology influences media constructions (representations), as well as the beliefs and values of the individual. Therefore, it also influences the view of the world that is constructed in the minds of audiences

ideology. In most cases they serve to reinforce it. Occasionally media material challenges it. Media students need to look for the challenge in the text. In this sense, decoding or textual analysis is about looking for value messages. So, it is about uncovering ideology, describing it and testing the validity of what it 'tells' us.

The major topics that we have views about tend to have those views implied through the kind of verbal and visual language that is used when talking about them – topics such as romance or parenting. The tricky thing about ideology is that it is like fluoride in the water: it's there, but difficult to detect. This is because your views on romance and parenting are probably in general the views of everyone else, which are the views of the dominant ideology. Most people, growing up with the views of friends, family and the media all around them, take them in with their cornflakes, as it were, so these views become naturalized. It is this **process of naturalization which makes ideology invisible**.

And we are certainly not saying that such views are wrong. We are only saying that they could be. We are saying that the phenomenon of naturalization works against questioning what the media (and ideology) 'tell us'. We are saying that being a communication student requires that questioning.

You could think about what your views are on the subjects of romance and parenting, for example, and where you think these views come from. Is romance depicted as a good thing? Do the media confuse romance and sex? If they do sometimes, what follows from this? Do you believe that all adults should become parents? What do you think about adults who don't have children? Are adults naturally able to be parents? What views of parenting are put across in TV programmes? In some of your answers to these questions you may find a difference between what you know is the accepted view and what you yourself think.

These 'topics' which have value messages attached to them are more formally known as **discourses**. One has a discourse when in a given topic area it is possible to recognize particular ways of using communication about the topic: language and codes. And this particular language gives out particular meanings. There are in fact many discourses within ideology. For example – and you would say quite naturally(!) – the verbal language we use about babies is very approving and affectionate. People will say things like 'isn't she sweet!' and 'you're so lucky' and 'they're so cuddly at that age'. People use words like 'sweet' and 'cuddly'. They don't say things like 'what a bald smelly lump!' and 'you're in for some rough nights'. The trouble is that babies are smelly as well as cuddly. But you won't often find the media presenting their audience with alternative views to the dominant ones. This is partly to do with giving people what they want to hear. But it also has a lot to do with selling baby products, and so also an idea of 'babydom'. Take a look at magazine adverts for baby products or those containing babies for some other reason. There is clearly a dominant view, a particular discourse, a certain set of values.

Are we victims of the media?

Hint: ask yourself how helpless you are as a consumer.

---

3 The media: particular examples

3.1 Advertising, publicity, marketing

A great deal of money is spent on the three activities of advertising, publicity and marketing: in 2004, UK advertising expenditure was £18.4 billion. They depend on communication. They use forms of communication, notably the media, as a way of persuading people to think or behave in ways that they might not otherwise have done.

Advertising is not a form of communication: it is way of using forms of communication.

Advertising has a clear price on it. The communication is charged for, whether it be through posters, radio slots or magazine advertisements.

Publicity is not charged for up front, though it may have hidden costs. A popular star may actually charge the media a fee for appearing on a television chat show. On the other hand, a launch lunch for that star's recently published biography could cost the publishers a lot of money to feed the journalists and personalities whom they would like to attend and to review the book well. Then again, a film company may get free coverage of some location work because the press believe this will help them sell newspapers.

Marketing is the calculated promotion of goods, services or even an individual. It combines advertising and publicity through a campaign. In the past twenty years the overall concept of marketing has come to dominate the advertising world. Even political parties will employ a marketing agency to help with everything from market research to the promotion of policies and of a public image.

Finance

Communication carried on in the name of advertising has enormous financial implications. It isn't just that advertising is an industry in itself which creates jobs and turns over huge sums for making adverts and buying media slots. It also fuels the other media industries.

Newspapers depend on their income from advertising to keep going. Commercial television couldn't exist without advertising. Magazines depend on advertising. To this extent the needs of the advertisers and the companies who use them shape media material. We get a lot of popular types of programme not just because they sell but because they sell the adverts around them.

Stereotypes

We have already explained the concept of stereotypes in the previous section.

Advertising tends to exploit the use of stereotypes because it has to communicate very quickly with its audience. As we have noted, stereotypes are immediately recognizable. If the advertisement has to sketch in a situation rapidly, then it helps to be able to slot characters into instantly recognizable roles. Stereotypes are all about instant roles.

Advertisers also like to identify their target audience as a group in the advertisement: 'busy housewives', 'Martini people'. So again, stereotypes help do this.

It is also arguable that advertising is especially responsible for maintaining and fixing stereotypes in the public consciousness. Very simply, advertising campaigns work across a range of media. Advertisements are repeated many times. Apart from genres, they are the most repetitious use of communication in the media. So, anything that they say, many times, is likely to get known.

And remember that the stereotyping is not just about role and appearance, but also about relationships and situations. There are no unmarried mothers in advertisements, no arguments between parents and children, and people are mostly at home or at play. There are a lot of large, well-appointed cars and large, well-appointed homes.

Covert messages

Indeed, these stereotypes of people and their situations also stand for messages about values, about a way of life and a set of beliefs that we in turn are invited to believe in. We have already given an advertising example for this concept. And we said then that the degree of covertness or overtness in these messages is a matter of observation and opinion.

But consider one more example. There is the value of 'newness'. Think of the number of advertisements that sell the product using the word 'new', or by emphasizing that this is the 'latest model', or by emphasizing the glossy new appearance of the product, or by giving some space-age context to the product. All this adds up to the covert message that newness is OK. If it is new, it must be good. This is, of course, convenient to manufacturers competing in markets that are already saturated with a given product and where there isn't much new to offer the public. But it does also mean that we may come to believe in newness for the sake of it. Something new is not necessarily a good thing. It is just – new.

Alternative realities

Apart from covert values, advertisements often communicate to us an idea of alternative realities. These are other situations and lifestyles. Some commentators have talked of an alternative world of the media. The idea of something manufactured is still there. But it is most accurate to recognize that what advertising communicates to us is a set of complementary fantasies.

These alternative realities are best recognized through the backgrounds in the advertisements. For instance, there is the 'beach in the sun' fantasy, including tropical islands, which has been used to give a context to the sale of products like holidays, crisps, drinks, sweets. Not all advertisements fit the patterns, but enough do to make the patterns valid. Again, there is the alternative 'ideal home'. This home has its downmarket and upmarket versions, and is usually shown in separate, disconnected rooms. But it is there, behind cleaning products for kitchen and bathroom, or types of fire and drinks for the living room, or furnishings for the bedroom.

Look for these alternative realities yourself. Construct them for yourself from magazine pictures. You will find other versions such as 'action in foreign parts', the traditional English countryside, the high-tech office, and so on.

The point is that the advertisements promote the illusion that these alternative backgrounds and situations are real. They are not. They are mostly myths about different worlds that the advertisers (and perhaps ourselves) would like to exist. The communication is the result of a careful process of construction, to enhance the illusion. Once more, it carries messages about values which are artificially enhanced by advertising. For example, the English countryside world is also about nostalgia for another way of life (which in any case never existed as it is depicted). We buy the dream of a lost world when we buy the product.

Advertising as communication

An advertisement is no more nor less than another piece of communication. It has an opening tease like any story to gain attention. It develops its own ideas and message in its main part, like a story. And it concludes with a punchline or a twist, like a story – anything to make its message memorable. **Advertising is an example of communication that is very consciously planned**. It is presented with the intention of affecting the audience.

Television advertising is an example of communication that is notable in terms of its costs. On British television a twenty-five-second advertisement can cost £40,000 or more to make, and £100,000 or more to transmit on peak-time slots over the whole TV network for a week. In terms of a campaign covering a range of media for, say, two months, it would cost at least £1.5 million to give a major new product in the domestic consumer market a proper launch. But still, advertising is only communication. The process by which it communicates is susceptible to analysis, as with any other example.

When we examine the **source** of the message we notice the interesting fact that it is in three parts. The advertising agency, or creative consultancy, may create the message. But the client for whom the advertisement is made also pays for it, and has some say about what goes into the advert. And the media that present the advert are also a source, so far as the audience is concerned. Their time slot or page space has to be paid for. And indeed, local display advertisements (the boxed ones with pictures) in local newspapers are mostly produced by the paper's own team. Similarly, local television makes solely local advertisements for local businesses.

If we examine the idea of **audience**, then we notice that advertisers, while bearing in mind that they want to communicate with fairly large numbers of people, still try to specify a typical member of their target audience as tightly as possible. The agency will produce an imaginative description of such a person. This will include all the attributes that we perceive in others: age, occupation, status, and so on, as well as ideas about their lifestyle. They are careful about who they think they are talking to, and adjust their communication style accordingly. Ineffective communication is expensive.

In the same way, advertisers think about the characteristics of the **medium** that they are using, about its possibilities.

And they are well aware of the social **context** within which they are operating. Advertisements fall within the consensus of our beliefs and values. They exploit them. They would never oppose them. In addition, they are sensitive to cultural nuances within the social mix, especially as they apply to particular groups of consumers. Advertisements for clothes for young people, for example, are alert to changing habits and fashions out in the real world. They follow at a safe distance behind, but they are there.

Categories of advertisements

Advertisements are usually divided into two broad categories: classified and display.

Classified advertisements are those lists of small ads in columns at the back of newspapers and magazines. They are used for recruiting staff as well as for selling and publicizing products and services. Job advertisements usually include the job title, duties and responsibilities, expected qualifications and experience of the person wanted, some idea of salary, and conditions, including any fringe benefits.

Display advertisements include all press, radio, cinema, TV and outdoor advertising that seeks to display the product or service to potential buyers. In general, classified advertisements are more factual and brief. Display advertisements may contain facts about the goods but are intended to be more persuasive and attractive. It has been suggested that a display advertisement should achieve four purposes:

- attract *attention*;
- arouse *interest*;
- create *desire*; and
- lead to *action*.

Look at and listen to some ads, to see how far they seek to do all four of these things. In most modern advertisements the action part is left unstated.

Brochures are also an interesting example of advertising and publicity. They are produced in a great variety of styles by almost all business organizations. We suggest you collect some and analyse them as pieces of communication.

Advertising and persuasion

We have said that all advertising seeks to persuade the receiver of something. **Advertising seeks to reinforce or shift attitudes and beliefs so that people will then behave differently**. For example, advertising might want us to believe that taking out certain kinds of insurance is a good thing. It might want us to feel positive about the image of some big company, and so perhaps to wish to buy its products.

There is plenty of evidence to show that advertising works in a general way for products and services but little evidence as to how it works. There is little evidence to prove one way or the other that advertising actually sells ideas (religion or politics).

The ways in which advertising may persuade us are much the same as those we use in everyday life when trying to persuade people to do something we want. In particular, advertising will communicate ideas of *reward or punishment*. There are various kinds of reward offered: material rewards like 20 per cent more soap powder free, fantasy rewards like the attention of women to go with the aftershave, moral rewards like the feeling of being a good mum for buying a certain sweet or candy for the kids. Punishment may go with the reward by implication: being a bad mum if you don't buy the candy; or it may be explicit, as when the deodorant advert suggests that one loses friends if one doesn't use the product.

A simple way of persuading people is through *repetition*. This is why a campaign is geared to saying the same thing many times across many media. It is why the same advertisements appear night after night on television.

Advertisements may persuade us by arousing the desire for *imitation* of what we read or view. This could mean imitating some famous person who is using the product, or it could mean imitating kinds of behaviour that we already approve of. For example, we approve of going to have a good time with friends or of going on holiday. It could be that someone will order that kind of drink next time they are out with friends, imitating what they have seen.

This reminds one that a good way of persuading people is to tie your real message to another one invoking *beliefs or values*. If those values are things that the receiver already agrees with, then they may agree with the advertising message as well. Everyone believes in romance and love, so a lot of advertisements are tied in with these values.

Humour is another good persuader. If the communication makes people laugh, it makes them feel good. If they feel good, they feel OK about the product and they are more likely to buy it.

Most of all, because advertisers are communication people, they know that their messages have to recognize people's *needs*. We went into this at the beginning of this book. There we noted that it is often psychological needs of various kinds which motivate people most strongly. They want to be loved, they want to have friends, they want self-esteem. If an advertisement promises you these things, you may be persuaded by it.

Look at some advertisements to see how the words and pictures may persuade in these various ways.

Marketing

Marketing plans to use a range of media to communicate particular views.

Marketing is about a whole strategy of persuasion, including devices of public relations. Its subjects may include the corporate image of companies such as Benetton or a collection of media products such as those sold under the Nike label. Marketing is about communication through many media on a national, even an international, scale. It is as much about indirect and soft selling of products as about obvious direct appeals. You can sell trainers by getting famous sports stars to wear them in public places, as much as by taking out adverts in magazines. It is about taking a broad view of what it is you want to sell and how. Films are a good example, because when a film is in pre-production and discussion the marketeers are right in there. They are thinking about selling the film on DVD and to television, as well as at the cinema. They are looking to the sales of spin-offs such as music albums, computer games and other merchandise such as toys. They are thinking about the image or persona of the stars, as much as the story. They are thinking about product placements – clothes and cars, perhaps – in the film.

Most interesting of all, they will be thinking, like all marketeers, about the impressions and value messages given off by the film in its various versions in different media. They will ask questions such as, how will people feel before seeing this movie, and how will they feel afterwards? How can we generate these feelings? What rating will we get from the censors? What rating do we want? You can apply these questions and our comments to many films – something like the *X Men* cycle of films would be an example.

3.2 Visual communication

Definitions

Many forms and media of communication are coded and decoded through the use of the eye, including writing. But in practice, by visual communication we refer only to those means of communication that use clearly pictorial or graphic elements. However, it must be recognized that media can contain graphic elements even in their treatment of the printed words. For example, popular newspapers are certainly visual media, not only because of the high proportion of pictures in them but also because of the intensely graphic treatment of print (banner headlines, varied typeface and type size, and so on).

Having made these points, we can divide visual communication broadly into **representational and schematic modes**. Representational visuals purport to look like the thing they represent. Most magazine and news photographs are of this mode. But schematic visuals, while they communicate visually, don't pretend to be anything but symbolic. A lot of what we think of as graphics are of this mode: bar charts, pie charts and the like.

This is a useful division, though it will not fit every single case. And some examples could seem to be a bit of both. You should look around you at the enormous variety of visual communication in our environment (street signs, for example), and make your own mind up about particular instances.

We want to concentrate here on representational and photographic images. This is because such images dominate the range of mass media, with the obvious exception of radio. Visual communication is a dominant experience in our culture. And, because representational images do look like the thing they stand for, they are absorbed into our consciousness with a kind of immediacy and force that the written or spoken word lacks.

This is not to claim that one form of communication is better than the other – merely different.

Image reading

Images are composed of signs as much as any other form or medium. We learn to decode these signs when we learn to decode those other sound signs made by adults, called speech. Visual communication does not possess the precise sense of grammar and syntax that verbal communication does. But it does have conventions that, for example, predict the order of shots in a piece of film. We want to concentrate on the single image.

The signs through which we read images fall into three areas. First, there are the **position signs**. These are signs given by the placing of the camera (or artist's point of view). How close the camera is to what it depicts (proximity), and the angle that it takes, define how we understand the image. This is about the meaning of the signs. The position of the camera defines our position as spectator. It becomes our position. For example, you will find that in many advertisements the camera actually directs attention to the product, though this may be a small part of the whole image. Or, if a woman is being used to sell the product, the camera directs attention to her sexuality. There is a fairly well-known advertisement for a bath product in which we are positioned in a room behind a half-naked woman in the foreground. The camera sign means, pay attention to this.

Next there are the image **structure signs**. These are elements from which the image is put together:

- *Composition* is about where items are placed in the frame.
- *Framing* is about the border, what it encloses, what it excludes.
- *Colour* is about overall hues, or the selective placing of colour within the frame.
- *Foregrounding* is about placing objects in the front of the frame, and

so making them larger. (This is also a sign of the supposed three-dimensionality of an image – a visual 'trick'.)

- *Middleground and background* is about placing objects in relation to fore-ground, and also saying something about their importance.

- *Lighting* is about things like picking out or diminishing objects according to how well lit they are. It is also about ideas of style.

- *Focus* is about what is made clear or unclear through choice and use of cam-era lens. This also may sign to us to direct our attention towards a certain object. Or it could sign something like, this is a dream or fantasy picture.

- *Perspective devices* (relative size of objects – lines of ceiling or floor) are about the illusion of depth in an image. We learn to read such signs as 'depth'. An image, of course, has no depth.

Next, there are image **content signs**. These are simply the objects within the frame. In fact, we have learnt to believe they are there because of various other signs that are part of the process of visual perception: shape, outline, hue, tone. But if we accept that they are so identified, then the objects themselves may sign to us, especially in combination. One visual cliché is the young girl and the apple, meant to sign health. This example is useful because it also reminds us that objects can become symbols in an image. In this case, there is an additional tinge of tease and sexuality because the two objects stand for more than just what they are. They also stand for the story of temptation in the Garden of Eden and all the associations that this has.

You may be able to add to these signs, and certainly to the examples. The basic point remains that the meaning of the image is not natural, but is constructed by the image makers through the use of these signs. We understand the code. If we didn't, we couldn't make sense of what we were looking at.

The overall meaning of the image is confirmed by our reference to all the signs. Two or three on their own may not be enough. In any case, the meaning of most images is actually quite complex. It can take many words to explain a picture.

The point of image reading is to get to the total possible meanings of the image. Often we are very careless about decoding images, either in not getting the full meaning or in not realizing that we are getting covert messages. It is commonly thought that pictures are 'easy to read'. This is questionable. But in any case, this doesn't mean to say that they are simple.

A visual medium like television can offer us multiple codes of commu-nication: visual, non-verbal, written captions, the spoken word, and so on. So, there is a complex variety of signs giving us the message.

Socialization and beliefs

Images are especially powerful in offering messages about beliefs because they are a dominant channel of communication in the media.

You should also refer back to what we said about the power of the mass media in general. For the same reasons, they are also a powerful agent of socialization. Socialization describes the ways in which we are taught or learn to fit into society. This includes society in general, as well as particular parts of society. Obviously, for example, one's family is also an agent of socialization – we learn from our growing experience in the family. We learn ways of behaving, a way of looking at the world, sets of beliefs and values.

Images on television or in magazines are influential because they offer direct models. That is, we can see what we could look like, how we could behave, how we could relate to others – everything is illustrated for us. It is all there in the pictures. For example, there are certain pictures that say a lot to us about the importance of security. Insurance company advertisements are inclined to promote this value because their business is based on it. But one would also be able to find a wide variety of other media material that represented the security of the home, the security of having savings, the security of having long-term relationships.

The idea of socialization relates to the notion of security as follows. One sees images of social behaviour and social relationships in which security figures. The insurance company advertisement may suggest that one is a good husband and a proper husband if one insures one's life, and the loving wife and family are there as a reward. DIY magazines present images of homes made more physically secure. Newspapers often represent disapprovingly those who appear to threaten security in the family or the workplace or in society as a whole – strikers are an obvious example here. 'Because ads are so pervasive and our reading of them so routine, we tend to take for granted the deep social assumptions embedded in adverts' (Robert Goldman, *Reading Ads Socially*, London: Routledge, 1992).

Denotation, connotation, anchorage

The three terms 'denotation', 'connotation' and 'anchorage' also help explain how images communicate and how we may analyse them. **Denotation** is about image content – see our 'Image reading' section above (pages 202–3). The idea is that one should look very carefully at everything that is in the image, and describe what it is and how it is treated. The idea is to stop one taking the quick and casual glance that we give to so many images around us – posters, for example. What is denoted is what the image refers to factually, in the material world – maybe an object such as an elephant.

Connotation is about deeper levels of image meaning. The idea is that one can then take the content carefully described and work out the meaning of the parts and the whole. The meaning will result from personal and cultural associations and experiences which we more or less share. Once more, the intention is to get the whole meaning, not just a partial one – to get the covert messages as well as the overt ones. These covert messages or connotations underlie the obvious 'facts' of what is represented in an image. So, a car in an advert will be more than a car. It may be a 'family pet', or a 'safe place', or 'the essence of technology'.

Anchorage is about particular aspects of an image that help pin down (or anchor) its meaning. Newspaper photographs are anchored by their captions. These help pin down, for example, who a person is and what they are doing. Advertisements may be anchored by a logo, a slogan, or the presence of the product somewhere in the image. Try cutting out newspaper photographs without their captions. How do the meanings change? Then add your own captions. Now what are the connotations of the image as anchored by your words?

3.3 News

Construction of reality

News and current affairs material is crucial in constructing our view of the world. It is ideological. This view is mainly a combination of information and beliefs: that is, what we think are the facts about the world we live in, and the beliefs and values we have that organize those facts. So, we are talking about what we believe the world to be like. But our country, other countries, other ways of life, all look different depending on what point of view one starts from. The media help shape that point of view. For example, one could easily argue that Western news machines represent Africa as a continent of war and disasters – war in Sierra Leone, starvation in Sudan, Aids epidemics in Kenya, civil conflict in Chad. Of course there are peaceful, happy places in that huge continent, but you wouldn't think so judging by news media.

Newspapers construct our view of what is going on and how we are meant to understand it in other ways. For example, the popular press is dominated by stories about personalities, the activities of media stars, by scandal and gossip. The so-called hard news of political and financial matters has little place in the British popular tabloid press. If you check on the news coverage on a given day, comparing such a tabloid with a quality paper (some are tabloid, some are broadsheet), you might be excused for thinking that the readers must be living on two different planets – or inhabiting two different realities. One can also look at this difference in terms of what is missed out in the tabloids. **What is absent is as significant as what is present.** Reality is selective.

Selection and construction: gathering a story

These sections on news overlap to some extent, but they build up a picture of news as something that is made, not found. Many news people tend to talk as if they are mining diamonds of truth 'out there' and bringing them back for the audience. This is not so. Some of those diamonds are entirely artificial, made-up stories, lies if you like, of the 'DJ ate my hamster' variety. But all the diamonds are cut and polished to suit the setting of the particular newspaper or news programme. Recently, a story about a 30-year-old woman running away with a 14-year-old boy figured in all the tabloids, but did not make the front page of most of the quality papers. Papers made different decisions about taking the story and about what they did with it.

The gathering of a news story like this one is an exercise in mediation (see section 2.2 of this chapter) – the way in which the act of communication changes its subject. With the news machine especially, there are many points at which this mediation, the shaping, the selection of a story can happen. The stringer, the news agency, the reporter, the photographer are at an initial stage. But then there are the sub-editor and the editor also shaping material at later stages of production. What you read is a very mediated version of what actually happens. Following sections amplify questions of how and why news communication is shaped in the ways that it is.

The news is especially influential, not only because it comes through powerful media but also because it is believed. And we believe television and radio news in particular because much of what is said is factually true, and because the news organizations have spent many years promoting their reputation for truthfulness and impartiality. However, given the necessary process of selection and construction that is part of news making, it is impossible for the news makers to provide the whole truth or a complete view of the world. They will interpret wars, disasters and affairs of state in the way that seems most truthful to them. This will be their view of the world. It is in effect offered to us and becomes part of our reality.

For example, members of some factions fighting in the Middle East have been referred to as 'terrorists' and the disapproving comments of politicians have been widely reported. But the news makers of some Middle Eastern countries have called those same people 'freedom fighters' and have quoted favourable comment. Neither view may be entirely right or wrong. But in both cases we are seeing views promoted, as much as facts reported. In each case the view of the world believed by the news makers becomes part of the communication to the audience. And in each case, they are contributing a little more to each audience's sense of reality.

They are helping construct a reality that is made up of beliefs as well as facts.

Agenda setting

By 'agenda setting', we mean that the **news makers in various media promote certain news topics more than others** (in the same way that an agenda of topics is set for a meeting). This list can be argued over in detail, but it certainly includes stories about political events, about disasters, about war, about the royal family and about popular public figures. You should also refer here to the next section on news values. With a little thought you can provide your own agenda as you read this.

If you can do this – identify those stories that are dominating the news media in a given week – then you are also identifying what the news makers consider to be important. In effect, they are telling you what is important. They may or may not be right. We don't know or don't notice those items that are dropped or given little space or time. Indeed, in this way they are 'said' to be less important. But still, the fact is that, positively or negatively, we are 'told' what is on the news agenda for the week. The idea that newspapers and news programmes simply communicate what is happening does not hold up. Messages, even news messages, are shaped in particular ways for particular reasons.

So, the idea of an agenda is useful because it helps us interpret news as communication. If we notice the pattern that is the agenda, then we may ask who sets the agenda and what effect this might have. These are questions about source and audience. In the first case we notice that it is an editorial team, influenced by its members' ideas of news value. In the second case we notice that the audience is affected once more, in the sense that their view of the world is being defined by communication that they receive from others. None of this is to suggest that news makers conspire to set the agenda. The fact that there is an agenda of broadly similar items most weeks is a result of their own similar backgrounds and views of what is 'real' and 'important'. Also, news reporters and editors use the same news agency sources and continually look at what other reporters and editors are presenting. For instance, radio and television editors always look at the newspapers first thing in the morning.

So, if the news does help construct our reality, we are finding out more about how and why this is done.

News values

News values are accepted by the people who make the news. **They are beliefs about what topics make good news and beliefs about how those topics should be handled.**

The topics are likely to be those that we have already seen on the news agenda. The same sorts of topics tend to appear every week in most media, because people in news organizations believe that they are the right sorts of topics to attract the audience into reading or watching. But we should also remember the point that, without trying alternatives, no one really knows what the audience might be interested in. Also, although there might be a kind of agreement about types of news story it is most important to present, this still doesn't prove that a particular story has to be chosen, or that it has to be treated in the way that news stories often are.

In fact, beliefs about the handling of topics are rather more important than beliefs about what is handled, we would suggest. 'It's not what you say, but the way that you say it.' Dominantly, news stories are handled in terms of drama, conflict and visual qualities.

Dramatization means that the creators of the story prefer something exciting, with a main character around whom the action revolves. So, in a disaster story in a popular newspaper, for example, one might get not only the drama of action as a fire is fought and people are rescued, but also a photograph and special story angle on the fireman hero who carried three children to safety. (Perhaps he was a hero, but then it is likely that so were some of his workmates who performed deeds with less emotional 'pull' than rescuing children.)

Conflict is introduced into stories by having two opposing sides, preferably villains to oppose the heroes. So, for example, many political stories on television are handled in terms of opposing views (as if there could not be more than two views on some event or issue). If the leader of one political party can be set up against the leader of another, so much the better. The tendency to handle news in this way – a belief that it is right to handle it in this way – excludes shades of opinion. Its misleading effect needs to be seen in the light of the fact that relatively few people watch the current affairs programmes that might fill in the shades of opinion. If you look at news stories around you now, you will find various examples of this treatment – perhaps the police in conflict with some social group, for example. In this instance it might well be demonstrators of some kind. Indeed, developing the old cliché that only bad news is good news, it could be said that peaceful demonstrations are bad news for the news people; there is neither drama nor conflict.

However, the third value of news handling might make a demonstration into a good story. It could provide lots of pictures. Television and popular newspapers have been made visual media, in a sense, because **there is a preference for using picture material**.

Television must have images of some sort, of course. But still, news makers will exploit this aspect of the medium by preferring stories with pictures and by sending out cameras to obtain picture material. Newspapers do a similar thing. As we have said, the story is put together; it doesn't just happen. Choices are made about how to handle it. And the use of a large picture of, for example, a personality arriving at an airport, with but a few words to say who and why, is definitely a choice. This choice represents a belief about what makes good news handling. This is the news value.

Gatekeeping

Among the team making the news, it is the sub-editor who has most respon-sibility for upholding news values, whether of content or of treatment. This person has the job of taking the general run of news stories, deciding whether they are newsworthy or not, and then cutting or rewriting them as necessary to suit the newspaper and its page or the broadcast and its time slot. Bigger newspapers will also have copytasters who will vet incoming material, especially from the news agencies.

People who handle information coming into an organization are called gatekeepers. The term also assumes that they have some power to decide who gets what information and sometimes to change some of it. People like receptionists and secretaries can be gatekeepers. In this case of the news, the point that is being made is indeed that newsworthy material can be and is filtered and changed to suit the policies of the paper or broadcasting organization – to suit its values.

Clearly, many other people can have an effect on the final content and treatment of the news. The editor, or section editors like the features editor, can also be influential and do some gatekeeping. But still the point is to draw attention to the fact that there is one group of people who are very influential in the selection and treatment of messages – of the messages that we receive from the news programme or newspaper.

Editorializing

'Editorializing' refers to the ways in which the broad opinions or points of view of the news-making organization are expressed through the newspaper or programme. Newspapers literally have an editorial – an article in which the editor expresses opinions on a number of news stories, or issues raised by such stories. There is no question that newspapers do have a point of view. They have points of view perhaps defined in terms of their support for a political position or a political party. They may also have a position or attitudes towards other matters, such as conservation of the environment, or the outcome of a major legal case. So, newspapers cannot pretend to be unbiased. The kinds of **bias** or opinion that they have can be explored through investigation of covert messages revealed in patterns of content or treatment. For instance, it is generally acknowledged that the *Daily Mail* in the United Kingdom is angled towards an audience including a high proportion of females, and towards a position on the right of the political spectrum.

In the United Kingdom the case of broadcasting is rather different. News broadcasting does not editorialize in the way that a newspaper does. There are no editorials. Presentation of news items pays attention to the ideals of **balance** and **impartiality**. Points of view should not be expressed on things that have happened, or on issues raised, especially political issues. The Acts of Parliament that brought into being the BBC and the Independent Broadcasting systems actually require this neutrality. Many countries also follow this line of 'telling the news like it is' in news broadcasting. However, perfect balance and impartiality is impossible to achieve. Someone has to make choices about what will be presented as news. There are reasons behind the choices that are made, and these reasons are based on values and opinions. So, we would argue that news broadcasting, not surprisingly, can editorialize covertly. The very notion of balance itself is a matter of opinion. It suggests the image of a weighing device called a balance. This has two sides. But we have already pointed out that many issues and arguments have more than two sides.

Certain news items, for example those to do with sensitive political or military matters, are likely not to be handled in a balanced way. One of the most obvious examples here in Britain relates to the situation in Iraq, where British troops are fighting Muslim insurgents, or (according to some) Al-Qaida. Previously there was a similar situation with relation to Northern Ireland, for which there was a long list of news items and current affairs programmes censored by the government or by the executives in the news organizations because they would have represented a Republican point of view. The point is that one cannot talk about balance if the views of one side are privileged and the other side suppressed. It may well be that many people would agree with this handling of the news in this case. But we should not pretend that it is balanced news. In an indirect and covert way the news broadcasters are actually editorializing. By leaving things out or by weighting picture time and interviews in such a news item, they can present a point of view or a way of looking at that situation.

3.4 New technology

The phrases 'new technology' and 'information technology' are often used to talk about the same things. Many of the devices one might discuss have a lot to do with communication. Often, old systems and means of communication have been changed. Sometimes a new form or medium has been created.

The camera has been transformed as an object used to create visual communication: now it can set focus and exposure automatically. The telephone system has been transformed as new equipment controls the routeing of electronic signals, passing via cables and satellites to most countries in the world, available from your home.

Communication devices like the CD/DVD replay/record machines are taken for granted. They have changed our lifestyles, our culture and our ability to send and receive communication. We want to draw attention to some of these devices and systems because they are having a considerable effect on our patterns of work and leisure and because, in many instances, these effects are taken for granted. For example, the size and computing power of a pocket calculator would have made it a miracle thirty years ago.

New technology has only just begun transforming our lives and our ability to communicate. Fresh surprises are round the corner, as scientists have begun creating objects such as the biochip that combines living tissue and electronics, and a computer that works with light rays instead of pulses of electricity.

Effects on mass communication

New technology has extended the range of many means of mass communication.

The development of the telephone system already referred to, the link-ups with satellites and new cable systems have made all this possible – for example, the Internet-based telephony systems typified by Skype. And the most important development that has made it possible to connect these systems with each other and with computers has been the creation of technology that makes them all speak in the language of number: **digital information**.

For example, another extension is that of electronic mail services, which connect computer users across continents, who can exchange electronic letters instantly and at any time. More dramatically, we now have the Internet and its subsidiary function, the Web. This spans the world, exploiting the explosion of cable and satellite links, and so far is virtually uncontrollable by governments or corporations (except in the case of certain very authoritarian regimes). It and electronic mail and fax systems are now fused into one worldwide communication system based on computers. It is used to 'talk', to provide free information, sometimes to disseminate 'stolen' information, to sell houses, to link organizations globally. It supplies pictures as well as words. It is sharpening a new cultural divide between 'haves' and 'have-nots'. For example, students who can access the Web can do their research globally from a chair. Those who cannot are hugely disadvantaged.

New technology has changed the production methods of many of the mass media in various ways. In general, it has made production quicker and cheaper, and has improved the quality of what is produced.

For example, newspapers are now put together by a few people using what is essentially a sophisticated word processor instead of, as happened thirty years ago, a number of people putting together pieces of metal. Colour pictures in magazines and books are now prepared with graphics programs (such as the ubiquitous Photoshop) that allow the printer to play around with the colours before deciding on the best version, instead of involving complicated efforts with photography and chemicals. Or a newspaper like the *Financial Times* (Europe) can be put together in Paris and the results sent along a wire to Frankfurt for printing.

New technology has brought new methods of distribution of material to the audience. In producers' terms this means they can often get to a bigger market faster. For example, movies are now distributed through cable systems such as Ten in England or Home Box Office in the United States, or through satellite channels.

New technology has created new products that are mass-produced for large audiences. For example, computer games are now being marketed on a huge scale. The technology for the present games and their computers did not exist even twenty-five years ago.

The medium of television makes a good case study through which to describe the effects of new technology on the media. For example, the very production of cameras, televisions and the equipment of the industry depends on new technology. Then again, the functions of a modern television set – electronic tuning, Videoplus, remote control unit – also depend on the microprocessor or chip. Ads and television title sequences depend on computer graphics. Electronic news gathering (using video cameras) is now taken for granted. Electronic editing in the newsroom or for home movies is now the norm. The norm changes fast.

Information

New technology has meant that systems of mass communication can handle more information faster than ever before.

Business organizations and governments have made the most use of this expensive information technology because it helps them save money or find new ways of making money. But still, all this affects us, even indirectly. It certainly affects most people in their work – for example, shop checkout tills can also keep track of what stock is being sold. Chips are inserted in goods such as clothes so that they can be tracked.

Communication corporations offer international services to business users, allowing them to pass written and graphic information from one business centre to another, via satellites. There is less and less paper moving around.

Banking is computerized. Not only does this mean that customers can do things like take out money and check their accounts without going into a bank, but also it will soon mean that banks can stop moving paper cheques around altogether. Online banking has taken off. Great changes in the communication of information have many effects, not all of them good. We are not going to make a lengthy analysis of social and economic effects, but two examples should indicate the scope of problems arising.

One point is that many people have lost jobs because of new technology. Some years ago, whole departments devoted to technical drawing in engineering firms simply disappeared as computer-aided design programs took over that work at a fraction of the cost. The jobs of car workers disappeared as computer-controlled robots took over some jobs on the production line. (Of course, new communications industries and jobs in these compensate for this situation to some extent.)

Another point could be the dangers of the computerized credit control agencies. These store information about many citizens, some of it personal and all related to their 'creditworthiness'. At the moment it is impossible to control what is put on file, and not that easy to get to see it and make sure that inaccuracies are corrected. The power taken by those who operate new information systems is great, and the lack of checks on this power is worrying.

The issue of who gets to use and control new communication and information systems is a major one.

Entertainment

New technology has extended the range of mass-produced or mass-distributed entertainment.

A number of examples already given help to prove this point. Entertainment is a big communications business. We pay for a lot of entertainment products. And, as we have suggested already, this has other consequences when one considers the covert messages about values, or the reinforcement of culture and attitudes, that come with this entertainment. For instance, video games are often designed around notions of competition, violence, war and the like: they are orientated towards young males and the values conventionally offered to this group through other media such as comics. In another example we can see how new developments tend to extend the scope and the tendencies of existing technology.

Portable personal MP3 and CD players (and the iPod) do for the music audio medium what portable radios did for that medium a generation ago. And all these extensions of entertainment are also an extension and diversification of the operation of existing media systems or media owners.

Entertainment has become more about personal control of private space than it was in the past. Apart from portable players, the personal computer has become a point of gaming, a point of global communication and information searching, out of that private and domestic space. The XBox game console is mostly used at home. DVDs are rented to watch at home. In 2005 global broadband use increased by 26 per cent (International Federation of Phonographic Industries).

Two issues

This brings us to the first of two issues with which new technology confronts us. **Are we going to get more of the same, or will we be offered something different?**

The immediate answer is that, on the whole, new technology hasn't done much to change patterns of ownership, means of finance or the marketing of entertainment. In this sense, new developments tend to be absorbed by the existing systems and used in the way that they always have been. For instance, the hugely successful Sony Playstation is owned by the same Japanese company that owns Columbia Pictures and one of the world's major music corporations. And the multinationals are engaged in ongoing battles to produce and control the world's next recording format. Currently (2006) the battle is over a format that can cope with new high-definition television, and the additional disk space need to record in this format (as well as store whole films).

On the other hand, there are particular examples of some difference emerging on the back of the technology of the Internet. The big corporations are struggling to hold on to copyright of all kinds of material, but of music in particular. There is no question that sales of CDs have diminished because of the spread of illegal (but apparently unstoppable) downloading via file sharing. The information company Google is moving rapidly into many related fields. It is digitally copying, and making available, for free, libraries of books that are out of print. It only stopped doing the same with in-copyright books after pressure and threats of legal action. This will affect the continuation of publishing as we know it. It provides free satellite images of most places on earth, down to the details of people's yards – including some details that authorities (especially the military) would like to be off limits. It has started a Web service that is the equivalent of classified ads in newspapers – and threatens the future of these. It is like an electronic free paper, in that it makes billions of dollars from its various enterprises because advertisers are keen to get access to domestic screens. They pay for its publishing and search services.

So, to what extent will new technology give us open access to information and entertainment? How much control we will have over what is offered to us?

Up to now we have been in a situation where mass-communications systems and products have been effectively directed or controlled by commercial organizations, with some intervention by government. In other words, the messages are framed and sent to us without our having much say about who does this and how. Given the large, complex and expensive operation of systems like a national telephone or television service (both terrestrial and satellite), this is not to suggest that everyone can have a direct part in running them or producing material. At the same time, it is also worth pointing out that, for example, the city of Hull runs a good, independent telephone service. Dutch broadcasting manages a system that gives minority groups some right to air time.

We do have the choice of TV viewing via hundreds of channels – but whether the material on them offers a real choice for different tastes is another matter. We can choose to buy DVDs, to rent them from a shop, to rent them via the Internet. But it would be fair to say that while we have access to a lot more material than even twenty years ago, control of content and distribution stays firmly in the hands of media industries. In most cases this means the same companies that have always run things.

The signs are that most access and control for the audience or user is happening with the new technologies of the personal computer and the Internet. It is possible to obtain a lot of freeware applications material over the Net. There are free sources of information on the Net, such as Wikipedia. Learning takes place via the Net, notably in the case of the Open University.

Many Western countries are wired up with fibre optic cable both within and between their major cities. These cables can carry vast quantities of digital information. It is in the continuing nature of mass communication that governments and companies are investing billions of pounds in this process because they see the advantages of being part of an 'information world'. Business sees a lot of money to be made. The same mixture of profit motives and political controls that brought in media such as television is still at work. In some respects, mass communication typically becomes cheaper, faster, more 'real' (e.g. video conferencing). But it is also typically in a state of tension between real availability and consumer control (cheap digital cameras and editing), and continuing dominance by international corporations that define what we get in terms of information and, especially, entertainment.

Is this the age of the image?

Hint: how much time do you spend with words or with images in a week? Count it!

Review

1   A MASS-COMMUNICATION SOCIETY

1.1   The word 'mass' refers to the volume, scale or speed of the system, product or audience.

1.2   The significance of mass production of communication is that it also means the mass repetition of messages. The messages are sometimes about ideas and beliefs. These may influence us because they are so often repeated.

1.3   The organizations of mass communication are not directly within our control as individuals, in contrast with face-to-face communication.

1.4   Mass communication has enabled more sending and exchange of information. But we are not necessarily able to control who sends what to us or what they do with information. The World Wide Web has revolutionized our access to information, and has given us services such as online shopping. But it has also created a division between those who can afford the technology and those who can't.

1.5 Mass communication has increased the range of entertainment available to us. But the choice of types of entertainment is not as great as it might appear, and we don't have much say in what we get.

1.6 The various means of mass communication can be seen as extensions of ourselves and of our abilities to do things like speaking, listening, writing, reading.

1.7 The media are part of our society in general. They help build up a picture of that society.

1.8 The term 'institution' refers to various organizations, most of them commercial, that control and run various aspects of mass communication, especially the media.

1.9 The media have power and influence within society because of their ability to duplicate and repeat messages and because of their ability to get to us, even into our homes.

2   INTERPRETING THE MEDIA

2.1 All kinds of media material, including visuals, can be described as texts, and can be 'read' to make sense of them.

2.2 The idea of mediation refers to the way that material is changed by the workings of the media organizations. This is particularly relevant to media material that is about matters of fact.

2.3 Realism, in its various forms, is important to audiences. It is made up from conventions. There is no perfect realism.

2.4 Media language refers to specific critical and descriptive terms, as used in this book.

2.5 Narrative is a part of all media texts, especially fiction. It is about story-telling, about plot and drama, about devices used to help us make up the story in our heads.

2.6 Selection and construction refers to the way that any example of the media is the result of a process where items are picked, left out and put together in a certain way. One should then look at who does this, and why.

2.7 The idea of product refers to the fact that much media material is mass-produced, like cars, and packaged and sold, like breakfast cereal.

2.8 Ownership and finance refer to the source of media messages and to where they get the money from to pay for the operation. Ownership of the media tends to be dominated by relatively few organizations, mainly commercial interests. They are concerned with profitability above all, and with increasing their dominant market position. In terms of finance, advertisers are especially dominant in influencing the kind of material we get, because they pay directly for a large proportion of media operations, even though the audience always pays in the end.

2.9 There are a variety of descriptions of audiences for the various output of the media. These audiences are targeted and constructed by shaping material to suit particular tastes. Audiences are active, not passive, in the way that they 'use' material. It is suggested by the uses and gratifications theory that this use is often to satisfy needs within us. The characteristics (profile) and lifestyles of audiences are researched by the media, especially advertisers, when trying to attract and persuade those audiences.

2.10 Scheduling is a device used to attract and hold audiences. It applies mainly to television and involves placing certain types of programme for certain audiences at certain times of the day or the year.

2.11 The idea of overt and covert values refers to the fact that, intentionally or unintentionally, not all messages in media material are obvious at first. They may be hidden. And the important messages are about values – beliefs and opinions.

2.12 People, their behaviour and their beliefs are often represented in a simplified and misleading way in popular media material. They are easy to understand, but encourage prejudice and misunderstanding. Stereotypes are created through repetition of representations.

2.13 The idea of genres is that there are certain types of media material, often story types, which are also recognizable through repeated elements that go to make them up. Genres are popular. So, one should look critically at covert messages that they may contain because they are also likely to be influential.

2.14 Most censorship of the British media is voluntary and run by the media industries themselves. The government influences media output in various ways, directly and indirectly. Any kind of censorship raises important issues about, for example, how far we should insist on the right of the public to know about things that organizations such as government do not wish them to know.

2.15 Effects of the media are much discussed, mostly in relation to sex and violence. But there is little or no clear evidence that the media have any specific effect on anyone.

2.16 Ideology is a view of the world whose values work in the interests of those who have power. The media tend to project that view because of their ownership and sources of finance, because they are 'in power'. When that view and those values are accepted as a matter of course by the audience, they are said to be naturalized.

3 THE MEDIA: PARTICULAR EXAMPLES

3.1 Advertising uses forms of communication in order to persuade. Marketing is about overall promotion; advertising is paid-for persuasive communication; publicity refers to promotion that is not paid for. Advertising uses and perpetuates stereotypes; contains covert messages and values; creates alternative realities for its products and services; is a use of communication and may be analysed through communication terms.

Advertising seeks to change behaviour by changing attitudes. The devices for persuasion through the media are the same in principle as those we use in everyday life. Examples of these are suggesting reward or punishment, using repetition, associating ideas with approved values, providing a context of humour, trading on people's needs.

3.2 Visual communication is a dominant means of communication in the mass media. In this sense it is mainly defined in terms of representational images, often the photograph. Images give meanings through signs which can be defined in terms of camera/viewer position, structure and content.

Images socialize us into the system of beliefs and values that dominates our society by presenting that society to itself. Images can also be understood through terms like denotation, connotation and anchorage.

3.3 News is important, among other media material, because it brings us information about the world which we use to construct our view of reality and truth. News makers set an agenda of topics which become the key issues and topics for us, the audience, at a given time. News makers have news values about what are important news topics and the 'right' ways to treat these topics. We tend to accept these values uncritically. The news machine illustrates the idea of gatekeeping in action, mainly through the selection and construction work done by sub-editors. News machines editorialize, overtly in newspapers, sometimes covertly in broadcasting: that is, they take positions on certain topics and issues. These points of view can represent kinds of political bias.

3.4 New technology is changing mass-communications systems, including the media and their products. It has affected mass communication by extending its range, changing its production methods, bringing new distribution methods, extending access to the audience and creating new products. New technology has greatly increased our ability to exchange and store quantities of information. This has benefited government and commerce more than the general public. It has also raised issues such as the question of data control. New technology has extended the range of mass entertainment. It has also raised many issues relating to media product, ownership and control. One crucial question is whether it can help bring us something different, or whether we will get more of the same. Another major question is whether or not we will have more access to use of communication systems as well as control of the material we get through them.

Debates

Where does one draw the line between mass communication and mass media?

- One point is that if there isn't any difference, then perhaps that says a lot about new technology and its effects.
- Another point has to do with the nature of audiences for communication or of users of communications – if there is a difference.
- Another point has to do with whether there is any difference so far as ownership is concerned.

WHAT DO YOU THINK?

Has mass communication taken over our lives?

- One related issue concerns whether we see ourselves as users or consumers, or possibly both.
- A similar issue has to do with control – whether we feel in control of communication technology and the media.
- Another issue turns on whether in fact we have simply assimilated mass communication into our lives – it is part of our life and what we want.
- This debate turns on how we live our lives, using communication. Also on whether we see mass communication as being constructive or destructive – and if so, in what ways.

WHAT DO YOU THINK?

Is there too much power in too few hands where the media are concerned?
The matter of concentration of power in the media has been talked about in this chapter, to an extent. It is such an important matter to debate that it is worth spending more time on the idea.

- You need to go back to the question of what kind of power.
- You need to go over the basics of media ownership: who owns how much in the different media industries.
- Then you need to consider the question of what 'too much' means. The main issue here probably relates to what is done or what may be done with that power.

WHAT DO YOU THINK?

Is our culture too much dominated by advertising and marketing?

This debate is also in one sense about power – financial power. But it also asks one to consider how, directly or indirectly, marketing may have taken over the hallmarks of our culture: our arts, our sports, even our religions.

- One point to consider is how far advertisements have become cultural artefacts in themselves.
- Another point is about how far marketability defines whether or not a media product is made in the first place.
- A further point is about the ways in which the practice of marketing affects what is being marketed – think about the presentation of football or of music groups.

WHAT DO YOU THINK?

Should newspeople be stopped from investigating and reporting on people's private lives?

This debate focuses on one aspect of the power of press and broadcasting news makers. It is about freedom of speech conflicting with a right to privacy. It is sharpened by examples such as the circumstances surrounding the death of Diana, Princess of Wales.

- One problem would be to decide who should or should not be investigated.
- Another problem would be to decide who would stop such investigations, why and when.
- Another problem is to decide what should be public and what should be private when one is talking about people who hold public office (politicians).
- Another problem is to square this debate with other beliefs such as that of 'the public's right to know'.

WHAT DO YOU THINK?

Assignments

Assignment 1

Three-dimensional image system

A leading Japanese company is going to market a three-dimensional (holographic) digital video system. This produces apparently real images in the space of a 70-centimetre cube. The company intends to sell the system like all previous ones, as a package, with a library of material on hologram discs. The discs play only. The company has deals with film companies and TV networks to access material, as well as to produce new material.

To reinforce your knowledge of ownership, finance and control, answer the following questions about what would happen with such a 3D system.

(a) Who is likely to own the technology and the discs?
(b) Who is likely to dominate the sales (retailing) of such a system?
(c) Who will make money out of it, and how?
(d) How might the player system be marketed?
(e) What kind of material is likely to be put out?
(f) Who is likely to control the distribution or renting or retailing of new discs to existing system owners?

Don't worry if you have more than one answer to each question.

Assignment 2

News

News Release – Al-Jazeera News   10.20 a.m. 13.2.07

Peace activist Elizabeth Brinckley, aged 28, has been kidnapped in the Palestinian Gaza strip. There is no information about the group which captured Ms Brinckley. No demands have been received by the Palestinian authorities or by the British representative, in relation to her kidnap. Ms Brinckley, who is a trained legal executive, had been helping teach Palestinian children. Unofficial sources suggest that she had also been providing support and advice to local communities.

It was known that the Israeli authorities had expressed concern about her presence, accusing her of supporting communities that harboured known terrorists. It is rumoured that she was under surveillance by Mossad, the Israeli secret service. The Palestinian Hamas authority has also previously expressed some irritation about her presence, because of her nationality and their view of the British as collaborating with Israeli oppression of the Palestinians. However, our sources indicate that local Palestinians have a high regard for Ms Brinckley, and are angry about the kidnapping.

A Hamas representative has told us that 'while we regret this episode, we are on record as advising Elizabeth Brinckley that she was taking a serious risk in remaining in Gaza, against our advice'. It was suggested that the Israelis, rather than Arab extremists, might be behind her kidnapping.

In a telephone conversation with Sir James Sutton, Elizabeth's father, our reporter was told that he was very worried and 'totally unimpressed' by the response of the British Foreign Office.

You may assume that there is available a family still picture of Elizabeth, plus a freelance photographer's image of her with children in Gaza (copyright Reuters). You may elaborate plausibly on the telephone interview with her father, and on the interview with the Palestinian Authority representative.

(a)   Produce an article on the incident for a popular tabloid newspaper.
(b)   Script an item for the lunchtime Sky news, running for ninety seconds.

Assignment 3: Case study

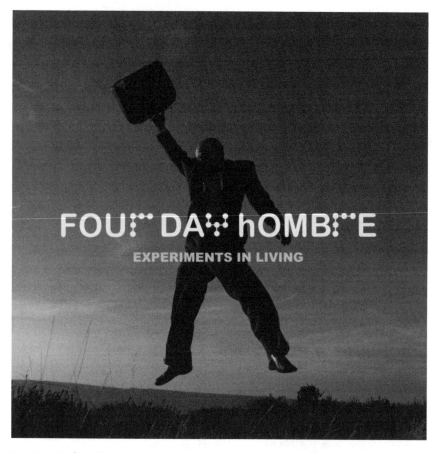

Four Day Hombre, Alamo Music, *Experiments in Living*, www.fourdayhombre.com

Four Day Hombre

You may refer to the CD cover image when completing this assignment.

This five-piece group produces music in roughly the same genre as Coldplay or Travis, but the sound is more experimental at times, the lyrics more wide-ranging (appealing to a wider audience) and their work ranges more broadly (between the use of two instruments and one voice, to full-on power numbers). The group has the looks and the musical skills to go further than a present appeal to a generally young but regional audience.

For the purpose of the exercise, you may make any other assumptions relevant to the tasks below.

You are working with a PR and marketing consultancy that is making a pitch for business with this increasingly successful group. As part of your preparation, you carry out the following tasks:

(a)   List possible product spin-offs that could be used to market this group and its image.
(b)   List four magazines or programmes in which the group might like to get coverage.
(c)   List five public relations devices for promoting the group.
(d)   Design a press advertisement for the CD.
(e)   Storyboard a fifteen-second video that will be used as the introduction to a segment of a television programme on rising groups, and about Four Day Hombre in particular.

Suggested reading

O'Sullivan, T., Dutton, B., and Rayner, P., *Studying the Media* [3rd ed.]. London: Hodder Arnold, 2003.
Wall, P., *Media Studies for GCSE* [2nd ed.]. London: Palgrave Macmillan, 2006.

Chapter 6

Communication and media skills

This chapter provides a general framework for practical production using various media.

There are guidelines for developing skills in writing for different formats and purposes, for effective listening, for being assertive, for designing leaflets, for making presentations, for conducting interviews, for devising questionnaires, for storyboards, for producing audio, for making digital video, for mounting exhibitions, for designing a website and using the Net.

FIGURE 49 Never miss a photo opportunity! Courtesy of Getty Images

1 Getting started: general principles for approaching practical work

Every communication production, of whatever length, complexity or simplicity, is likely to come from two sources. One is the inner creative needs and visions that you have. The other is external forces – educational demands for you to make a communication project, or perhaps even because it is your job. This is a mixture of self-expression and desired outcomes from people or organizations who may have commissioned your production. You need to be well organized and clear about what you are trying to do.

If you are creating a communication project for A level, this remains true. You are expected to treat the activity as if you indeed have a job that depends on it. You have to develop a brief for your work, as would anyone who is working for a client. You have to keep a log evaluating what you are doing, especially in relation to your use of the medium, achievement of your aims and satisfaction of the needs of your audience. You have to research your subject matter, the medium and the audience – to a greater or lesser degree, depending on what level you are working at. Pay attention to the specific requirements of a specific syllabus.

Organization and preparation help successful communication and the process of creation. We recommend that you look at the chart summarizing guidelines for successful practical production (figure 50). The skills that you use are not just about the mechanics of designing a wallchart or using a digital video camera. There are other face-to-face skills used, for example in interviewing people, explaining your work in progress, presenting your completed work to others. So, in this chapter we are offering some coverage of interpersonal skills to supplement what we have written earlier.

Of course, some examples of communication and audience are more or less creative and technically complicated than others. But remember that even writers of novels, for example, will do things like research their topics and background. They have a reader in their mind's eye. They block out sections of their novel so that they know in principle where the narrative is going. You will find that communication projects that focus on a particular audience with specific needs are usually the most effective in the end. The kind of project that is a 'guide to local clubs', for instance, often lapses into self-indulgence. If a local newspaper is going to publish an insert on this topic, the readers don't want a limited survey of what you get up to at the weekend. They want a range of real information, attractively presented.

So, ask yourself questions like – who wants to hear what I want to communicate about? What do they already know about the subject? What am I really trying to do through this communication – to inform, to warn, to entertain, to explain? It may be a mixture of these points, all of which form your aims. What is really the best medium for putting across my ideas? Who

FIGURE 50   Guidelines for practical production

would sponsor or pay for my communication, at least in principle? How would it actually get to the audience? You need to ask yourself both practical and creative questions – and never assume that you know the answers already!

2 Interpersonal skills

Chapters 2 and 3 contain information on a variety of interpersonal communication skills. These include using non-verbal communication, perceiving other people effectively and working in groups. You could refer back to these. This section develops other skills areas which should help you deal with other people.

2.1 Listening

All of us at some time must have accused other people of not listening to us. Since we spend virtually all our waking hours listening (we cannot close our ears), it's worth learning to do it effectively. There is obviously more to listening than meets the ear. We listen not only with our ears but also with our eyes and mind, using our experience and knowledge. In that sense we often do 'close our ears' by not engaging our attention and our thinking.

Hearing simply refers to our consciousness of sounds. Listening refers to our attempts to make sense of what we hear. It is an active process that demands effort on our part. There has even been quite a lot said in recent years by various organizations about the importance of listening. The most famous of these has probably been the business that used to proclaim itself to be the 'listening bank'.

Successful listening and listening skills involve one not only in being seen to listen but in doing something about it. Try filling in the brief listening questionnaire that follows (figure 51). It should cause you to think about your own listening behaviour. This and the checklist chart (table 1) will help you realize that skilled listening to others requires action, such as giving non-verbal responses to show that you are paying attention; not shutting off when what is being said doesn't immediately grab your attention; asking for elaboration if necessary; and not ignoring what people say simply because of who they are (or what you think of them!). It could be argued that not listening is a mixture of lack of skills and degrees of laziness and self-centredness.

We hope that you recognize that effective listening is something that you can control. It is as active as talking and it is something you can learn to do. There are ways you can develop your listening skills. The checklist may help.

Whatever the context – for example, a personal conversation, a group meeting, a lecture, a radio or TV programme – these elements all apply. It is not easy to maintain concentration to listen effectively. It is tiring, because it calls for active attention and may demand a response.

WHEN YOU ARE TALKING TO OTHERS OR HAVING TO LISTEN TO A SPEAKER, HOW GOOD ARE YOU AT REALLY LISTENING?

Answer the following few questions – and then reflect on what your answers mean.

	NEVER	SOMETIMES	OFTEN
Do you find yourself thinking about something else?			
Do you want to ask them questions?			
Do you interrupt them?			
Do you pretend to be listening?			
Do you think about what you want to say next?			
Do you talk a lot about the speaker's clothes and mannerisms afterwards?			
Do you talk about others being boring?			
Do you pick up on what the other person has been saying?			

FIGURE 51   Questionnaire for listeners

A psychotherapist from the United States, Carl Rogers, devised a strategy for enabling people to check how effective their listening skills are. He suggested that the next time you are in an argument with someone, stop the discussion and try this experiment. Each person can speak up for him- or herself only after he or she has first restated the ideas and feelings of the previous speaker accurately and to that person's satisfaction. If you try this, you may find that most of the time in our daily life we do not really listen to and understand what the other person has said to us. We may not have really placed ourselves in their position in order to recognize what they feel or believe.

Being able to do this goes a long way to enabling us to be effective communicators. Our skills at receiving spoken messages from people from the media are as important communication skills as being able to present our own ideas.

2.2 Assertiveness

Being assertive comes into many situations where we communicate with others, not least when putting together a communication project. We want to open your mind to basic ideas about this topic, but recommend that you take on further reading if you are really interested. The main thing about being assertive

Table 1 A guide to effective listening

Key to effective listening	The poor listener	The good listener
1 Find areas of interest	Switches off if the material seems dry or dull	Says 'what can I get out of this?'
2 Concentrate on content, not delivery	Switches off if the delivery is poor	Judges content and ignores errors in delivery as far as possible
3 Be patient	Tends to jump in and argue, or (mentally) disagree or reject ideas before hearing the speaker out	Doesn't judge until understanding is complete
4 Listen for ideas	Listens only for facts even when the topic does not require this	Listens for central themes
5 Be flexible	Takes intensive notes using only one system. Tries to write down every word	Takes few notes but uses four or five different systems, depending on the speaker
6 Work at listening	Shows no energy output, any attention shown is faked, confuses 'hearing' with 'listening'	Works hard, exhibits active body state, engages with what is heard
7 Resist distractions	Is easily distracted	Fights or avoids distractions, tolerates bad habits, knows how to concentrate
8 Keep your mind open	Reacts to emotional or emotive words	Interprets or translates emotive words; does not get hung up on them
9 Capitalize on the fact that thought is faster than speech	Tends to day-dream with slow speakers	Challenges, anticipates, mentally summarizes, weighs the evidence, listens between the lines to tone of voice, verbal give-aways, etc.
10 Ask questions	Adopts a passive or bored attitude	Seeks to make sense of what is heard and to make clear what seems confused

is that it involves you in communicating clearly about what you want without being rude and without assuming that you will always get your own way. We think that assertiveness has a lot to do with effective interpersonal communication, because it involves knowing what you want to say, saying it plainly, and not being evasive and manipulative in how you deal with others.

Assertiveness is very much related to what we have said about self, because it requires you to look at who you are and what you want in a given situation. It means that you stand up for your rights and beliefs without despising, ignoring or riding over the rights of others.

Assertiveness is often confused with aggression, especially where females are concerned. One common reason for this is that people, not least men, tend to assume that females should be submissive. One of the most common submission phrases which people use at the beginning of sentences (usually responses) is 'I'm sorry'. Often we have nothing to be sorry about and nothing to apologize for. Aggression is no better, of course. Telling someone to 'push off' if they ask you for something, even if they are being unreasonable, is a good way to start an argument. If someone asks you to lend them money (and you don't want to), the best assertive response is to say briefly 'No, I don't want to.' If pressed, you might say, 'I really don't think I can afford it.' But after that, just keep on saying no. Be firm. Don't give in to attempts to blackmail you in some way. You have a right to say no, and you don't have to justify yourself. So, to sum up, assertiveness skills are:

- Deciding what you really want out of a given situation (particularly if it is to say no).
- Saying what you want.
- Being brief and to the point.
- Using 'I' statements such as 'I want', 'I like', 'I think'.
- Looking for ways round a potentially difficult situation if compromise is really OK for you – 'I can't lend you thirty pounds, but I'll lend you fifteen if you're able to pay it back next Monday.'
- Trying to find out what the other person wants – 'Is there something else I can help you with, if not the money?'
- Being careful to sort out fact from opinion in the way that you talk. If you refuse an invitation to go to a club with a friend on the grounds that you think it is a boring place, then that is not a fact. It is your opinion. So say so. Or it may be a fact that you were bored the last time that you went there.

2.3 Interviews

There are many books and leaflets that provide advice on how to be interviewed, especially for a job. The essential advice they all give is to be prepared and to anticipate as well as possible what you are likely to be asked and how you want to present yourself.

An interview is best seen as a formal conversation: that is, it has a clear purpose and is approached systematically with a beginning, a middle and an end.

This section is going to concentrate on how to conduct an interview rather than on how to be interviewed. Imagine that you need to interview someone to find out something he or she knows.

Conducting an interview

PREPARATION

1   Be clear what you want from your interview.
2   Ensure that the person to be interviewed is willing and has the information you want. If you are getting a news story, the person may not be willing to give the information he or she has. In this case, you have to use your persuasive powers and to spend more time developing their trust in you.
3   Devise likely questions in advance. Use open questions and avoid leading to a yes/no response. Always be clear and unambiguous in your questions. Try to anticipate the responses you will get.
4   Decide how you want to record the interview: written notes, audio, video, and maybe photographs.
5   Decide what you will do with the information afterwards.
6   Arrange the interview – clear date, time and place. Explain the purpose to the interviewee and how it will be recorded and used. Perhaps you might want to send questions in advance.

AT THE INTERVIEW

7   Introduce yourself and explain the purpose of the interview. Build up the trust and confidence of the interviewee.
8   Seek agreement on how it will be recorded and used. (If you're using audio or video, check that it is working properly.)
9   Conduct the interview – clear questions, clear voice, use of non-verbal communication and layout of the room.
10   Conclude clearly, express your thanks and explain to the interviewee how the interview will be used.

AFTER THE INTERVIEW

11   Review the questions and answers.
12   Has it provided what you want? If not, do you need to return?

13   How can you now use it?

14   What have you learnt about effective interviewing from this experience?

2.4 Making a presentation

'Have something to say and say it well . . .' It sounds easy. But you may have memories of, or dread, the awful nerves when you have to stand in front of a group to give a talk. The most effective ways of dealing with nerves or fright are, first, to plan and prepare so you know what you are doing; second, to practise giving the talk (the more you do, the easier they become); and third, if necessary, use actors' techniques to relax and deal with stress. These might include testing your voice before you start; doing something totally different just before your talk to distract yourself from it; gently swinging your arms and rolling your neck to ease muscle tension; breathing deeply a few times; and thinking about the task and not thinking about yourself.

We suggest you review the early part of this chapter on getting started. All the information there, surrounding the questions of why, what, to whom, where, when and for what result, is important for making a presentation.

The following is a checklist of how you might set about giving a successful presentation.

1 Planning and preparing

1.1   Brainstorm for any ideas you may have on the topic. Make a list or a spider diagram with as many aspects as you can think of. Don't select or filter them at this stage.

1.2   Select and structure these jottings into the main ideas in an appropriate sequence. Think of 'hooks' for the audience's interest; decide on examples that you know will appeal to the intended audience.

1.3   Think of an interesting opening and a conclusion that your audience should remember. These could include some unusual fact, or an anecdote about something that happened to you.

1.4   Write up notes on one side of small cards, number each card and hold them together by punching a hole in the top left-hand corner and using a treasury tag. There is nothing worse than dropping your notes in confusion. Avoid continuous sentences that you will read out. Make main headings, subheadings, use numbers, use different-coloured pens – anything that you think will be helpful in giving the talk.

1.5   Use visual aids such as transparencies for an overhead projector or a flipchart, or video and audio inserts – and, of course, PowerPoint. Keep your aids simple and try them out in the place beforehand. Pre-prepared overhead transparencies or flipchart sheets can be a great aid to the talk and a support to you. But don't use too many and do keep them simple and uncluttered. Where you can, use diagrams or pictures. If you want people to take specific information away, prepare a handout that they can take with them. If you are using PowerPoint, by all means include some effects, such as the text sliding in from the side. You can also insert images. But don't use so many effects that they distract from the words. Don't simply repeat words on the screen, but speak to them. Control the pace of the frames, so that your presentation doesn't seem to be driven by the technology. There is a strong argument for not using PowerPoint for the whole of a presentation, because the illuminated screen distracts an audience and stops them listening to you.

1.6   Rehearse and practise for timing. This can help with nerves, but over-practising the same speech can make it seem dull when you give it.

1.7   Think of your audience. Are the content, style and length of the presentation appropriate for the audience and the place?

2 Delivering your talk

2.1   Preparation is vital. Don't stand up and think, 'if only . . .' Being well prepared gives you confidence and keeps down nerves.

2.2   Use the space that's available. Make sure you are visible and any aids you are using are visible. Think about the relationship you want to create with the audience.

2.3   Don't be afraid to overact. What may seem very slow and overdramatic to you won't seem like that to the audience. Keep your expression, both in speech and in the way you present yourself, lively. Try to vary the speed and the pitch of your voice. Make sure everyone can hear you.

2.4   Use non-verbal communication, such as eye contact; smile at people; move about – but not too much; keep particular mannerisms in check. Try to be yourself and be natural. Other things that may help you are looking just over people's heads if you are very nervous about eye contact; it is not helpful to sit behind a table, but if you are worried about standing, then it is OK to sit on the edge of the table – but avoid sitting on your hands; hands can be occupied with your check cards, but let them be free enough for use in emphasizing points.

2.5   Use audio-visual aids. They brighten up your talk and help explain things. Sometimes it is possible to use items such as a section of video by way of example. But the most common devices are overhead displays, flipchart displays and material that is handed out. Displays should be big and bold and brief. Remember the dangers of getting in the way of your checklist or diagram when standing near them. It is OK to use a pointer if you need to draw attention to details. Switch off overhead projectors when not in use. If you use handout material by way of example, then do decide what you want the audience to do with it. Point out what is relevant in the material and give the audience a little time to take it in. But then tell them firmly to leave the handout and that you are going on with the talk.

3 Reviewing the presentation

3.1   Seek feedback. You should be able to tell if people become bored or fall asleep! But ask people afterwards about your strengths and weaknesses.

3.2   Reflect on your successes and failures and analyse what went well or went badly. Had you prepared enough? Did you judge your audience accurately? Were your notes good enough? Did the aids you used work successfully? – and so on.

Some people may appear to be natural public speakers. But sometimes these people can seem to be doing it for themselves rather than for their audience. You may not feel like a natural public speaker, but through careful planning and practice you can gain these skills.

3 Writing skills

Many textbooks, especially for business communication, deal at length with conventions of letters, memos, notices, agendas for meetings, reports, press releases, and so on. We are not going to repeat this information here.

The key to successful writing skills for communication is the appropriateness of what and how you write for the context and the audience. Be clear about what you want to say. Be clear about how it will be received.

The great advantage of written communication is that it leaves a record. It stores the message for future reference. Writing does not necessarily depend on high technology, although written communication is now likely to be produced and reproduced through information technology. Using a word processor or a desktop publishing system can ensure that whatever is produced is carefully prepared and designed for the effects you want.

Your style of writing – the choice of vocabulary, the length of sentences, the tone of language you adopt – reflects the relationship you want to create with your reader or readers. Often, reading out loud what you have written can help capture the tone that you want. Tone is really about the relationship between you the writer and your reader. It comes out of the kind of voice that you can 'hear' when you read a piece of writing. This notion also helps define what is called style. If something is written in an ironic way or a serious way, then this is evident in that voice.

3.1 Questionnaires

A questionnaire is a set of written questions designed to collect information from individuals. This information may include their personal attitudes. The questionnaire may be completed in the absence of the person who wishes to collect the data. A questionnaire can also be used as the basis for a face-to-face interview.

As always, be clear about what you want to achieve. Is a questionnaire the best way of obtaining the information you want? Make sure the questions do ask what you want to know. Make sure the results will be suitable to analyse and present. Are you asking the appropriate people?

Once you have decided to use a questionnaire, take care in designing it. Time spent in careful writing and layout, and in piloting the questionnaire with a few people, will save a lot of time later on. The way in which the information is collected will make a lot of difference to how easy it is to analyse and to summarize.

Designing a questionnaire

1   HEADINGS

Make clear at the top of the questionnaire where it is coming from. State who is conducting it. Make clear how the information will be used. You may want to guarantee people's anonymity and confirm that the information will not be published. State the purpose of the questionnaire.

2   TYPES OF QUESTIONS

There are two types of questions: open and closed questions. An open question simply leaves the respondent to make a free statement in reply. For example, you might ask, 'Why do you read a daily newspaper?' This leaves it free for the reply to cover whatever the person wishes.

There are various types of closed questions. These can lead the respondent to make a particular reply. They are much easier to analyse afterwards. There are five major types of closed questions, as shown in the following examples:

(a)   *Tick one box*
      I feel that the news coverage of X was:
            biased in favour   ☐
            neutral   ☐
            biased against   ☐

(b)   *Yes–no*
      Did you find X helpful during the production?
          YES   NO
          ☐   ☐

(c)   *Rating*
      Did you find X helpful during the production?

Very helpful	Helpful	Neutral	Not helpful	Not at all helpful
☐	☐	☐	☐	☐

(d)   *Checklist*
      Tick as many boxes as necessary:
      What did you like about the project?
          More freedom than usual   ☐
          Being able to work on my own   ☐
          Being able to get on with my work   ☐
          Discussing my work with the teacher   ☐

(e)   *Ranking*
      The following statements have been suggested as relevant to project
      work. Put them in order of importance: put 1 alongside the statement
      you consider is most important, 2 alongside the next most important,
      etc.
          Improves practical skills   ☐
          Makes work more interesting   ☐
          Helps you become more independent   ☐
          Improves ability to work under pressure   ☐

It is worth noting that open questions are quicker and easier to write, they
give more freedom in answering, and they do not have predetermined answers.
But they are more difficult to analyse, especially when you have a large
sample.

3   WRITING QUESTIONS

It is important that questions are:

      Easy to understand
      On one specific point
      Concise
      Clear and unambiguous
      Not in negative form
      Without bias

The instructions for completing the questionnaire must also be clear, concise and unambiguous. The layout must be open and attractive with plenty of room for replies. You should also make questionnaires easy to process and analyse afterwards.

4 TRIALLING

When you have drafted a questionnaire, it is essential to test it out with a small sample of the target audience before you actually use it. You may find that questions you thought were clear, unambiguous and without bias were not. You may pick up useful hints for improving the questionnaire from the reactions of other people.

Although the responses you have may not be statistically valid, they can often provide you with useful information as part of producing a communication artefact.

5 COLLECTING AND PRESENTING THE RESULTS

When you draft the questions, always keep in mind how you will bring together and present the responses. If you have a hundred or more responses it can be a big task.

With open questions you will need to summarize the general points and indicate how many of the total respondents agreed with the ideas.

With closed questions you will need to count the responses and convert to percentages: for example, 60 per cent said yes and 40 per cent said no. It is also useful to convert these percentages to a diagrammatic presentation with bar charts or pie charts.

3.2 Writing scripts (radio)

You should link this section with what we say about producing audio, below. Before trying to write a script, listen to radio – maybe tune into your local commercial station. Listen to a selection of the advertisements.

What have you heard? We think you may have heard a mixture of music, some variety of voices, and some dialogue or drama. . . . You may have found the use of an accent or dialect or the selling tone of a voice annoying. The best radio advertisements are carefully scripted for maximum impact in thirty or sixty seconds. Words are chosen to create a quick positive impression and for ease of listening.

Listen to radio trails; pay attention to how segments of magazine-type programmes are put together.

Checklist for writing a script

1   As always, be clear about what you want to say and how you want to say it. See figure 50. Look at the sample radio script (figure 52).

```
MUSIC:    Bright, faded on musical phrase, held under speech.    5"
SPEECH:   Obtains interest.                                      10"
          Provides information on content.
          (Music edit at low level under speech)
          Gives transmission details                            5"
MUSIC:    Fade up to end.                                        5"
```

```
(American voices)              Fx hiss of space circuit, bleep
MAN 1 (on filter):            OK base, I'm on the ladder now. (Music:
                              majestic, low level) This is one small leap
                              for man …

MAN 2:                        Hank, er, just hold on there will you.
                              (Music cuts) That's 'one small step for man,
                              there.

MAN 1 (filter):               Er, yes sir. (To self) One small step – OK
                              base. (Music begins) This is one tiny
                              (Music cuts) – oh rats.

MAN 2 (laconic):              Relax, Hank, just take your time now.
                              (Music begins)

MAN 1 (filter):               This is one big, small, step here, for one
                              man to take off a ladder – (Music cuts)

MAN 2:                        OK, Hank, you're getting warm. 'One giant
                              leap for mankind.'

MAN 3 (filter):               Hank, I'm getting cramp on the ladder up
                              here, will you hurry it up please. (Music
                              begins)

MAN 1 (filter):               This is one small leap for a giant (Music
                              cuts)

MAN 2 (interrupting):         One giant leap for mankind. (Music begins)

MAN 1 (filter):               This kind man is a small giant. (Music cuts)

MAN 2 (testily):              Giant leap. (Music begins)

MAN 1 (filter):               This leap year is gonna be the best (Music
                              cuts) – aah.

MAN 2:                        Chuck, will you unload the Heineken bay and
                              refresh that man's speech please?

FX (close):                   Pouring liquid into a glass

MAN 1 (filter):               OK, I'm ready – run the music. (Music
                              begins again)
                              This is one small step for man – one giant
                              leap for mankind.
                              FX applause up
                              Music: man's voices sing slowly in the
                              style of 'Space Odyssey'

                              'Heineken refreshes the parts other beers
                              cannot reach'.

MAN 1 (filter;
triumphant):                  The Blue Tit has landed.

MAN 2:                        The Eagle, Hank, the Eagle.

(85 secs)
```

FIGURE 52   Radio trail and advert example. Radio trail reprinted from Robert McLeish, *Radio Production*, fifth edition, 2005, p. 126, with permission from Elsevier. Radio advert reprinted from the same source, pp. 202–3, courtesy of Lowe Howard – Spink Marshall, with permission from Elsevier

2   You are not writing an essay, so the conventions of properly structured sentences and paragraphs with a beginning, a middle and an end don't apply.

3   Be direct, clear and simple. Write for a speaking voice. Use short sentences, natural speech rhythms and easily understood language. Obviously, if it is a technical topic, you will have to use appropriate words to describe it. But only use jargon if you know that the target audience will understand it.

4   Keep paragraphs short.

5   Read out aloud as you write it.

6   Use more than one voice if possible. You can simply use a different reader, or you may be able to create some dialogue between two voices, or a conversation between more than two voices.

7   Use sound effects and/or music. Remember those radio adverts that you listened to. They may have crammed lots of different sound effects into just a few seconds.

8   Use vivid language. Stress the ideas you want to convey. Repeat main ideas to make sure people hear them.

9   Be prepared to leave gaps. You may want to use music to fill them.

10   Annotate your script with instructions on how you want it to be read or recorded. You can obtain published radio scripts or TV scripts which you can look at to see how they are set out. You can use your own notes for yourself so you know what you intended.

11   Record it and listen to it. Play it to one or more of the intended audience to get their response. Amend it in the light of their feedback.

As with all the communication skills we are discussing here, the more you practise it the easier it will become and the more effective you are likely to become at producing a script.

4 Design skills

In this section we are not attempting to provide an introduction to graphic design or desktop publishing. We are simply seeking to provide a checklist of guidelines for producing formats such as booklets, leaflets or brochures.

The creation of a successful brochure requires the combination of words and pictures to form an attractive effect and to convey the ideas that are needed. As always, being clear about your purpose, your target audience and how the brochure will be used is essential.

We suggest that you collect some leaflets and brochures from shops and offices and from community centres, and analyse what you believe are their successes and failures. Look at the typefaces and the lettering as well as the visuals and the general layout.

It is very useful to create layout sheets to help you visualize what the finished product will be like. Indeed, these can be a part of your design package, because however good your mock-up is, it is unlikely that you will be able to get it to professional printing standard. Layout sheets are usually bigger than the finished page size. This size is drawn on the sheet, and the space around the real page size lines can be used to put in notes. Areas of text and graphics are just sketched in outline on the page, so that their proportions and placing are clear. These blocks can be keyed by numbers (or letters for illustrations) to the writing and pictures which you have on other sheets. Big headings may be written out. The surrounding notes, perhaps with arrows pointing on to the page area, say things about intended final qualities, such as typeface and type size, use of colour, design of logo, and details of graphic devices such as borders. This approach emphasizes the fact that you are designing, and do not necessarily have to have artistic or technical skills in order to communicate your vision of the particular print format.

For all the availability of desktop publishing packages such as Front Page, the hand-produced and annotated layout sheet still has a lot to recommend it. It is easy to produce, whereas DTP packages have limitations, and don't necessarily allow you to make something that is perfectly authentic and professional-looking. Some practical work looks as if it is driven by what the DTP package can do, rather than being informed by the imagination of the creator. A layout sheet is a good way of communicating the look of a magazine or newspaper page, or indeed a Web page (see below).

Checklist for brochures

1   Decide on the *content*, including words, pictures and diagrams. These may have to be amended in the light of the practicalities and the cost of reproduction, but it is worth beginning with the impact you want to make. Try out rough scribbled versions to visualize how you want it to look. You may want it to be a formal, carefully laid out document, or you may want it to be much more personal and quirky.

2   Decide on *the format and the layout*. These include the size of the page, the number of pages, how they will be folded or stapled. It's useful to try a mock-up with blank sheets to get the look of it and to get the page sequence right.

3   Be clear about *the front and the back*. Have some sort of introduction and some sort of conclusion. People want to know how to use it. In textbooks on advertising it's often suggested that an effective advertisement attracts attention, holds interest, creates desire and leads to action. It's often worth thinking what your brochure is doing to attract attention and what action you want from the people who have read it or seen it.

4   Decide *how it will be reproduced*. Will it be black and white or colour? How

many copies will you print? Will you be able to print photographs effectively? There are a whole lot of practicalities to deal with. It is worth experimenting with your masters and a photocopier.

5   *Be sparing with colour* (maybe use coloured paper, which is cheaper than colour printing or copying).

6   *Leave space around images or blocks of text*, so that they stand out against the background colour, and do not crowd the page too much, especially at the borders.

7   Think how you will handle *the text on the page*, e.g. colours, type size, typeface, borders.

8   *Create the final master*. Use one side of the paper. Always use the same size of paper for the masters. Make sure the sequence is clear and leave wide margins, especially where it may be stapled or folded.

9   Experiment with any photocopying that you want to do, especially to get material round the right way, and to get it facing properly if you are printing both sides of a sheet (as opposed to doing a straight paste-up).

10 Test a *pilot copy* of the brochure with your intended audience.

One thing you can do with technology is to use any basic word-processing program to print out text, even to arrange it, up to a point. You can then cut and paste what you have produced. The advantage of using word processing is that you can go on experimenting and printing until you get the size and the look of it as close as possible to what you want. You can do a lot just with Word for Windows, including the production of boxes around text, graphic features such as arrows, and putting in colour.

5 Storyboarding

Storyboards are sketches of picture sequences, perhaps with some written notes on the visuals and sound (see figure 53). They are relevant to creating items such as title sequences, adverts, action sequences, tape-slides. Storyboards come in two versions of detail. The looser is where the storyboard frames illustrate key shots in a longish sequence. The tighter (and easier to handle) version is where every frame is a shot, or even two parts of an elaborate shot involving a moving camera. Professional film storyboards may have only the pictures for the sequence. But we recommend a version more like television storyboards, where you write notes on the shot and the scene to the right of the sketch frame (see figure 55, later in the chapter).

This approach enables one to use words to make clear what the visuals intend. Of course it helps to be able to draw, but storyboarding – especially for communication/media courses – is about visualization and design. It is OK to draw stick people. If you can't sketch the right angle on a scene, then describe it alongside. This brings us to visual language.

1 Establishing wide shot (WS) of a Gents' toilet door inside a cinema. The camera slowly tracks in as tense, eerie music begins.

2 Int. toilets. Low angle mid shot (MS) of a man's legs in black trousers. We pan up …

3 … to reveal the man dressed totally in black standing at a sink.

4 Close-up (CU) of a man's belongings beside sink.

5 CU of blood being washed down sink.

6 CU as man bandages his bleeding hand.

7 MS of reflection in mirror of man clenching fist. Pan up and pull out of focus to …

8 … man's blurred face as he turns his head. We hear the door opening.

FIGURE 53 An example of a storyboard

You do need to be able to use basic descriptive terms, and abbreviations of these. Everyone 'knows' this visual language because you see it happening every day – including in most comics. With your storyboard you should number every frame, explain how 'close' the shot is, explain the camera position/audience point of view if necessary, explain any camera movements, explain links between shots. The next sections describe these items.

Proximity/framing

- Extreme close-up (ECU) – eyes
- Close-up (CU) – head
- Medium close-up (MCU) – head and shoulders
- Medium shot (MS)
- Medium long shot (MLS)
- Long shot (LS)

Shot types

- **Establishing shot** – shows a scene/location and establishes where characters are within the scene.
- **Cutaway shot** – shows some significant detail off to one side of the main scene, like the face at the window behind a character.
- **Two shot** – describes a conventional framing of two characters, probably in conversation.
- **Subjective shot** – is one where the viewer believes they are seeing what a character sees.

Camera position

Camera position is about the angle of the camera on a scene and the point of view (POV) of the viewer/camera. Usually this is commented on only when it is quite dramatic. So, if the POV is from a balcony down into a square, then it could be described either as, say, Evita's POV from balcony to crowd below, or as high camera angle past balcony and down on to crowd.

Camera movements

- **Pull in/pull out** (also **zoom**) – strictly, the lenses moving, not the camera. Brings the subject closer or further away.
- **Track in/track out, track sideways** (also **dolly**) – the camera moving on a trolley and rails. Gives a different effect from zooms and pans.
- **Tilt up/tilt down** – the camera pivots vertically up or down something like a skyscraper.

- **Pan right/left** – the camera pivots horizontally across a scene.
- **Crane shot** – the camera is on a crane, and so – 'camera cranes across square and into hotel window'.

Shot links

These terms are in effect about editing. Professionally it is assumed that there is a cut between shots unless it says otherwise. You can write your instructions between one frame and another. Electronic video allows one to do many complicated changes, such as when one picture zooms towards us out of the middle of the previous one. But the basic repertoire of links are these:

- **Cut to** – the sequence 'jumps' from one picture to another.
- **Dissolve/mix** – one picture merges into another.
- **Fade in/out** – the picture goes slowly to white or black, and the next one comes in.

You can learn a lot about storyboards from watching adverts and titles on TV. But basically we would advise you to learn to vary your proximity and angle; it is boring to watch a whole sequence of medium shots.

6 Taking photographs

We are assuming that most students and media/communication departments in education will now be using digital cameras for their photography. We have revised this section accordingly. However, if you are using a digital SLR, then much of what we wrote in the last edition still applies. But because these cameras are relatively expensive – they still cost more than their roll film predecessors – we are assuming that you will be using a lower grade of digital. Therefore, we are not talking about changing lenses. We are assuming, however, that you will use a digital camera with some kind of optical zoom lens (and not fixed focus).

In the details that follow, we comment on the key characteristics and functions of digital cameras in general. For individual models, you will have to use the manual. What you do need to understand is that the very cheapest models are not particularly useful for practical work. For example, digital zoom gives poor definition, whereas optical zoom is good. You pay more for optical zoom.

We are talking about stills camera-work here. This accounts for the nature of our advice. But much of what we say is relevant to shooting moving images as well.

The main problems that you need to understand about digital cameras are:

- They don't cope very well with action shots/movement. It depends on what you pay for the camera!

- Their lens tends not to be that 'wide angle' (unless they are expensive) – so you may have trouble getting good shots of buildings and other large subjects.
- Their sensors can attract dust. Keep them clean and away from dirty environments.
- They get through batteries – always carry charged spares with you.

One of the great things about digital is that you can manipulate and print your own images via a computer. We are not going to try to cover this side of picture production in the space we have got. It isn't that hard to learn the basics. There is a range of proprietary software that comes with items such as Hewlett-Packard scanners, and which is easy to use. Obviously we do advise you to practise using a program such as Photoshop before you start on an important project.

The quality of your printout photos depends on the quality of your printer and on the paper you put through it. It is easy enough to buy photo-quality paper. We suggest that if necessary you get advice about essentials such as the definition that your printer and computer program can offer. It is no good having a high-definition camera if the rest of the hardware isn't up to it.

6.1 Things to watch out for about the camera

Shot quality

- Has it got 4-megapixel resolution or better? You need this definition to be able to produce clear prints of a reasonable size, e.g. 20 × 25 cm. (Camera details should always tell you about this electronic quality, e.g. 4.2 mps.)
- Check out the shot definition; cameras give you a choice of settings which affect how good your shot is, and how many shots you can store on the memory card. You need to go for fewer shots stored, better quality, but then watch out for the increased demands on the battery.

Flash

- Has it got red-eye reduction on the flash? If not, your human subjects will have 'Dracula' eyes in your image. Also remember that any ordinary in-camera flash can't do more than illuminate nearby subjects, so you can't get night shots of crowds or scenes or buildings without extra equipment.

Viewfinder

- What you see through your viewfinder is not exactly what the lens sees, and this affects the framing of your subject. Usually, cameras put some lines on the viewfinder which help you frame what the lens 'sees'. Only an SLR truly lets you see through the lens.
- Try not to use cameras with a liquid crystal display (LCD). They burn up batteries, and they have to be held away from you to see them properly, so then the camera is likely to shake.

Memory/image storage

- Sort out what format is being used to store your images, and make sure that you have spares. One common format is called CF. But then Sony, for example, use their own memory stick. These formats are not interchangeable.
- Make sure that you have the leads and gizmos that allow you to download images to your computer, and perhaps to some other storage device that you carry around.
- In general, it is better to use smaller memory cards storing fewer images, and change them more often. They have been known to fail!

Batteries

Always carry spares (see above).

More technical points (but they're really useful!)

- Get to know what your camera can and can't do – its *functions*. For example, has it got a setting that helps you photograph moving targets? (This needs a faster shutter speed.) Has it got a setting that helps compensate for photographing subjects with at least some of the sky in the background? (This needs a larger aperture.) So, can you control the shutter speed or the aperture (see below) on your camera? Or are there general settings for types of shot, such as 'moving' or 'distant' or 'close' – often shown by little symbols?
- The *shutter* controls how quickly or slowly light is let through on to the sensor in the camera; darker conditions need a slower speed. Shutter speed is measured in fractions of a second; 1/125 of a second will freeze most movement. But remember, no one can hold a camera perfectly still for 1 second.
- The *aperture* refers to the size of the hole behind the lens, which lets more or less light through when the shutter is released; this also affects the

sharpness of the image. So, early or late in the day your camera may automatically open up the aperture because there is less light. But be aware that the images may then lose some sharpness. Aperture is measured in *f* stop numbers. Something like *f*16 is a smaller hole and a sharper image. Not many cameras are going to offer a larger hole than the one measured at 2.8.

- Think about what *standard* of electronic image file you are going to use, where you have a choice. JPEG files are OK – the 5/6 setting is acceptable for general use. But the best-quality image file is called TIFF, even though this quality means fewer images on your storage device.

- Consider whether it is worth getting hold of some *portable storage device*; an HDD is best. This gives you back-up to the camera card. It means you don't have to worry about how many shots you are taking – especially if you are a long way from 'base', and you will never be able to get back to that location again.

- If you come across a reference to ISOE for the camera, it may be useful to understand that this describes the *light sensitivity* of the camera (i.e. of the sensors). The better the sensors, the more sensitive to light – and this is useful if you have to shoot in fairly dark conditions. (There are now some cameras that can film indoors without needing flash.) A sensitivity measured at 200 is average and acceptable. But a higher number (e.g. 400) means more sensitivity.

- If you are using a *scanner* to acquire images (especially from transparencies or negatives used by traditional roll film), then make sure that it is up to the job. You will need a special adaptor for transparencies. Technically, you will need a scanner that can achieve a density rating of 3.6 or better.

- If you are using a *CD writer* to store images, then make sure that it is a proper standard: that is, ISO 9660 badged, which means that it is compatible with both PC and Apple computers.

- Regarding your *computer*, remember that images and their manipulation through a program like Photoshop use up lots of memory, so you need a machine with plenty of megabytes (MB) on its hard disk. It is useful to have Firewire, as well as USB ports, for connecting devices to the computer.

6.2 Using the camera

The following points are designed to help you get reasonable-quality images, and to avoid messing up shots. There is nothing like *practice* to find out what your camera can and can't do. It is cheap enough to try different kinds of shot under different conditions, using different functions on the camera. Keep a log of what you have taken, look at the results, and learn what is possible and what not to do.

Preparation can save a lot of grief later on. Check out locations to see what you can and can't get in the shot. Make sure you have permissions where necessary. You can stand on public land to take shots – but the military might get upset if you film their bases. You can't film in a bus station without permission – it's private land. Don't try to take pictures of children in playgrounds – you might get arrested! Preparation also involves checking – where people are involved in photos – that they know exactly when and where they are supposed to be. You may only be able to get them one time. Rehearse and practise shots, and especially their framing, before going for a final take. Of course you can film as much material as you have memory. But it is possible to take too much material. It is very tiresome having to go through unnecessary dud shots.

Carry a *tripod* with you where at all possible. Of course you can't use it for spontaneous quick shots. But otherwise it helps get rid of camera shake, keeps the camera level, and holds on to the framing that you have set up. You don't want to have to reframe everything via post-production. And remember that the slower the shutter speed and/or the bigger the aperture, then the more likely it is that camera shake will show up.

Movement can be a problem in filming – not with moving film, of course! With stills shots either you want a fast enough shutter speed to freeze the motion of the subject – a race perhaps. Or you can try moving the camera with the direction of the moving subject, so that even a slower shutter speed (e.g. 1/60th) will probably freeze it. In this case you should get a clever effect in which the background blurs but the subject is clear.

Think about *light*. Natural light is best. Avoid sharp shadows and sunlight. Light coming in from an angle or the side helps 'mould' your subject and emphasize the three-dimensionality of it.

Avoid *backlighting*. This means, don't take shots against a window or the sky. Most cameras can't cope. You end up with the foreground subject looking black, and all you see properly is the light bit. Good cameras allow you to try to compensate by 'holding open' the aperture, but in our experience even this rarely works properly. And if your camera is highly automated, then you don't have a choice.

If you have to film against a light background (even white walls), then get close to your subject and reduce the amount of background. Your auto camera will set its controls to light the subject properly, not the sky.

If you are determined to try this kind of shot, and *if* you can control aperture and shutter speed on your camera, then set these standing close to your subject. Then, when you move back and include more sky, the subject should be properly visible, though the sky will tend to 'white out'.

Watch out for *flash* (see above). It can be pretty harsh on its subject. Don't be fooled into thinking that lots of artificial light will compensate. The light from bulbs or strips is different from daylight (all about something called colour temperature, but don't ask, at this level!), so it affects the colour and brilliance of what you are filming. Only expensive cameras are able to compensate for this. The best advice is to check out and practise in places where you want to shoot in dim or dark surroundings.

Think about *framing*. Even though you can crop and resize material electronically, this may involve problems such as losing definition. Better to get it mainly right in the first place. The frame should contain the subject and concentrate the eye upon it, not least when the subject is a person. Generally speaking, it is better to frame the subject more tightly than you think you have to – without chopping off heads! Our brains have an amazing ability to cut out clutter surrounding a figure – the camera won't.

Remember that with stills work you have a choice between the usual 'wide' frame (landscape), and turning the camera through 90 degrees to get a 'tall' frame (portrait). This is called portrait precisely because it is often used when taking pictures of people.

It can also be good to have a relevant *context* to figures. If you are filming a go-kart race, say, then you don't want all head shots (or all long-distance shots). It is good to see some of the kart around the person, and sometimes to see the track or the pits around the kart. Learn to see what the lens is seeing – not what you would like it to have seen.

Consider *composition*. How are elements arranged within the image? You might want to use a road or a wall to carry the eye from front to back of the image. This might help it seem more three-dimensional and 'real'. This helps what is called *perspective*.

Where is the *horizon line*? Too much sky doesn't seem 'right'. As a rule of thumb, don't let the sky take up more than a third of your image. Keep single figures centre or even slightly left in the image. Notice what is in the *foreground and background* of your shot. You might be able to create a nice shot, for example, where your front figure is head and shoulders and in focus, but a back figure is slightly out of focus. You might be able to balance them, one to the left, one in the right of the frame.

And most of all, watch out for the elements that your brain censors: the drainpipe growing out of your subject's head; your friend's dog in the background of the shot.

Remember that every camera shot creates a *point of view* (POV). This is about where the camera is positioned with relation to what it is filming. This will then become the position from which the viewer of the image sees it. It will affect the impression created by the image. In general, avoid shots that are all about the POV of someone just standing there looking at the subject – for example, all head height.

It isn't hard to kneel down, to stand on a set of steps, to take the subject from a side angle. It isn't hard to vary shots between close-up (CU) – a head shot – or medium close-up (MCU) – say, head and shoulders or a half-body shot. It is deadly to have to look at a lot of MS or MLS, taken from the front, where the images look like a lot of boring postcards or paintings.

Think about why you are using the *zoom* – or telephoto. A decent digital camera will have at least a ×3 optical zoom, which allows you to fine-tune framing without keeping moving the camera, and which allows you to get near a subject without having to be physically close to it. The least zoom position allows you to get the most in frame. The most zoom can allow you to home in on detail. But remember that if you have zoomed in on a subject, it plays visual games with our sense of the difference between back to front of the image (depth of field). In this case it makes foreground and background objects seem closer together than they actually are. Also remember that the bigger your zoom, the more camera shake shows up, so the more you need a fast shutter speed and/or a tripod.

We have saved the simplest and most important thing till last: *focus*. Highly automated digital cameras – and a lot of them are – will do the focusing for you. This sounds convenient, but can be a problem. For example, how quickly can your camera get the subject into focus? Cheaper cameras take time to measure distance and drive the lens round. So, if something is moving into frame it may be better for you to have pre-set your focus manually before the car comes round the corner – and then just click when it does. Otherwise the car may be halfway out of shot by the time a cheap autofocus has done its job.

Another problem relates to how the focusing is done and where in the lens area the camera does its focus reading. Your camera may not be 'reading' the object in the frame that you want to stay in focus. You might end up with a sharp background but a blurred figure, when you wanted it the other way round. So, there are arguments for switching off autofocus if you can. Once more, pre-checking shots can save grief.

7 Audio-visual production

Here, what we are seeking to do is to give you guidelines for creating your own productions. One of your main reasons, as a student of communication, for producing materials is to experiment with equipment and to experiment with conventions of communication. For example, if you and a group decided to produce a news magazine or some advertisements, you might 'naturally' follow broadcast conventions. But you might want to seek to challenge those conventions and to create your own individual style of presentation.

Technical limitations may cramp your style. What is important is your creative planning and individual ideas. Access to the means of home production is now easier than ever before. Most schools and colleges can now give access to audio and digital video recording equipment. In our experience, there are usually frustrations between the ideas we want to create and the limitations of technical equipment and our abilities in using it. This does not prevent the whole practical production from being great fun and enabling us to learn a good deal about how mass-media products are created.

This section is not going to give technical details about a range of equipment. You can obtain that elsewhere, indeed from equipment manuals. We aim to provide some basic checklists that will help you to use audio-visual equipment more successfully.

7.1 Producing audio

It is almost certain that if you are recording audio, and it isn't for dubbing on to visuals, then your exercise is aimed at either radio simulation or music production. Music is another specialist story, not least in respect of the types of mike and their placing in a given space. So, we will briefly consider audio in relation to radio. If you are thinking about digital video (DV), then link these comments with the section below.

Obviously you need a cassette recorder and a microphone, or the same thing in a solid-state recorder using CD or minidisk. You can get recorders that have internal mixing facilities (two mike/line inputs, so you don't have to mix in a computer). If you are recording outside, then you need an omni-directional microphone with a decent windshield. It is also useful to have a lip mike, which will give you voice but cut out a lot of surrounding noise.

Alternatively, a lapel mike will do something similar – though many users would prefer to have this as an addition. It is useful to have a little mike stand for supporting your mike on a table when interviewing someone. But remember to put it on a book or something that insulates it from the vibrations of a bare wooden surface. It is also helpful to have a full microphone stand for 'studio' work.

You should use a pair of headphones so that you can monitor what is actually being recorded, whether it is an interviewee or some specific sound at a location (though of course effects CDs can give you many of the sounds that you might want to mix in).

It helps if you have a second direct-link player to record from one machine to another.

Listening to pre-prepared disks and radio broadcasts, particularly from local radio stations, will provide you with ideas of how to produce your own. You may, of course, seek to do it differently from the broadcasts. Think about small formats such as trails or adverts. Or try to make a segment for a larger programme. Combine elements such as the vox pop (interview with a member of the public), music lead-ins, natural sound, voice-over.

If you have access to digital editing, it is much easier to combine sounds, music and voice-overs, but you can still do this with one or two recorders. For example, you can play music and speak over it so that both music and voice are

FIGURE 54 Flow diagram for making an audio production on your local area

picked up by a simple recording mike. However, it isn't hard to get hold of cheap audio software through which to mix FX and voice, and then burn on to a CD. If you can edit multiple tracks, then consider the use of wild sound and atmosphere – 'open' recordings at a location that would give you the background noise to a room, or perhaps to a location such as an airport. In life, sound is never digitally clean. There is always either background noise or that intangible sound quality to any space. It is like the difference between a 'pure' digital music recording and one that has been made at a venue. In making your production, pay attention to existing conventions, most of all the fade-in and fade-out used at the lead-in and exit to your whole piece, or as a way of telling the listener that you are changing location or time within the piece.

Practical checklist

- Check your batteries – recorder and possibly the mike (e.g. condenser mikes).
- Check your microphone and sound source (using headphones) before you record for real.
- Check that record is engaged.
- Avoid outside noises as much as possible.

7.2 Mounting an exhibition

An exhibition provides a permanent or temporary presentation for large numbers of people in a variety of locations. It does not necessarily depend on access to technology for its use, and it can have good visual impact as well as providing verbal information.

Here we shall confine ourselves to the design of a few easy-to-handle panels. However, professional exhibitions may be the creation of a complete environment in, say, a museum, a gallery or a trade exhibition, where a stand may consist of a complete room using a whole range of technical inputs.

Any exhibition requires the design of images and words and the design of a physical layout and space to engage the attention and participation of visitors. An exhibition can include posters, photographs, cartoons, diagrams, text, slides, sound, video input, computer data display, leaflets or questionnaires to take away, people to talk to, food to taste, and so on. There is almost no limit to what can be provided if resources allow it.

With these ideas in mind, the producer of an exhibition needs to address the following issues:

- The *stand* itself: size, weight, location for display, the materials it is to be made of, whether it is self-sufficient or needs people to manage it and display it. Use arrows or layout to show people how they should follow the items.

- *Text*: keep words to the minimum; capture key ideas; these should be carefully written, and use an eye-catching graphic layout to create interest. Type size is obviously crucial and will vary according to the scale and location of the stand.
- *Pictures*: photos (not small snapshots), captions, cartoons and line diagrams all need to be bold and eye-catching at the right scale. You need to think about how far away people will be when they view them. You may be able to build in an image projector or video player as part of the stand.
- *Sound*: use of pre-prepared material with sound, music or voices is useful to capture attention. Be wary of using voices, however, since the stand is likely to be surrounded by noise anyway.
- *Things to take away or things to do*: a summary leaflet may be useful; a questionnaire could be appropriate; you could have a game or quiz, or you may have free samples. All of this will depend on the nature of the exhibition and the impact you want to have after the exhibition has gone.
- *Layout* in exhibition space: it is useful to make a ground plan so that you can experiment with what goes where. Think about where people come in and what they first see – probably a display that explains the whole exhibition, and directs them in some way. Think about the space needed for people to circulate around safely and comfortably. Think about giving people enough room to stand back from a display board and to see things properly. Think about the direction or sequence that you may want visitors to take. This can help to stop crowding in a confined space. It may be about making sense of the whole thing.

In producing exhibition boards, your access to large-scale printing or photocopying will dictate the possibilities.

Since people will be moving around the exhibition, the issue of safety is important. You must make sure that if someone touches or knocks any item, it will not fall down.

The overall theme for mounting an exhibition should be to keep it uncluttered. Think of exhibitions or displays that have made an impact on you. Probably they were simple and direct with a few key ideas well expressed, with strong images and strong use of lettering. Detailed text is best put on a sheet for people to pick up.

7.3 Making films (digital video)

This section assumes you have access to a digital camcorder (e.g. mini DV) and at least basic editing facilities. You might, for example, be using Windows Movie-Maker. If your computer is powerful enough, you can use a program like Pinnacle. For the Apple Mac, the proprietary program provided is I-Movie. For visual digital work generally, most people argue that Apple systems are superior to Windows. Another program called After Effects is popular with MAC users, though we cannot speak from experience. And a common program, in versions for both Mac and PC, is Adobe Premiere. There is a cheap version of this, Adobe Premiere Elements 2.00, which can also be used with that increasing number of digital cameras that have a video function added on.

We are not seeking to introduce technical jargon or to cover movie production at anything like a professional level. You will find some of the material under sections 5 ('Storyboarding') and 6 ('Taking photos'), above, also useful for this section.

Producing videos can be great fun and good for experimenting with interesting ways of presenting material. But video productions can also be very disappointing when what gets recorded bears little relationship to what you intended. This may be a result of your own lack of experience, the limitations of the equipment, or your need to manage other people more effectively when you need their help. The interpersonal and group skills required for producing video productions should not be underestimated.

A successful production depends on detailed planning and careful preparation at every stage as well as a range of technical and social skills. The most important single piece of advice is to be well organized.

The following is a checklist of steps that will help you towards the final production you hope for, starting off with comments on learning to use the equipment.

1   Get to know how to use your equipment. The basic quality of picture and sound determines the final outcome. Use your instruction manual and have lots of practice. Make sure that you carry out a quick check before you go out. Check that batteries in the camera (and in the audio recorder and the neck of an external microphone, if you are using these) are there and charged. Have spare batteries with you. Check that the camera is set up; until you get confident, put all the relevant buttons on auto or leave them alone. If you are using a separate audio recorder as part of your shoot, then do a voice check to make sure it is working. If you are plugging a separate microphone into the camera, then try taping it firmly to a strong bamboo garden cane. This gives you an instant boom mike!

2   Experiment with using the camera in a range of shots, for example long shots and close-ups on people. Try a range of angles, at eye level, for example, and from a high or low angle. Try techniques of panning (sideways movements of the camera) and tilting (up and down movement). Observe the effect on the viewer when you review your camera work; if you are using a low angle, it probably suggests some sort of looking up to authority. Use the in-camera playback facility to look at your shots instantly. Often when people first use a camera there is a tendency to

move it around as if it were a hosepipe; the effect on the viewer can be irritating. Think about the frame of your picture and what you are putting into the shot. When you are filming for real, use a tripod if at all possible; no one has a totally steady hand.

Run through each shot in terms of zoom or pans and framing, before the take. Note that zoom is the [W]ide–[T]ight rocker switch on your camera. Remember that digital zoom is inferior to optical; a blown-up image degrades, and at worst starts to expose pixels. If you make your camera movements in what you think is slow motion, it will look fine on screen.

3   Experiment with lighting. Get to know the effect of different light direction. Basically, keep your light sources behind the camera unless you want special effects. This means that you should never shoot people against the sky or a window, because they come out as black silhouettes. Even backgrounds such as large areas of white wall or a display of white roses could be a problem here.

4   Experiment with sound through the camera and, if you have them, through different sorts of microphone. Remember that the inbuilt camera mike is only good for sounds up to about 2 metres away. This is why it is good to have a separate mike plugged in, if that is possible. The camera mike is not bad for a half-body shot on someone talking. But further than this and it 'chooses' to pick up other sounds around that you may not want. With some cameras you can plug in headphones to monitor the sound that you are getting. If you can, use these. If you can borrow a rifle mike, you will find this is excellent for selecting sound in a certain direction and from a distance – very useful for voices.

If you can't do any of this, don't panic. But realize that you will have to structure your work so far as sound is concerned, by using narration, sound effects and music. You will put these on in post-production.

5   We assume that you will have access to editing equipment, so practise with it. Similarly, experiment with sound editing and dubbing (putting new sound over the visual image). It's a good idea to allow a little overrun in filming at the end of each shot. This means you won't have to be split-second perfect when making the edit (or effects link) between one shot and another.

6   Once you have some confidence in using your equipment and you know its capabilities, then you can think about producing material. Don't try to make TV programmes or feature films. In any case, the requirements of syllabuses are specific and more limited. You can be thinking of *formats*

FIGURE 55 Sample storyboard blank

such as titles sequences, promo shorts, trailers, music videos, adverts, information films. Look at real media examples to get ideas and to see how they have done it.

Talk about the *audience* – the kind of person who would want to look at your work, what they would expect, what they wouldn't like.

Talk generally about your *medium*, how you are going to put over what you want to 'say'. Don't be afraid to rely on voice-over/narration, music, text on screen. You don't have to get clever just because you have technology in your hands.

All we have said elsewhere about getting started and about using storyboards and scripts also applies to video productions. Ideally you need three people to shoot DV: camera operator; sound person, probably holding an external mike; and production assistant to log everything that is recorded (what it is and how long).

The essential sequence of planning and producing a piece is likely to include:

- **Brainstorming for ideas** and discussing them with other people.
- **Carrying out research** on topics, people, places for filming, possible sequences and a variety of visual and sound input.
- **Preparing a storyboard** to visualize the total sequence. This is very important in respect of visualizing what you want to end up on screen. Filming doesn't work if you turn up at a location with a camera and expect directorial brilliance to just happen.
- **Preparing an outline script**.
- **Preparing a plan/schedule** for producing the whole sequence, which will include dates, times, places and people involved.
- **Logging** (writing systematically) everything that you have recorded: timing, shot numbers, shot/location description
- **Producing a final (post-production) script** with any necessary titles or captions as well as sources of material. Also, **producing a post-production storyboard**, to help with the editing process.
- **Editing recordings**: this can be a very time-consuming activity. It will most likely take longer than the filming. Never underestimate how much time you need for this post-production part of the process, especially if you are trying to dub quite a lot of sound.

It is usually best to play safe with links or transitions between shots. Cuts and fades are common in real media examples. Clever mixes and travelling wipes (which may be offered by better programs) can be difficult to achieve and actually distracting for the viewer. Obviously a specific example such as a music video is more likely to include elements such as jump cuts, colour effects, digital drag-on shots, tilt frame, and so on.

Keep your cutting tight. There is always a tendency to hang on to shots too long: not to want to abandon shots that were tough to get but which actually don't work for the final production. Look at what media professionals do in short formats, and notice how if a shot is held for more than two seconds, then there is something about it (dialogue, camera movement, narrative sense) that justifies this.

- **Dubbing sound** against your pictures, from various sources such as music, narration and effects. This can be quite difficult, especially with the more basic computer programs. But it can make a lot of difference if you get, for example, your entry and exit points, your fades, your pace for a music track just right against the shots.

Finally, you will need to copy your work on to a DVD.

Especially if you are working to the requirements of a syllabus, you will find that some of the items above are required for your final assessment – so you can't cut corners.

8 Into the Net

Use of the Internet and the World Wide Web is now so well established that we hesitated about including this section at all. If you are in education you will have access to the Net. And many people have access at home. However, not every home in Britain has a computer, and only a minority of homes are connected to broadband. And some people are using the Net without having set it up themselves. So, there may be some use in what follows.

To access the Net, you need a telephone connection, a computer, a modem to link the last two (one may well be built into the computer), and an Internet Service Provider (ISP). This business, such as Tesco.net or hotmail.com or NTLworld.com, will give you an email address and probably some Web space. Some providers give a free service, some (especially for broadband) will charge you per month. When you sign up to a provider, you will be given a disk with a program on it. All you have to do to make it all happen is to follow instructions as they appear on screen. If you are likely to be sent emails with photos, then you need to be sure that your mailbox is of sufficient size (several MB) to be able to hold pictures, which use far more space than words. If you go for broadband, you can expect your provider to give you different user options – essentially about the size of the 'pipe' through which your electronic traffic will pass. For most people, 1 MB is enough. Things will change as computers change and as the more of the United Kingdom gets properly wired up with fibre optics. But at the time of writing it is generally useless to have bigger broadband capacity, because the average computer can't cope or 'go any faster'.

Once you are connected, you will rapidly get into the various possible uses of the Net. Apart from emailing and going on to websites (see our list under 'Resources'), people find out about sites like MySpace, where you can 'talk' to other people and set up your own personal little Web space, such as an open diary plus pictures of you. You might want to become a blogger. You are likely to buy things online; apart from high street stores' websites, the famous huge example of an online store is amazon.com. Some people get into online games. Many of us have favourite sites, perhaps to do with music. You can add these to a Favorites list (or Bookmarks for Apple) attached to the program (from your provider), which allows you to get on the Web in the first place – for many people this is Internet Explorer. And you will then be able to go to a browser site that allows you to search for information and other sites on the Web.

Google.com has become the world leader in this respect. It is also now providing other services, including its own email.

Some sites are especially useful because they also provide links to further sites.

9 Designing a website

In this section we are going to give you some advice about the production and design of Web pages. We cannot give you detailed instructions for using programs. There are plenty of detailed self-help books out there; see our recommendation at the end of this chapter. But we hope that our advice will get you into being able to set up your own website, and to make it look attractive as well as usable.

9.1 Why a website

Apart from the possible reason that it is because of some project that you have committed to, there are other pretty obvious reasons for websites being out there:

- They are promotion points for goods and services.
- They are information and exchange bases for almost anything, including interest groups.
- They may be home sites for organizations or individuals (see also weblogs).
- They are accessible from any computer with an Internet connection, any place, any time.

9.2 Setting up a site

- You need a computer connected to the Internet, and software that serves your Web pages. Most people use their ISP if it also offers Web pages. So, if you have an email account, the odds are that this provider will already offer you the possibility of a site and space for a few pages; but you might decide to go for another provider. The ISP that you use will ask you to choose and register a domain, and this will be used as your Web identity. In the case of blogs, or sites such as MySpace, you are talking about something called a hosted account, in which your Web address is the URL for the company site, plus your Web identity.

- The cost of registering your domain name runs from about £3.00 a year upwards (see http://www.123-reg.co.uk/ or http://fasthosts.co.uk/domains/). If you do use registration sites such as these, then note that it doesn't matter who you register your domain through, so long as they offer DNS management, which means that you can direct your domain name to any Web server.
- You need to think about how big your site needs to be, what it is going to 'talk' about and how it might need to be organized.
- You can either set up a single directory site on a Web server, or a multiple directory site which establishes different functions or sections from the outset.
- The single directory is simple but small. You can still link pages.
- In the case of multiple directories, these carry separate sections. The main directory might carry only your front page. This is the kind of site you are probably used to seeing on the Net. It is easier to grow this kind of site, and to navigate it. You can do things like repeat the main site categories on each of the section pages, as you can with single directories. This means that a user doesn't have to keep going back to the main page to work out where they want to jump to next (persistent navigation).
- You can buy proprietary packages to help you to set up and design a site, but they do take away your control over what you set up and how you design the site. But whatever, you are going to have to use a program to put words and pictures out there.

Now for some slightly technical stuff . . .

- To put up text on your site, you will need at least a text editor program. This is because what you write has to be in plain text; ordinary word-processing programs can put information into documents that can confuse Web browsers. But there are disadvantages to such programs – read on! You can use Notepad (part of the Windows PC package), or SimpleText in the case of Apple computers. These programs will work in the Web 'language' of HTML. You can also look at sites such as download.com for access to shareware and freeware.

    But this kind of editor program is just a text editor. It won't have HTML options or helpers. You will need to save your files with the HTML suffix. So, a program like Textpad for Windows is not a proper HTML editor. If you want editorial control, you need to use an HTML editor. (If you see references to XHTML, don't worry: this is fine; it is an improved version of HTML.) This means you can edit in HTML source code. In this case, you can add the commands. Examples of such packages are HandyHTML for Windows, or Webdesign for Apple (see also iWeb for Apple or editplus or bbedit – all code editors).

- Finally, there are useful HTML editors like Dreamweaver which in effect add the code for you, but let you see your work on screen as it will appear on the website. Although we are told there are limitations to this program, we would say that it is a good one to go for, and worth learning how to use. This one is described as a 'what you see is what you get' editor (WYSIWYG).

- With relation to putting images in your Web pages, you will probably want to edit these images through programs such as Photoshop, or PaintshopPro for Windows, or The Gimp (http://www.gimp.org/ – which is free and powerful. It is also worth noting that Adobe offer cheap alternatives to Photoshop. You can import images into a program like Dreamweaver (Macromedia), which operates like a desktop publishing program. Macromedia offers a program such as fireworks, which of course integrates with Dreamweaver and is aimed specifically at Web image editing.

- It is also possible to put up moving images through programs like Quiktime or Flash. But we would advise against trying to do too much too soon. There is also the question of why you would need to use animation on your site, anyway. If it doesn't serve a purpose, it is irritating. And it takes time for the user to download, always assuming they have a program that will do so.

9.3 Designing your site

- The main thing to do overall (see directories above) is to have a clear overall organization for your site, so that it is easy for anyone to navigate. Don't be reluctant to copy good ideas from successful sites.

- Think about who your site is for, and what you are trying to do for your audience through the site. It won't work if it is about you showing off technical skills, or if it isn't easy to move around it and find what one wants.

- Think about what file type directories you need – for example, images, pages, downloads. These cover the functions of your website, not the content. It is your HTML instructions that are going to pull material such as images out of their file and into the correct place on your page (JPEG for photos, GIF for graphics).

- Think about the titles you give to files and folders. These need to clearly indicate use and/or content.

- It is well worth keeping a clone folder on your hard disk, so that you have a protected copy of your Web material. Also, this means that you can test the addition or replacement of file names and links if you want to change the site.

- You can design a style sheet for the whole site; every page can be to a standard format if there aren't too many of them. You can put page links on the toolbar. There must be consistency of links on every page, with an indication of the link that got the user to their current page.
- You can design pages with interactive menus, action buttons, and so on; but these will require more investment in technical learrning.
- Content is king: so plan out what each page is about, how the pages connect with each other in respect of what they are saying, how each page breaks down in terms of what item is where. For example, one of the most important items of content is about how you can be contacted

9.4 Designing your pages

- You could do a lot worse than design the pages themselves around the look of a magazine, with boxes, margin bars, sub-headings, and so on.
- Keep the pages short, clear and graphically attractive; it is irritating to have to scroll on and on, down pages of text. Better to put in a hyperlink to a separate page, which breaks up the amount of text that has to be read all at once.
- The text itself can be broken up with graphic devices such as colour sections, boxes around headings, bar lines, margin changes, and so on. Again, you can get ideas from newspapers and magazines. Anything is better than lines and lines of text, however neatly justified on both margins.
- The best Web pages have qualities of variety, clarity and not too many images. Pages that have colours, boxes and content items all over the place are actually hard on the eye and hard to sort out.
- You can use devices such as background colour and standard format to link pages together visually.
- You can use contrast of colour or graphic devices to distinguish one area of a page from another – perhaps especially on a front page.
- But most of all you need to think about content and audience. What is your site about? Why would someone want to visit it? Could you describe or define the kind of person who would want to use your site? What would they get out of it? How easy it for them to navigate the site? What kind of technology are they likely to have, and how would this affect your site design and presentation of content?
- Don't forget the practical elements of content: what this site is about; what you can do with this site; how this site works; how you can contact us.
- Think about your medium. Your audience may be looking at your page on a 15-inch screen – so small print and fine graphic detail are not on. They have to do some scrolling, so what is at the top? (first impressions), and what is at front page bottom? (may be hidden).

- We've said that you shouldn't overload on graphics, but using at least some graphics will lift the look of a page. You can import photos from a digital camera.

In general, if you are going to design and build a website, then you have to invest time and practice, and have a long deadline by which to achieve a finished result.

If you are designing content for some other, more technically capable person to put up for you, then you have to understand the organization of a site. You need to plan content, links, the structure of the whole thing, by talking to your site designer.

If you are designing a Web page as a short practical exercise, then you need to think about content, layout, audience, purpose, the medium, and what other material one could navigate to, in principle at least.

For further information, especially about specialist terms and acronyms, you can go to the online encyclopedia www.wikipedia.com.

Assignment

Case study

NATIONAL SOCIETY FOR ROAD SAFETY
Barnham House
Colwell Terrace
London NW16 5NM

Tel: 0121 5827966

Press Release: immediate

30 June 2007

CARMAGEDDON: Computer game

This game has been referred to the Society for comment. It has been the subject of much discussion in the press. Players drive simulated cars at high speeds and gain points for knocking down people and animals.

The Society regrets that the Video Standards Council has awarded this game a 15 plus certificate. We find the game disturbing. It is not an appropriate message to be sending out. People endure much pain and grief because of reckless driving. Glorifying such behaviour can deliver a dangerous signal to future and current drivers who use the game.

END

Contact: The Press Secretary

To complete these tasks, you should refer to the press release from the National Society for Road Safety.

You are a researcher/production assistant for an 'issues'-based radio programme entitled *Now Britain*. The producer has decided to run an edition on sex, violence and sexism in computer games.

You obtain an interview with the marketing manager of the company selling the game Carmageddon. He says of the graphics and game victims:

> We have made slight cosmetic changes . . . giving the characters zombie-white faces and red eyes. When they are hit they emit a green gunk as opposed to blood . . . we are not trying to offend people . . . the idea of cars deliberately hitting people is not new: it was aired by the film *Death Race 2000*.

You also interview the editor of *PC Magazine*, who says:

> We liked it. Mowing down pedestrians clearly isn't something we would like to encourage but it is so obviously over the top as to be pure fantasy. It may not be morally correct but it is fun. There is no question that it will sell well.

Now complete the following tasks:

(a) List who else you might interview in the course of your research, and why.

(b) Draft a blurb to go in one of the listings magazines such as *Radio Times*, describing this programme edition.

(c) Script the voice piece introducing the edition. You may use sound from the game and an interview clip. The piece should not run over thirty seconds.

(d) Write a draft for a script segment to be used by the programme presenter which puts forward arguments for and against censorship of video games – to last no more than one minute.

(e) Script a radio advert for Carmageddon lasting fifteen to twenty seconds.

Suggested reading

No one book covers the whole range of practical communication that we have referred to. But in the Resources list that follows the Glossary, we have suggested some individually useful books and websites for particular topics that we have dealt with. There is of course an extensive literature that covers specific interpersonal skills such as assertiveness or giving presentations.

Glossary of communication terms

This list provides a brief definition of how some important terms are used in communication studies. We also suggest you consult the Index of this book. For further references and information, see *Communication, Culture and Media Studies: key concepts* by J. Hartley (2002) and *A Dictionary of Communication and Media Studies* by J. Watson and A. Hill (7th edition, 2006).

Agenda setting refers to the process by which the news media define which topics (the agenda) should be of main interest to the audience. Hence, the media have a significant influence on issues for public discussion.

Assertiveness refers to skills through which the communicator asserts her/his needs without imposing on others.

Audience Those persons who are the receivers of a message, particularly of a mass-media message. (Also called **receiver** or **destination**.)

Barriers to communication Factors in the communication process that impede open communication between source and destination. (Also called **filters** or **noise**.) They exist within individuals (psychological filters), within the sign/message (semantic filters) and within the context (mechanical filters).

Channel The means of communication through which messages flow from source to destination. Most examples of the communication process include multiple channels.

Code A system of signs bound by conventions. The English language is a primary code (see also the notion of secondary codes, page 29).

    Encoding refers to the process of translating ideas, feelings, opinions into signs following the conventions of a code (e.g. speaking or writing).

    Decoding refers to the understanding and interpreting of signs (e.g. listening or reading).

Communication The process of creating and sharing meaning through the transmission and exchange of signs. This process requires interaction within oneself, between people, or between people and machines.

Communication skills are about the ability to control various means of communication in order to produce effective communication. Skills are to do with managing social interaction successfully, rather than to do with technical expertise.

Consensus refers to the centre ground of beliefs and values agreed within a society. These are broadly held and proposed by the mass media. As expressed by the media, consensus tends to exclude the notion of alternative or multiple views of a given topic or issue.

Context is the environment or surroundings in which communication takes place. Contexts may be physical or social/cultural.

Conventions are rules defining how signs are used within codes and how these signs, collectively, may be understood.

Culture A collection of beliefs, values and behaviours distinctive to a large group of people and expressed through various forms of communication. It is common to identify culture in terms of nation (e.g. French), or area (e.g. European), or race and religion (e.g. Jewish). Culture is represented through dress, religion and art forms in particular, as well as through language.

> **Popular culture** generally refers to popular and commercial forms of art and media entertainment.

> **High culture** generally refers to the culture of an educated and dominant class.

> **Folk culture** generally refers to the culture that is created by people for themselves. It usually relies on oral traditions.

> **Mass culture** generally refers to the popular culture shared by a mass media/consumer audience.

Discourse is a term that is used in a variety of contexts to describe how certain kinds of understanding are created and perpetuated within various institutions in society. These discourses are about ideas and meanings that are made apparent through the use of communication. While the word originally referred to patterns of speech, it is now used to refer to patterns of communication processes in education, the mass media or television or a particular type of television, such as news.

> **Discourse analysis** refers to the ways of trying to identify the elements in the communication processes of a particular medium. It is usually used to refer to the analysis of the output of mass media and how the audience interacts with that output.

Feedback is communication in response to a previous message. It includes the idea that the sender adjusts his or her communication style in response to feedback. Feedback is continuous in conversation. It may be a deliberate response (e.g. a spoken reply) or an unintentional response (e.g. some non-verbal behaviours).

Gatekeeper refers to an individual within an organization who has some power to control and direct the flow of information into and out of that organization. This power may include the right to select information or even to interpret it (e.g. a news sub-editor).

Genre A term describing a recognizable body of work with common characteristics (e.g. science fiction). Genres are thus usually recognized within popular narrative fiction and art forms.

Group A collection of people who interact in some way and share common goals or interests. A **virtual group** refers to a collection of people who do not meet face to face but communicate via electronic means, such as emails or the World Wide Web.

Ideology is a term for describing a particular view of the world constructed from certain sets of values. The twentieth century was much influenced by a conflict of two ideologies, capitalism and communism, not to mention those ideologies we call religions. There is usually a **dominant ideology** in a given culture. The values and beliefs of this dominant ideology come to us through major agencies of socialization: family, school and the media. The value messages concerned are contained in media texts. From one view, these messages are 'packaged up under topic headings' such as family, or crime, and can be called **discourses**. These messages/meanings often come across implicitly, through the ways that the media text puts things across, as much as through what it obviously says.

Image A picture, as seen in a photograph or single frame of film. In literary criticism an image is an extended metaphor. More broadly, image can refer to a mental conception of a person, place or thing (e.g. a brand image of a particular consumer product).

Information refers in the first place to factual communication, including verifiable and objective facts about the world. More broadly the term can include anything that adds to our sum of knowledge about the world and people. In this case, beliefs and opinions given and received could be described as information. Information serves to reduce uncertainty; you know more than you did before gaining the information.

Institution describes a great range of organizations, usually commercial, that own and control media industries. Most obviously, one is talking about businesses like Carlton Communications. But Reuters news agency or Microsoft could also be described as institutions.

Internet describes the worldwide network of communication based on computers and existing cables and satellite links. The Web, which is what most people use, is a system that uses the network. The Net, or the Web, is unique in that no company owns it. It lives through its users. Some companies (e.g. Demon or Virgin) can make money selling you a connection to it and an email address, and others by owning particular websites with things for sale.

Language is a widely used term referring to a system/code for organizing signs according to conventions. Learning how to use our native language is fundamental to becoming a social being. We use language for personal purposes (to think, organize our ideas and perceptions, and to imagine), for social purposes (to exchange messages with one another) and for cultural purposes (to record the past and to transmit ideas and values to the future).

Meaning What is signified by a message conveyed through the signs that we give or receive. The meanings of messages are in our heads, not in their words or pictures. What a sender means by the signs offered may be different from what the receiver understands by the signs received. Levels of meaning are often distinguished in signs: for example, a sign serves to **denote** a generally agreed basic meaning within a culture and it also serves to **connote** broader personal and cultural associations (e.g. words like *slim, slender, thin, lean, skinny* have similar basic denotations but also suggest different connotations).

Medium/media A channel or means of communicating. A medium usually comprises more than one form of communication. The word **media** has now come to refer to mass media.

> **Mediation** refers to the process of selection and interpretation that transforms material passing through the media.

Message A unit of information, whether of fact or of opinion, passed via a channel. In most examples of the communication process, more than one message is passed. It is the **content** of a piece of communication.

> **Overt messages** are those that are apparent and obvious.

> **Covert messages** are those that are concealed, intentionally or otherwise. They may well be messages about beliefs, opinions and attitudes.

Model of communication is a consciously simplified description of a communication process which is usually expressed in graphic form as a diagram showing the elements of the process and how they relate to each other.

Narrative describes the story functions that exist in most media material. It covers aspects such as the unfolding of the storyline (plot) and the treatment of the story (drama). The term most obviously relates to items such a radio drama or a novel. But the news or a magazine travel feature, for example, also has narrative.

NVB Abbreviation for **non-verbal behaviour**. This phrase refers to all the actions people display, apart from speech, from which other people may draw meanings.

NVC Abbreviation for **non-verbal communication**. That is, the means of communication that includes body language, paralanguage and dress.

Perception refers to the process by which we make sense of the world and other people. It involves selecting, organizing and interpreting what we receive through our senses to create our own mental reality. Perception is a fundamental aspect of decoding meanings and depends on our knowledge, beliefs and experience.

Process refers to the act of communication, including the various factors that contribute to communication. Examples may be taken within any one of the four categories of communication (i.e. intrapersonal, interpersonal, group, mass). Communication is described as a process because it is not static.

Radio trail A short segment between programmes, designed to trail or market a programme in advance of its broadcast.

Realism refers to the quality of realness in a media text. This quality is the result of our reading certain conventions from the text. There are different kinds of realism, some described by titles such as documentary or fiction.

Representation is the act of re-presenting something through the media. Generally, one could have representations of anything – London, family life. In particular, the term is often applied to representations of groups/ types of people. It does lead one to the study of stereotyping, but this is not all that it is about.

Role A part played by an individual within a given group and situation. This part includes selected personality traits and kinds of behaviour that help define that person's relationship with other people in a group (e.g. work roles or family roles).

Semiology The discipline or area of study that examines signs and their meanings.

Sign A single unit of communication which conveys a meaning (or meanings) that is learnt through education or socialization. Most examples of communication include a flow of signs, perhaps through more than one channel, all of which interact. Anything that we can say has a meaning may be defined as a sign, whether it be a word or an object.

Socialization The process through which we learn the dominant beliefs, values and behaviour acceptable within our society. So, it is also concerned with learning to communicate. The family, work, school and the media are significant agents of socialization.

Stereotype A simplified depiction of a person or group, in writing or in a picture, usually represented in the media. The type has a few dominant characteristics that make it easily identified (e.g. the nutty professor).

Strategy A piece of communication with a purpose. The term usually refers to interpersonal communication in which we use strategies, learnt through experience, to achieve a purpose such as the breaking-off of conversation.

Subculture A cultural group within a dominant larger culture. The subculture nevertheless has its own distinctive characteristics and behaviour and beliefs (e.g. West Indian communities in Britain, Hell's Angels).

Team refers to a group of three or more people who work together, combining different and complementary skills, and operating in different roles to achieve a set of agreed aims.

Text describes any piece of media material using any form of communication. TV programmes, newspaper articles, computer games are all texts.

> **Textual analysis** is the process of looking into a text to see what messages are in it. The most important messages are to do with values and beliefs – ideology.

Transaction A communication exchange, usually with functional connotations (e.g. withdrawing money from a bank). Two or more people agree to deal with one another (interact) to develop a relationship that will enable the exchange of meanings.

Resources for Communication Studies

A great deal has changed since our last edition. The Web has come into its own, hence the following section identifying Web addresses as resources. On the other hand, publishers have cut reading and resource lists. GCSE Communication Studies has disappeared, though the A/AS level remains. But Media Studies has boomed in educational terms, hence the situation in which media dominate a definition of mass communication. Film Studies is an established cousin of Media. And Cultural Studies has given a new dimension to communication and media.

So, we have revamped this section to cover books, websites, magazines and journals, and other resources.

Books

General and reference

Beck, A., Bennett, P. and Wall, P. (2004) *AS Communication Studies*, London: Routledge.

Beck, A., Bennett, P. and Wall, P. (2004) *Communication Studies: the essential resource*, London: Routledge.

Ellis, R. and McClintock, A. (1994) *If You Take My Meaning: theory into practice in human communication* [2nd ed.], London: Hodder Arnold.

Hartley, J. (2002) *Communication, Culture and Media Studies: Key Concepts*, London: Routledge.

Wall, P. (2006) *Media Studies for GCSE* [2nd ed.], London: Collins.

Watson, J. and Hill, A. (2006): *A Dictionary of Communication and Media Studies* [7th ed.], London: Hodder Arnold.

Interpersonal and group communication

Argyle, M. (1992) *The Social Psychology of Everyday Life*, London: Routledge.

Argyle, M. (1994) *The Psychology of Interpersonal Behaviour*, London: Penguin.

Aronson, E., Wilson, T. and Akert, R. (2004) *Social Psychology* [4th ed.], Upper Saddle River, NJ: Pearson Education.

Baron, R., Byrne, D. and Branscombe, N. (2005) *Social Psychology, the international edition* [11th ed.], London: Pearson Education.

Berne, E. (1973) *Games People Play*, Harmondsworth: Penguin.

Brown, R. (2000) *Group Processes* [2nd ed.]. Oxford: Blackwell.

Burton, G. and Dimbleby, R. (2006) *Between Ourselves: an introduction to interpersonal communication* [3rd ed.], London: Hodder Arnold.

Goffman, E. (1990) *The Presentation of Self in Everyday Life*, London: Penguin.

Hammersley, R. and Reid, M. (2000) *Communicating Successfully in Groups: a practical guide for the workplace*, London: Routledge.

Hargie, O. [ed.] (2006) *A Handbook of Communication Skills* [3rd ed.], London: Routledge.

Hargie, O. and Dickson, D. (2004) *Skilled Interpersonal Communication* [4th ed.], London: Routledge.

Hartley, P. (1999) *Interpersonal Communication* [2nd ed.], London: Routledge.

Honey, P. (1988) *Face to Face: a practical guide to interactive skills* [2nd ed.], Aldershot: Gower Publishing.

Montgomery, M. (1995) *Introduction to Language and Society* [2nd ed.], London: Routledge.

Pennington, D. (2002) *The Social Psychology of Behaviour in Small Groups*, London: Routledge.

Pennington, D., Gillen, K. and Hill, P. (1999) *Social Psychology*, London: Hodder Education.

Schneider, M. and Corey, G. (2002) *Groups: process and practice* [6th ed.], Pacific Grove, CA: Thomson Learning/Brooks, Cole.

Stanger, C. (2004) *Social Groups in Action and Interaction*, London: Routledge.

Watson, J. (2003) *Media Communication: an introduction to theory and process* [2nd ed.], London: Palgrave Macmillan.

Wilson, G.L. and Hanna, M.S. (1993) *Leadership and Participation in Small Groups* [3rd ed.], New York: McGraw-Hill.

Communication in organizations

Belbin, R.M. (1996) *Team Roles at Work*, Oxford: Butterworth-Heinemann.

Furnham, A. (2005) *The Psychology of Behaviour at Work* [2nd ed.], London: Psychology Press.

Goleman, D. (1998) *Working with Emotional Intelligence*, London: Bloomsbury.

Handy, C. (1993) *Understanding Organizations*, London: Penguin.

Stanton, N. (2004) *Mastering Communication* [4th ed.], Basingstoke: Palgrave Macmillan.

Theobald, T. and Cooper, C. (2004) *Shut Up and Listen: the truth about how to communicate at work*, London: Kogan Page.

West, M. (2004) *The Secrets of Successful Team Management*, London: Duncan Baird.

Woods, C. (2003) *Everything You Need to Know at Work: a complete manual of workplace skills*, London: Pearson.

Mass communication (media)

Bignell, J. and Orlebar, J. (2005) *The Television Handbook*, London: Routledge.

Blandford, S., Grant, B. and Hillier, J. (2000) *The Film Studies Dictionary*, London: Routledge.

Branston, G. and Stafford, R. (2006) *The Media Students' Book* [4th ed.], London: Routledge.
Briggs, A. and Cobley, P. (2002) *The Media* [2nd ed.], London: Pearson Education.
Curran, J. and Seaton, J. (2003) *Power without Responsibility: the press and broadcasting in Britain*, London: Routledge.
Devereux, E. (2003) *Understanding the Media*, London: Sage.
Harrison, J. (2005) *News*, London: Routledge.
Lacey, N. (1998) *Image and Representation*, Basingstoke: Macmillan.
Lacey, N. (2002) *Media Institutions and Audiences*, Basingstoke: Macmillan.
Lacey, N. (2005) *An Introduction to Film*, London: Palgrave Macmillan.
Myers, G. (1999) *Adworlds: brands, media, audiences*, London: Arnold.
Newbold, C., Boyd-Barrett, O. and van Bulcke, H. (2002) *The Media Book*, London: Routledge.
O'Sullivan, T., Dutton, B. and Rayner, P. (2003) *Studying the Media* [3rd ed.], London: Hodder Arnold.
Phillips, P. (2005) *Film: an introduction*, London: Palgrave Macmillan.
Starkey, G. (2004) *Radio in Context*, London: Palgrave Macmillan.

Finally in this section, we recommend taking a look at many of the products from Auteur Publishing, which specializes in film and media, including classroom resources and guides for teachers. As we write this, the website – www.auteur.co.uk – is being reconstructed and due to open soon. There are many products that might interest you, including some geared to the controlled test topics of GCSE Media Studies. Among titles that could be mentioned are *Narrative in Film and TV* (both a teacher's guide and resources), *Teaching TV Advertising*, *Contemporary British Cinema* and *Radio for Media Studies*.

Practical communication

McLeish, R. (2005) *Radio Production* [5th ed.], Oxford: Focal Press.

In general, the Focal Press is a source of expertise and information about the range of practical media. Some of its productions are difficult, since they are written with industry standards and practices in mind. But you will find the following of its books more accessible: The Easy Guides; the Hands on Guides; and the Photography, essential skills series.

Stauffer, T. (2003) *The Absolute Beginner's Guide to Creating Web Pages* [2nd ed.], Indianapolis, IN: QUE Publishing.
Weston, C. (2004) *500 Digital Photography Hints, Tips and Techniques*, Hove: RotoVision.

You will also find the media practice Handbook series, published by Routledge, London, very useful for their mixture of practical and background information to various media, as well as their outline of critical approaches to understanding the medium concerned. These are:

Holland, P. – *The Television Handbook*
Wilby, P. and Conroy, A. – *The Radio Handbook*
Keeble, R. – *The Newspapers Handbook*
Brierley, S. – *The Advertising Handbook*

Wright, T. – *The Photography Handbook*
McKay, J. – *The Magazines Handbook*
A number of these books are in second editions.

There is a useful website relating to digital video and digital video skills across the national curriculum, namely www.oxdv.co.uk, which offers clips and notes, and which covers areas such as theory, planning and shooting.

In terms of the 'soft' skills in the earlier part of chapter 6, there are a few websites that you may find useful. They are often based at universities.

For example, you can find something on presentation skills at www.le.ac/slc/presentation.html. This site includes study guides, and PDF files on aspects of presentation; and it offers a DVD to purchase.

There is material on questionnaire design at www.sharedlearning.org.uk.

There is material on assertiveness at http://hcd2.bupa.co.uk/fact_sheets/html/improving_assertiveness.html. This is contextualized within caring professions, but none the less useful for that.

Websites

The websites listed here are mostly to do with mass communication and practical communication. They are useful for information and other resources. Websites of course provide postal and email addresses if needed.

Advertising Association www.adassoc.org.uk
The professional body for advertising in the United Kingdom. The site has an information centre, and offers student briefing. Like the authority below, it informs briefing about regulation, and offers, for example, a pack on advertising.

Advertising Standards Authority www.asa.org.uk
The UK watchdog for advertising. Provides information about aspects of regulation, about cases and judgements regarding adverts, and various links.

Audit Bureau of Circulation www.www.abc.org.uk
The audit watchdog for the UK print industries. There is a certain amount of information offered at the front end.

British Broadcasting Corporation www.bbc.co.uk
Everyone knows this one. But still it is a major site, receiving more hits than any other in the United Kingdom. Much information about the BBC, but also useful links. The front page has an extensive directory of topics such as music, plus a browse facility, plus for example streamed radio.

British Rate and Data www.brad.co.uk
The online version of the printed resource, which offers some information for free up front.

British Film Institute www.bfi.org.uk
This will give you access to a range of resources, mostly to do with the moving image, of course. There is material for media in English courses. Other examples include

'scanning television', 'moving images in the classroom', 'images and reality', teaching film and media studies', and 'media briefing'. The teaching series cover topics such as digital video and music video.

Campaign for Press and Broadcasting Freedom www.cpbf.demon.co.uk
Offers for instance sections on its policies, on publications, articles, and items on topics such as ownership and Ofcom. (At the time of writing, CPBF was building a new website, but had a link from this address.)

Cinema and Media Directory cinemedia.org
This is an industry site, an online directory of businesses in the sector. As such, it is specialized, but can be interesting, to get a picture of the huge range of providers out there.

Education sites
There are at least a few sites based in universities and elsewhere, which are useful for information and links. The 'difficulty' of the level of materials varies, of course.

www.aber.ac.uk/media
Based on the University of Aberystwyth and run by Daniel Goldman. Provides a range of materials and topics.

communication, culture and media studies
www.cultsock.ndirect.co.uk/MUhome/cshtml
This is Mick Underwood's Australian site, which includes summary definitions and descriptions for various topics. The front page opens with a subject index.

www.theory.org.uk
Based at Bournemouth University, this is David Gauntlett's site, containing a mixture of reviews and articles. It is strong in areas such as identity and gender.

www.byteachers.org.uk
This will be more useful for readers of this book, and their teachers! This one connects the Association of Teachers' sites. A good starting point for searches. Go to Members' Sites and then scroll down to the English & Media list. This gives links to, for example, RSS Media Studies or Filton College Media, as well as to:

www.start.at/media studies
This is Steve Baker's media site, aimed at GCE level.

English and Media Centre, London www.englishandmedia.co.uk
Resources on 'doing news', a media magazine for students, and much more.

www.filmeducation.org

The Guardian newspaper www.media.guardian.co.uk
A range of materials about the media, as well as the online version of the newspaper. Options include a media magazine section or media briefing.

Government Film Archives www.national archives.gov.uk/films
Provides information about archived films, and some access to these; also education sections and news about exhibitions.

Internet Magazine (Future Publishing) www.netmag.co.uk
Includes, for example, sections on webcams, Web Builder and news.

ITV plc www.itv.com
ITV is Britain's largest commercial broadcaster. The site provides information about the company and its activities. It has an A–Z list, ITV main genres and weather.

Media Production www.mch.co.uk/southwest/videofilmproduction.shtml
This one is rather specialized, in an industry sense. But it is informative to access a list of audio-visual AV producers and support services in your region. Any region of the country can be accessed from any other.

Media UK www.mediauk.com
A Web provider that covers news, resources, business lists, and links. There are, for example, sections such as a media directory, streamed radio and TV, blogs and Google Earth.

National Museum of Photography, Film and Television, Bradford
www.nmpft.org.uk.
Provides access to resources and information, as well as information on what is going on at the museum. It has, for example, an education site link to sites such as C4 schools or Media Educ, as well as access to educational materials and packs.

News Corporation www.newscorp.com
An example of one of the big media corporation websites, which provides a range of information about the company's interests and activities.

Office for Communication www.ofcom.org.uk
The government-created regulator for the broadcasting industries. There is a lot of information about the regulatory work of the body, as well as other material such as facts sheets on careers in broadcasting.

Press Complaints Commission www.pcc.org.uk
Provides information about the work of this body, about cases and judgments. Sub-sites include codes of practice, case examples and statistics.

Undercurrents www.undercurrents.org
An important independent and radical provider of news covering issues around the country. Apart from periodic alternative news productions, it provides other materials, including *The Video Activist's Handbook*.

Voice of the Listener & Viewer www.vlv.org.uk
Voice of the Listener & Viewer (VLV) represents the citizen and consumer interest in broadcasting and works for quality and diversity in British broadcasting.

Wired News www.wired.com/news
This site provides news on the Net, and covers areas such as technology, culture and a magazine.

Journals/magazines/reference works*

The following are mainly to do with mass communication. You should find at least some of them in school, college or city libraries. Many of them are now available online. Details and addresses are available through libraries and through Web searches. (Note: an asterisk before a title indicates that it is a reference work.)

*Benn's Press Directory
BFI Film and Television Handbook
*BRAD [British Rate and Data]
*British Humanities Index
British Journalism Review
Broadcast
Film Quarterly
*The Guardian Media Guide
Journal of Popular Film and Television
Journalism Studies
Marketing
Marketing News
Marketing Week
Mass Communication and Society
Media, Culture and Society
The Moving Image
New Media and Society
Popular Music and Society
Press Gazette
The Radio Journal
Sight and Sound (film and TV)
*Social Trends (HMSO)
Technology and New Media
*Who Owns Whom

Index

Related titles from Routledge

Communication Studies
The Essential Resource
Andrew Beck, Peter Bennett and Peter Wall

Communication Studies: The Essential Resource is a collection of resource material for all those studying communication at university and pre-university level. The Resource brings together a wide array of material ranging from academic articles to film scripts to websites, to illustrate key topics in Communication Studies.

Each extract is introduced and contextualised by the editors, and followed by suggestions for further activities and reading, to help kick-start students' autonomy.

ISBN 13: 978-0-415-28792-0 (hbk)
ISBN 13: 978-0-415-28793-7 (pbk)

Available at all good bookshops
For ordering and further information please visit:
www.routledge.com

Related titles from Routledge

Introduction to Communication Studies
Second Edition
John Fiske

How can we study communication?

What are the main theories and methods of approach?

The discipline of communication studies is now firmly established in the academic market-place. This now classic text is a lucid introduction to the main authorities in the field, aimed at students coming to the subject for the first time. It outlines a range of methods of analysing examples of communication, and describes the theories underpinning them. Thus armed, the reader will be able to tease out the latent cultural meanings in such apparently simple communications as news photos or popular TV programmes, and to see them with new eyes.

This second edition includes new material on the theory, methods and applications of structuralism, ideology and audience ethnography.

ISBN 13: 978-0-415-04672-5 (pbk)

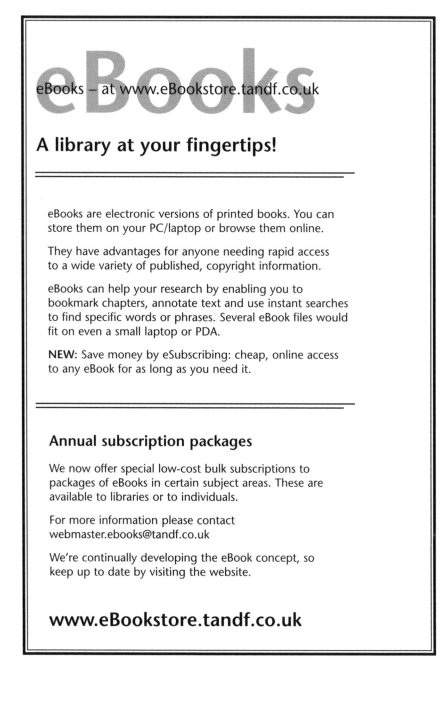